P9-AOO-052

HD9506.A2 S58
Negotiating Third World mineral agr
Kennedy Sch of Govt   ACP8431

3 2044 014 920 474

**Negotiating Third-World
Mineral Agreements**

Negotiating Third-World Mineral Agreements

Promises as Prologue

David N. Smith
Harvard Law School

Louis T. Wells, Jr.
Harvard Business School

Ballinger Publishing Company ● Cambridge, Massachusetts
A Subsidiary of Harper & Row, Publishers, Inc.

3536

P-110

HD
9506
.A2
S58

RECEIVED

AUG 26 1982

KENNEDY SCHOOL OF
GOVERNMENT LIBRARY

 This book is printed on recycled paper.

Copyright © 1975 by Ballinger Publishing Company. All rights reserved. No part of this publication may be reproduced, stored in a retrieval system, or transmitted in any form or by any means, electronic, mechanical, photocopy, recording or otherwise, without the prior written consent of the publisher.

International Standard Book Number: 0–88410–041–3

Library of Congress Catalog Card Number: 75–29274

Printed in the United States of America

Library of Congress Cataloging in Publication Data

Smith, David Nathan.
    Negotiating third world mineral agreements.
    1. Underdeveloped areas—Mineral industries.
2. Underdeveloped areas—Concessions. 3. Underdeveloped areas—Investments, Foreign. I. Wells, Louis T., joint author. II. Title.
HD9506.A2S58   338.2'09172'4   75–29274
ISBN 0–88410–041–3

For Robin and David, the products of two
other highly successful, but quite independent,
joint ventures.

Contents

Foreword

A perceptive essayist once wrote that when Al Smith urged voters to look at the record he had no idea how large the record would eventually become. The literature on multinational corporations and foreign private investment is now assuming a size which might even draw from the late Governor of New York the admission that a point has been made.

At the same time, the numerous books, articles, United Nations reports and Congressional hearings on the subject display a curious gap. They are rich on all sides of the question in assessing the costs and benefits of multinationals and foreign investment, and in analyzing the practices and characteristics of firms over a wide range of industries. What is missing, however, is a solid understanding of how developing countries and foreign firms actually agree on who gets what and how much. The relative void is in a comprehension of the bargaining process as it takes place every day in the year; it is in an appreciation of the complexity of constraints and opportunities which operate on both sides of the bargaining table and which produce a wide variety of outcomes.

David Smith and Louis Wells have chosen to step into the breach by making concessions agreements in the mining industry their modest but illuminating means of entry. Their knowledge is based on more than fifteen years of joint experience working with governments in Asia, Africa and Latin America, analyzing and studying agreements around the world and teaching what they have learned.

Perhaps because of their numerous close involvements in helping developing countries sort out policies and procedures relating to foreign investments, the authors adhere to a canon of technical assistance more honored in the breach than the observance. They know that western concepts, technologies and institutions cannot be automatically transferred to developing countries. Their experience confirms that Western notions of contract are subject to substantial adaptation in environments that have different histories and are changing rapidly.

They observe that the forms contracts take are set in large part by the economic, political and social environments in which they function. They also observe that concessions agreements are themselves a dynamic process, changing as perceptions and power change.

While these basic perceptions on which the authors build their analysis are by no means novel, the richness of empirical detail which they employ to describe the concessions process conveys a model of reality which parties on both sides of the bargaining table often fail to perceive. Originally, the book was intended to help governments of developing countries arm thenselves to strike better bargains on the basis of accurate knowledge of the opportunities and constraints they face. As the writing progressed, it became apparent that the authors' emerging views also had considerable bearing on the foreign investor's perception of reality.

This should, therefore, be a useful volume for governments interested in foreign private investment and for firms seeking investment opportunities. Whether it will in fact be useful will doubtless depend on each party's capacity for assessing the limits faced by those across the green baize table top. Such capacity is comprised of more than an appropriate attitude, mood or ideology. As this volume displays with careful reasoning and detail, the contract bargaining process entails matters of economics, law, technology and politics which call for a high order of technical analysis. It is on this score that the developing countries are generally at a disadvantage. One happy consequence of this pioneering work might be to encourage international aid agencies to support relevant courses of instruction and technical assistance for developing countries. At the moment, such assistance is largely absent from their programs.

Louis T. Wells is Professor of Business Administration at the Graduate School of Business Administration, Harvard University. David N. Smith is Assistant Dean for International Legal Studies, Harvard Law School. The Harvard Institute for International Development (HIID) and its predecessor, the Development Advisory Service of Harvard University, afforded the authors exposure to the problems on which they write by attaching them at various times to its advisory groups abroad. The Institute also provided support for preparing this volume.

Lester E. Gordon
Director
Harvard Institute for
International Development

Acknowledgments

The debts owed by the authors of a book based on a number of years of field experience are so numerous that all cannot possibly be acknowledged. Many of these debts are to clients we have advised, or to negotiators on the other side of the bargaining table. These contributors must, unfortunately, remain anonymous.

The largest debts we owe are to Professors Raymond Vernon and Milton Katz who got us, *faut de mieux,* into the subject of natural resource negotiations when they heard of a country that desperately needed help. They have been a major source of our education in the field all along. Also of importance in the creation of this book was William Hollinger, former advisor of Harvard's Development Advisory Service (now Harvard Institute for International Development). In spite of his problems with our "staff standing ready," his patience with us was a major contribution to our gaining more knowledge in the field.

We are also very grateful for the comments of a number of friends who were kind enough to read earlier drafts of various chapters of this book. Among these were Richard Baxter, Dwight Brothers, Malcolm Gillis, Lester Gordon, Michael McIntyre, Cornelius Murphy, Oliver Oldman, Elizabeth Owens, Michael Roemer, Robert Stobaugh, Stanley Surrey, and Detlev Vagts. We corrected several errors that they pointed out; our stubbornness may have kept us from altering other points.

Harvard's Business School, Law School, and Institute for International Development believed our annual claims that we were actually nurturing a manuscript, and they continued to give financial support until it finally emerged in this form.

**Negotiating Third-World
Mineral Agreements**

Chapter One

Changing Relationships in the Concessions Process

Improving the bargaining position of developing countries in their negotiations with foreign investors interested in access to natural resources was the original intent of this book. In many developing countries, concession agreements with foreign firms—for mining, petroleum, plantation, or timbering operations—account for as much as a third of government revenue. In a number of countries the percentage is considerably higher. Concessions provide, for many countries, a major source of foreign exchange and employment, as well as stimuli for economic growth. They are frequently major points of internal and international political conflict. It was our original assumption that most developing countries, no matter how long they have been in the natural resources business, need some help in dealing with the foreign firm interested in the extractive industry.

Our initial goal of aiding the developing countries stemmed partly from the fact that most of our field experience had come from work for governments of these countries. This experience led us to believe that many host countries were at a disadvantage in dealing with foreign firms. The lack of bargaining skills and technical know-how on the government side, and the control over technology, capital, and markets on the company side, made the going rough for many government officials. Although the benefits that host countries have received have probably outweighed the costs in most cases, many agreements appear to have been skewed in favor of the foreign firm.

In recent years the situation has changed somewhat. In some countries and in some industries, bargaining powers have shifted in favor of the host country. Changes in industry structures and improvements in skills in the developing countries have done much for the host country cause. In fact, in some cases there is a new peril: that the host country, flushed with its new-found power, will force its advantage to the point that it will suffer in the long run. This is, of course, a striking reversal of the hazards of a few decades ago, when similar warnings to the extracting companies would have been appropriate.

Yet one must be cautious in generalizing from the well-publicized examples. Although, in the wake of the notorious OPEC successes in the early 1970s, a number of observers proclaimed a major shift in bargaining power from the companies to the developing countries, the change has, in fact, been uneven. There are still many industries where the balance of power has not shifted in favor of the host country. And in cases where the balance of power has shifted, this shift may not be recognized by the potential beneficiaries. There are still a signficant number of countries that do not have the knowledge and skills to perceive changes and to negotiate effectively with foreign investors in light of these changes. While the oil wolf may be at the door of the consuming countries, many developing countries of much gentler characterization have not yet started up the path. The need for help has not disappeared.

Despite our concern for the developing countries, our book is not directed solely to them. As our consulting and writing have progressed, and as we have continued a dialogue with representatives of private industry, we have become increasingly convinced that much of what we say here will be of interest and importance to the investor. *Mirabile dictu,* there are still some private firms that lack the skills necessary to negotiate effectively with the developing countries. And there is a much larger group of firms that remains remarkably ignorant of the forces affecting their bargaining positions in the developing world, as well as regrettably unaware of the concerns and motivations of host governments.

Our intention is to bring an element of realism to a subject that has long been clouded by mythology and misunderstanding. The common illusions are myriad: host country belief that maximum concession income will materialize without maximum concession supervision; investing company belief that it can carry on business-as-usual in the face of changes in the host country and in the international forum; host country faith in the panacea of nationalization; investing company fear of concession arrangements that provide for equity or other participation by the host country; lawyers' jousting with *pacta sunt servanda* vs. *rebus sic stantibus,* and lawyers' discussions of "economic development agreements" that may have little to do with economic development. Many of the issues we discuss are at the heart of the question of whether agreements for the development of mineral resources will play an important role in what became, in the mid-1970s, the developing countries' quest for a "new economic order."[1]

In an environment as complex and as changing as that in which minerals agreements are negotiated, simple rules are of little value. The underlying forces must be understood. And that understanding must be applied to the case at hand to arrive at an appropriate decision. Thus we have abandoned our initial attempt at creating a handbook on concessions. At the same time, however, we have tried to remain practical and to confront in some detail those issues that seem to cause the most problems in negotiations.

Although we intended at the outset to deal only with the "hard minerals," we came gradually to realize that what we had to say applied, in many cases, to other natural resources. So we have retained a focus on the hard minerals but have not hesitated to draw liberally from experience with timber and plantation concessions, and from the well-documented petroleum industry.

We hope then that this book will be useful to both sides in a range of natural resource industries: to developing countries by providing them with new perceptions, perspectives, and skills; and to managers of the firms by giving them a clearer view of where they are and where they are going in their relations with host governments. We hope that by explaining what we have seen of the total concessions process, we can help both parties end up with better agreements and more congenial relations.

STATIC AND DYNAMIC BARGAINING MODELS

Many practitioners of the concessions art, both investors and host governments, are operating with outdated and misleading notions about the nature of the concession arrangements into which they have entered or are about to enter. Anyone analyzing these arrangements must start with a central concept—that the concession contract cannot be understood in isolation from the economic, social, political, and bureaucratic forces at work in the host country and in the particular industry. The initial negotiation of the contract is merely one step in a process of unfolding relationships. The contract itself may set off a chain of events that will alter the ultimate shape of the relationship. The "concession contract" should be viewed as a part of a "concessions process."

Traditional notions about concession arrangements have tended to reflect a static bargaining model in which a fixed set of rewards is divided in a single set of negotiations between two parties. On specific issues one party "wins" and the other party "loses" for the life of the contract. This traditional view may grow out of Western concepts of the adversary process and out of tendencies to view agreements as legal documents divorced from economic, social and political influences.

The static bargaining model has some utility. For purposes of comparing concession arrangements at a particular moment, the model offers certain insights. A comparison of Indonesian oil and copper concession contracts negotiated in the late 1960s tells one a great deal about the relative bargaining powers of the government vis à vis oil and copper investors in that period. In oil arrangements the effective tax rate was around 65 percent; title to equipment imported by the company vested in the government; and investors were restricted to production-sharing agreements. In contrast, the tax rate for copper agreements began at 35 percent; the foreign firm held title to all equipment; and agreements had most of the characteristics of very traditional concession agreements. The differences in Indonesia's bargaining power in the two industries was dramatic, and the contracts revealed the differences. The underlying factors influencing these differences were clear. In the late 1960s Indonesia was a proven source of low-sulphur oil. It was close to a major market, Japan. On the other hand, Indonesia was an unproven source for copper in a region with a number of other supplying countries.

What the static bargaining model does not reveal, however, are the changes that occur both within the industry and within the host country, which ultimately alter the shape of the agreement. Nor does it reveal the presence of other potential actors in the concessions process—consuming countries, other firms, other countries— whose actions may lead to a reshaping of the particular concession. As a planning model for investors and governments the static model is deceptive. It is a rare agreement of the post-1950 period that has not been altered at least once, or even several times, since.

Not only do individual agreements change over time, but new concessions may also differ dramatically from those negotiated for the same industry and in the same country in an earlier period. The forms and substance of oil contracts negotiated in the 1970s are, almost without exception, dramatically different from those negotiated in the 1950s. Differences are apparent for other mineral industries as well.

While we do not wish to exaggerate the need for a bargaining model to understand the concessions process, any analytical construct must incorporate three basic concepts: (1) the process of on-going negotiations over the life of the contract; (2) changing sets of rewards for each party; and (3) the interests and influence of parties other than the host country and the investing firm, whose influence is often felt only after the concession agreement has been negotiated. The essence of this model is change.

Some observers have characterized the changes that occur in the life of individual contracts and the changes within an industry from one contract negotiation to the next as "evolutionary" or "generational." In this view, oil contracts have usually been described as being a "generation ahead" of hard mineral and timber contracts. Frequently, the evolution has been characterized in terms of a movement from "concession to contract" (implying the development of more equitable contracts) and, for oil agreements, from "concession to service contracts." These characterizations do capture some sense of the nature of the changes that have typically occurred. Yet, for some industries, such a description overstates the changes that have occurred or that may take place. The economic and industry forces that affect concession arrangements vary considerably from industry to industry and from region to region. That agreements in a particular industry will move inexorably into another generational form is not necessarily the case. And, even where the change in contract form is real, the benefits accruing to one party or the other may not move in step with the changes in contract structure. A movement from a traditional concession arrangement to a service contract may not, in substantive terms, mean a significant shift in the allocative benefits. In terms of financial benefits or control, the host country can end up in a worse position under an equity-sharing or service contract arrangement than under the traditional form of agreement. An exploration of the relationship between form and benefits is the subject of the second chapter.

We prefer to limit the use of generational terminology to specific situations in specific countries. The Indonesian hard mineral agreements, for example, have generally been regarded as having moved through three "generations" since 1966.[2] The second generation of agreements has incorporated provisions regarded as more restrictive in terms of benefits for the investors than the first-generation contracts. The third-generation contracts are said to bear a similar relation to the second-generation contracts.

MUTUALITY OF INTERESTS: WINNING AND LOSING

In addition to adopting a dynamic bargaining model for concessions analysis, we discard the view that, on specific issues, one party necessarily "wins" or "loses"—particularly over the life of the contract. On specific issues today's loser may be tomorrow's winner. Or, there may be no winner or loser on specific issues; wins and losses may be shared.

The traditional conception of the concessions process is that of a zero-sum game in which two parties negotiate about the division of a fixed set of rewards. This view is one frequently adopted by company and host country negotiators and one that may lead to terms less beneficial to both parties than some alternative set of terms. Rather than seeing the concessions package as one in which the parties have certain mutual interests, a negotiator frequently sees each move by opposing negotiators as an attempt to undermine his rewards. In some cases the result is a breakdown in negotiations. In others, the firm may lose potential profits while the host country obtains less revenue than it could have gained. A company's position favoring an income tax to a royalty arrangement may, for example, have a sound and reasonable basis in light of the tax provisions operative in the company's home country. An appropriate tax arrangement that enables the company to receive tax credits at home may enable the company to have higher after-tax profits, even after an increased payment to the host government, than would some alternative arrangement. In such a case, both parties may benefit from a tax structure other than the one originally proposed.

Such problems are not easily solved until each side has a thorough understanding of the bargaining interests and position of the other party. In many instances an analysis of the economic interests and strengths must be reinforced with an understanding of the political and organizational forces at work in the private company or in the host country. Many negotiations have broken down not because the investor and host country no longer had a common interest in the agreement, but because one party was unable to adjust the politics or organization of his side to respond to the political or organizational drives of the other.

On the company side, negotiators have sometimes been unable to accept terms less favorable than previous investors received, not because the investment would no longer be attractive, but because the negotiator feared that he might lose his reputation within the company as a good bargainer. Similarly, departures from conventional concession arrangements, which would satisfy political needs in the host countries, have been rejected out-of-hand by companies, even though the economic effects of the novel provisions might be minimal.

Governments have not acted very differently. Host countries have on occasion been unwilling to make essential trade-offs. In one case we observed, the government was unwilling to relax its insistence on a joint venture relationship for a particular potential investor. Yet this form of doing business was inconsistent with the strategic needs of the firm. The firm was willing to give up its claim on tax holidays in exchange for the right to a wholly-owned subsidiary. The government refused to yield. After the breakdown of the negotiations, the government officials realized that they would have preferred the exchange to the loss of the investor, but had been unable to agree among themselves during the negotiations.

Often the inability to put together a satisfactory package on the government side is, as in the case just cited, the result of the conflicting interests and jurisdictions of various ministries concerned with the negotiations and a failure to perceive the parties' mutual interests.

Multimillion-dollar bargaining can be a heady business. Too often those involved in concession negotiations have become so fascinated with the process of international negotiation that they have failed to perceive or take into account economic and political realities. Bargaining becomes an end in itself. Yet economic and political factors act inexorably on the bargaining process. The negotiator who understands them well can often improve the outcome for his side. And the government or company that understands that economic, political, and other factors do not retain constant values, but change over the life of a mining agreement, can better defend its interests in the concessions process.

FACTORS INFLUENCING CHANGE

While we avoid labels such as "generational" and "evolutionary" in describing the changes that occur in concessions generally and within particular industries, some elements of change in concession arrangements are to an extent predictable. The bargaining powers that influence the concessions process appear to be influenced by three major factors, all influenced by a fourth: (1) the structure and evolution of the particular industry concerned; (2) the position and interests of a particular firm within the industry; and (3) the economic, political, bureaucratic, and social forces at work in the host country. Cutting across each of these factors is: (4) the relative negotiating and administrative skills of each party. If, for example, changes in one of the three major factors improves the bargaining power of the host government, these changes will be translated into revision of the concession arrangement only if the host government has sufficient technical competence to recognize that a critical change has taken place. It appears that Liberia's bargaining strength vis à vis a number of its concessionaires was substantial in the early 1960s, but this strength was not reflected in the agreements. Lacking a concessions unit to supervise and review concessions arrangements, Liberia did not undertake major revisions until the early 1970s. Negotiating skills took ten years to catch up with bargaining powers.

In most cases none of the four factors listed above remains constant over the life of a concession arrangement. The structure of the industry, or the firm's position in that industry, may change dramatically in the years following the signing of the original contract. In the host country the goals and skills of government policymakers and negotiators may change, often as a direct or indirect result of the increased income generated by the concession activities.

Revisions of contracts to reflect new bargaining powers and perceived interests have come, in some cases, with little rancor and fanfare; in other cases change has been accompanied by considerable acrimony and publicity. Much seems to depend on the extent to which both the investors and host countries have recognized the forces leading to change.

In many cases, once changes in any of the four basic factors are perceived, changes in bargaining powers and interests will be more clearly comprehended. For example, the demands for and eventual success of the oil-producing countries in obtaining equity participation in petroleum operations in the early 1970s should not have been surprising, given the changes that occurred in the oil industry in the 1960s. An analysis of the markets for metal-grade and calcine-grade bauxite can help to explain how Guyana was able to move from a rather traditional concession arrangement to a takeover of a major bauxite firm, while Jamaica was not able to accomplish the move in the same period. An understanding of the 1973-74 conflict over terms in the Bougainville copper arrangements, and a prediction of the likely results, could be achieved only through an understanding of the changes that have occurred in the copper industry and of the evolving political aspirations of the nation that was to emerge from the Territory of Papua and New Guinea.

As suggested above, changes in Liberian iron ore agreements have resulted from changes in industry factors, but only after there was an increased awareness on the government's part of its bargaining strengths and an increase in negotiating skills. The first iron ore concession was granted in 1945 to the Liberian Mining Company. The principal financial arrangement in that contract was a straight royalty based on a ton of ore. That agreement eventually evolved into an arrangement based primarily on an income tax. The 1960 Liberian American Company (LAMCO) agreement and the later (1967) agreement with Liberian Iron and Steel Corporation in the same country incorporated profit-sharing principles, but the government's take remained small. In the late 1960s steps were taken to reform existing contracts to establish a clearer delineation of the rights of the Liberian government and the obligations of the various companies. By 1973 a general review of iron ore concession arrangements was under way in Liberia with a view to increasing the benefits accruing to the government. The result was to be a further revision in the terms under which iron ore mining was to be undertaken in that country.

Although the direction of change within particular industries and within particular countries has generally favored the host government, there have been exceptions. Indonesia in 1966, after a decade or more of nationalization and rejection of foreign investment, reversed its policies and once again opened its doors to foreign companies interested in investing in oil, hard minerals, and timber. The early post-1966 agreements for mining may be regarded, on any impartial basis, as highly favorable to private investors, with provisions for extended tax holidays, low tax rates, and other investment incentives. Six years later, after the reestablishment of the country's favorable investment environment, concession terms were becoming slightly less liberal, again illustrating the more common movement toward terms that reflect the enhanced bargaining power of the host country as the strength of the private firms is gradually eroded. There have been cases of renegotiations that favored the company. Years ago in Malaya there were shifts in royalties to favor the private tin firms. Averell Harriman's manganese concession in the Soviet Union was renegotiated in his favor in 1927.[3] And in 1974 the Colombian government was considering a foreign mining firm's request to revise its contract to increase the firm's profitability.

Although the factors underlying the concessions process are not difficult to understand, they are frequently ignored. Many companies within various mineral resource industries have failed to monitor changes and take precautionary measures. Many have clung to the concept of "sanctity of contract" like ships' captains clinging to the helms of sinking vessels. Indeed, some companies fail to learn from their own experience. We have observed petroleum companies that have attempted to diversify into other industries as their bargaining power in oil declined. An intuitive understanding of what was happening to their position in the oil industry appeared to be insufficient to cause them to undertake a thorough analysis of developments in other industries. In a number of cases they have attempted to diversify into other mineral industries in which the position of foreign firms was being eroded equally rapidly, rather than selecting industries that promised some hope of counterbalancing their lost powers in oil.

A comparable disregard for the basic factors underlying the concessions process has led some countries to counterproductive policies. Eager to emulate

Zambia, Peru, and Chile, some copper-producing countries in weaker bargaining positions initiated steps that could prove very costly in terms of needed technology and capital in the future. Some parties in the Papua New Guinea (PNG) government, for example, urged a takeover of a significant portion of a major copper mine in early 1974.[4] A thorough analysis of industry structure and PNG's role in the industry suggested the need for less dramatic and less costly action until the country's bargaining position was stronger.

In the following pages we deal with the three factors that appear to be critical in the concessions process: industry structure; the interests of the company and its position within the industry; and the interests, strengths, and weaknesses of the host government. We deal briefly with the role of negotiating and administrative skills in the context of the host government's position, but we reserve a detailed discussion of this subject to Chapter 6.

The Industry Structure

One of the most important determinants of the outcome of the bargain that can be struck between the host government and the foreign firm is the structure of the particular industry that is involved. Where the organization of the industry is such that the country is dependent on a small number of firms that do not bid against each other for the development of its resource, the bargain is likely to be relatively favorable to the foreign enterprises. On the other hand, if the country can develop its resources itself or can turn to any of a large number of foreign firms for this task, the host government is likely to be in a better bargaining position than it is when the options are more limited.

The simple fact that the options available to a country vary considerably from industry to industry has often been overlooked. In some industries the barriers to the successful entry of new firms are substantial. In others it is relatively easy for the number of firms to swell, or for producing countries to enter the market even without the participation of foreign enterprises.

The number of options is usually limited where competing firms are kept out of the business because of the capital needs, the managerial and technological know-how, or the access to markets for the products that are controlled by firms already in the industry. These same factors can keep governments from developing profitably their own resources without foreign investors. And they limit the number of bidders for a particular project.

The capital needs are large for many mining operations. In most mineral projects, investment far exceeds $100 million. In some industries the sums required in the past have presented formidable barriers to a new firm or a government. However, by the 1960s, where the other resources were available, a potential new entrant, whether a private firm or a state development enterprise, could usually borrow the required capital. International institutions would sometimes lend for such development. And an increasing amount of mining investment was being financed on a project basis, without the guarantees of a private company from a developed country. Of course, a government might prefer to use its capital or credit for other purposes, especially since most mineral ventures are seen, at the outset, as being risky undertakings.[5] But the ultimate barrier to the local development of raw materials was proving only rarely to be capital by the late 1960s.

The requirements of managerial and technological know-how vary greatly by industry. For some mining operations the technology is simple. Little more is required than the ability to operate large shovels and to run a transportation system. Foreign managers and engineers can be hired for such operations if domestic resources are not available. Direct foreign investment is not necessary. But for other industries the managerial and technological skills are complicated and closely held by a few foreign enterprises. To acquire the skills the host country may have to accept direct investment, if that is the price the existing firms insist on imposing in exchange for their technology.

In the 1960s and 1970s the greatest barrier to domestic development of natural resources without foreign direct investment has probably been access to markets. Where sales of raw material must be made to a small number of foreign firms that have generated a vertically integrated structure and prefer to buy from their own captive sources, the host country is dependent on ties to foreign investors. Even where an independent market does exist in an industry characterized by vertical integration, it may be thin and subject to widely fluctuating prices that reflect only marginal supply and demand. In such a case the host country may see the market ties brought by the foreign company as a very valuable asset.

Certain conditions influence the importance of vertical integration in an industry. One stage in the processing of a particular product may be under the control of a small number of firms because of the large scale required for efficient operation or because of the technical skills required for that stage. In this case the firms that control the processing may be concerned about maintaining regular flows of quality supply into the processing facility. Concern is likely to be especially significant if the operation has high fixed costs and if the quality of the input is particularly important to the efficient running of the facilities. If there are many potential sources of supply, the firms that control the processing stage are not likely to try to control sources. But if there are few independent sources of satisfactory inputs, an individual firm will worry that its sources might be curtailed. The threat of a shortage is especially worrisome if a competitor begins to control sources of supply. In an industry where such fears are real, vertical integration—with attempts at "balancing" supplies and processing facilities—is likely to be the result.

The cases of coffee and aluminum provide illustrations of two resource-based industries in which the degree of vertical integration has been very different. In both instances, the processing stage (roasting for coffee, smelting for aluminum) has been relatively concentrated. This concentration has been perhaps somewhat more in aluminum, but even in coffee four companies have supposedly accounted for 80 percent of U.S. imports and sales. The strength of the major coffee firms has been based on access to final markets. Marketing operations require a large initial investment and a package of skills that is not easily put together. The strength of the major aluminum firms has been based both on the huge capital requirements needed to build a smelter and perhaps also on the availability of the technical know-how to a relatively few firms. But although both industries have been concentrated at the processing stage, they have differed dramatically in the degree of integration into the "extractive stage"—the growing of coffee or the mining of bauxite.

There are many independent sources of coffee beans in the world. Entry into coffee growing is easy; it can be done by farmers on a small scale. Many countries have the weather and soil needed to grow coffee. Moreover, an individual roaster needs coffee from several areas to obtain a properly blended mixture. In such a fractionated market there is little danger that an individual company in the processing business would be unable to buy coffee beans at a price similar to those that his competitors must pay. And should the roaster decide on vertical integration anyway, he would have to have several sources to obtain all the coffee types that he would want. There is little reason for him to proceed with such a complex strategy, since there is little threat of a shortage of beans that would put him at a disadvantage compared to his competitors.

Aluminum has provided a very different story. Bauxite, like coffee, has not been a significantly scarce commodity. But the development of a bauxite mine usually requires a substantial amount of capital both to remove overburden and to provide access roads and ports. The output from such an operation, if the mine is to be efficient, comes in large quantities, in contrast to the small scale on which coffee can be grown. So, relatively few sources of bauxite are likely to be developed at one time. To assure a steady supply of bauxite, aluminum companies have sought to control sources of mineral supply. An individual aluminum company with a smelter has been unwilling to depend on a small number of independent sources when most competitors have their own sources. The goal of the firm in such a case has generally been to reach something of a balance between sources and processing capacity. In such a market a country that chooses to develop its own deposits may find it difficult to sell its output to aluminum firms that have their own captive sources of bauxite.[6]

Such an analysis of industry structure is relatively simple and straightforward, although it has been done too infrequently by negotiators. The analysis is complicated, however, by the fact that most industry structures change. The trend in most instances is toward a weakening of the position of the foreign firms. Closely controlled oligopolies tend to break up as new firms gain the technology or access to markets.

As raw material industries mature, the most common pattern is a decline in the control that a particular foreign firm exercises. As the technology spreads, new firms enter the industry. As new entrants appear, the bargaining power of the host country usually increases. Unconstrained by commitments elsewhere, the new entrants may be willing to bid more than the established firms to gain access to raw materials, or they may be willing to buy from sources of materials that they do not control. Both possibilities open up new options for the developing countries with minerals to exploit.

Still other developments in particular industries have tended to strengthen the position of the host country in the bargaining process. The development may be a purely local one. Sometimes the need for the access to markets provided by the foreign firms has been lessened because of the growth of the local market. If the lack of access to foreign markets was the critical barrier before, the host country can now undertake the project alone. The growth of a local market in the 1960s seems, for example, to have influenced Peru in its decision to nationalize the International Petroleum Company. As Peruvian consumers began to absorb most of the petroleum output, the foreign firm was no longer essential. Discoveries of additional oil in the 1970s, however, changed the situation. This oil had to be exported from Peru. As a result, new invitations were extended to foreign investors. The strength of foreign firms was restored as their marketing inputs were again needed. With some assurance that their marketing contribution would leave them a number of years of profitable operations, foreign firms were again willing to enter Peru. This was true in spite of the unsettled International Petroleum Company case.

The change in relationships is not always simply a function of autonomous economic factors. Government policy can play a role in reducing the dependency of producing countries on foreign firms by weakening the hold of the traditional companies on the market. A few countries have attempted to short-circuit the foreign firm in the export marketing process by integrating forward into foreign markets themselves. An example is Iran, which in the 1960s concluded an agreement with India to construct an oil refinery there. With its own refinery in the final market, a producing country draws one more bargaining card from the hand of the foreign firm. No longer is the presence of the foreigner essential for access to the particular overseas market.

More complex was the proposal of Saudi Arabia to invest in oil facilities in the United States.[7] Such investment would guarantee an outlet for Saudi oil. But it would also provide the United States with a bargaining hostage if Saudi Arabia were to cut off oil to the United States or if Saudi Arabia were to nationalize American enterprises.

Even when the country is dependent on foreign investors and cannot develop its own resources, it has the option of delaying development of its resources until its own bargaining position has improved. The fact is, however, that greater benefits which might be available at a later time have rarely appeared attractive to a country with known mineral deposits. The analytical problem is not complex. It is to discount, at an appropriate rate, one stream of benefits that begin at a future date and another stream of benefits that begin now. The calculation (often not explicit) of most developing countries seems to result in favor of the earlier rewards.

The decision to develop now has also been based on the uncertainty of a future market for its resource in an age of rapidly developing product and resource substitution. The marketability of copper or oil from a particular source at one time may be far greater than the marketability of these resources twenty years hence. By the time Sierra Leone, for example, finally decided to exploit its Tonkolili iron-ore deposit, the project was no longer feasible because economically superior deposits in Africa and Australia had been discovered in the meantime.[8] While a resource that is already in the process of development may be able to compete with new technology or new finds elsewhere, an undeveloped resource may be unable to do so. Analysis in this context has often been influenced by simplistic catch-phrases. Raw materials are alternately "abundant," with declining terms of trade, or "scarce," with ever-increasing prices projected into the future. The short-term characterizations have usually turned out to be wrong for the medium term. Decisions to delay based on ever-rising prices often result in mines that begin to produce just about the time prices are depressed.

Uncertainty about markets may also take the form of uncertainty about the continuation of the current industry structure. Although the oligopolistic position of the firms generates more bargaining power for them in relation to the host country, the oligopoly may also serve as the basic support for high prices for the mineral products. It is possible, for example, that oil prices in the 1960s and 1970s would have been lower if the oil oligopoly, with its interest in stability and high prices, had broken down. The decline of the oligopoly in some mineral industries may mean that the country that waits to develop its resources will obtain a larger share in a financially smaller package in the future.

Given the uncertainties, it is not surprising that most countries have opted for the earlier returns instead of the possibly larger—but uncertain—returns at a later date.

Interests of the Company and its Position within the Industry

The interests of a particular firm are not necessarily identical to those of others in the industry. Host countries can profit from a careful analysis of the companies most likely to agree to favorable terms. Some firms have been more eager to gain access to additional resources than have others, and have consequently been willing to bid more. In industries in which control over sources of supply has been critical, managers have generally sought a balance between processing capacity and resource reserves. Firms that have a disproportionately large capacity for processing have generally been eager to expand their reserves of raw materials. To obtain reserves they have sometimes been willing to offer more to the host country than the firm with a greater degree of "vertical balance."

More important, generally, have been the firms that are just beginning to enter a particular industry. As an industry matures, firms outside the traditional oligopoly obtain the technology and know-how. Eager to obtain resources, they have sometimes been willing to offer more to the host country than the traditional enterprises. In fact, the terms accepted by new entrants have sometimes led to renegotiations of the contracts with the traditional enterprises.

In most cases the new entrant is not really a new firm. Generally it is an old firm from another industry that is diversifying into a new line. Relatively secure because of its other lines, such a firm is in a particularly good position to breach the norms that govern the behavior of the members of the oligopoly. Not dependent on the new raw material, it can undercut the traditional firms. The strategy of such a firm is different, for example, from that of Aluminium, Ltd. (ALCAN) in its negotiations with Guyana in the early 1970s. In that case, the firm appeared to fear that any yielding from traditional concession terms in Guyana would result in a domino effect in other countries in which ALCAN had bauxite activities. For the established firms, such fears have usually been overwhelming. The new entrant has no such fears.

There are numerous examples of the change of terms that may result from new entrants. The oil "independents" were often the first companies to break the solid front, when under pressure to renegotiate in countries such as Libya. Significant change was introduced in the realm of nickel agreements as Hanna entered Colombia in 1970. Hanna, already in nickel, was not, however, one of the major nickel producers. To gain access to sources in Colombia, it agreed to 50 percent voting power for the Instituto de Fomento Industrial, a Colombian government agency, although the agency's financial contribution was only 33 percent. The agreement called for reversion of the operation to the Colombian government after 25 years, and for access to the refinery for the output of the government's wholly-owned ferronickel deposits in the area. These were not provisions typical of nickel agreements at the time.

In some cases, where the project has appeared risky, firms that were outsiders to the oligopoly have not been willing to accept terms that departed significantly from contracts of a traditional nature, but have been willing to enter countries where established firms might not. The perceived risk may be associated with questionable political stability in the country or with the uncertain potential for the particular raw material in an unproved region. Both kinds of risk faced Freeport Sulphur when it expanded into the copper market as the first major U.S. firm to enter post-Sukarno Indonesia and as an early entrant into a new region for copper mining, Southeast Asia.

No matter what brings the new firm into the industry, its entry is likely to have a destabilizing effect in the industry. The result is usually a series of countermoves by the established enterprises. The entry of a new firm into an area in which the mineral has not been actively exploited in the past, as in the case of Freeport Sulphur in Indonesia, has often stimulated other firms to follow the new firm into the same area. The entry has in many cases resulted from fear that the outsider may find a particularly cheap source of raw material. It might be tempted to cut prices. If the traditional firms respond by moving into the same areas, they would be in a position to cut prices if necessary. The importance of a strategy of following other firms into a region has been well documented in a recent study of the investment of U.S.-based multinational enterprise.[9] Some countries have been successful in imposing on these later entrants terms that were tougher than those agreed to by the outsider.

Interests, Strengths, and Weaknesses of the Host Country

Host countries differ from one another as much as the firms do. Of major importance to the bargaining process have been the differences in the attractiveness of the raw material that they offer, their bargaining skills, and their politics.

The country evaluating its bargaining position has rarely neglected to consider the value of the raw material it offers and the comparative costs of developing the source. The country with high-grade ore located close to a port, for instance, usually recognizes that it is in a stronger position than a country with a low-grade ore that requires investment in transportation facilities.

The value of a mineral is, of course, a function of its scarcity, as well as of its quality and cost of extraction. Some minerals, like bauxite, seem to be abundant. Others, like high-grade copper, have been considered scarce. Governments have usually recognized scarcity value, but they have not usually noted the rapidity with which "scarce" minerals have sometimes become "common," as new technologies are developed to handle, economically, low-grade ores. In copper, the result of technological change has been the development of low-grade deposits in many countries that have not previously been copper producers. Some of these countries offered much more favorable terms to the investor than had become the norm in the traditional copper exporting nations. The scarcity value of high-grade copper was being challenged in the early 1970s.

Risk and uncertainty are additional significant factors. The country in a region of proven ores, for example, is in a stronger position than a country in which exploitation is new. The quality of the ore and the costs of development and extraction are easier for the private investor to forecast where the experience of others can be examined.

Similarly, the country that is perceived by the investor as being politically stable is generally in a better position than one that is viewed as politically risky. The investor who feels that his future is uncertain has tended to require a compensatory high rate of return, usually in the early years.

Host country experience and skill are also factors. Government negotiating skills differ according to their experience in dealing with concessions problems. The country with limited experience is usually at a serious disadvantage in its negotiations with foreign firms. The government may be unable to organize an effective bargaining team, its negotiators may not have sufficient information available, and its ministries may not be able to administer adequately the agreements that are reached.

Organization of the negotiating team has proved to be an important determinant of the outcome of mineral negotiations (see Chapter 6). Countries that have not had experience with concession negotiations have often had teams with frequently changing membership and no clear assignments of responsibility. The teams have not had access to critical data or to a staff of industry specialists on whom they could draw. On the other hand, the experienced countries have usually had well-organized negotiating teams supported by an accumulation of industry data, tax information, and local and foreign industry specialists. These specialists know the structure and interests of the industry and the terms of agreements negotiated by foreign firms for similar projects in other developing countries.

Although, at the outset, many governments have few skills in dealing with foreign investors, these skills may be brought in from outside or developed within the country. Obviously, experience helps the country. But experience is not always transferred from one government agency to another. We have served as advisors in one country where the state petroleum organization's extensive experience in negotiation had led to very sophisticated skills and personnel possessing a depth of understanding of the issues. Yet hard minerals agreements were being negotiated in the same country by a government ministry that could not, for political reasons, receive help from the state petroleum entity. The particular ministry was beginning as if the country had had almost no experience with the negotiation of mineral agreements.

Investment in improving skills generally begins as the government perceives the importance of the concessions. Usually this occurs when the taxes from raw materials represent a significant item on the income side of the government budget. Slowly, resources, in terms of money and skilled manpower, are assigned to the concessions problems. Again, our experience suggests that this reallocation of resources can occur far too slowly. In one country, a small number of concessions represented over 40 percent of the government's budget, yet no one was assigned to full-time administration of the agreements. We calculated that the government was missing several millions of dollars of collections that would have been identified through the most elementary improvements in administration of the existing agreements. Not only were the agreements not being adequately enforced, but the agreements had not kept pace with agreements in the same industry in other countries. No one was assigned the task of following the developments in the industry and in other countries so that the agreements could be kept up to date. It is clear that small investments in man-power could have yielded tremendous returns to the country.

Although expectations of increased income play a role, local political opposition is often the catalyst in inducing improved government procedures. It is perhaps significant that the country to which reference was just made was one with no active overt political opposition. In other countries, opposition parties or opposition elements within a single-party government typically criticize those in power when terms of concessions do not keep pace with those in other countries, or when administration is patently poor. Coups may bring changed attitudes toward existing investment agreements.

In addition, as an industry matures, cooperation among the producing countries sometimes plays an important role in providing newly entering countries with consultants and information about agreements in other countries. The Organization of Petroleum Exporting Countries (OPEC) has provided the most important example of a cooperative effort of producing countries to help each other. While there are other organizations with the potential for increasing access to information essential to effective negotiations, their influence, to date, has been relatively limited (see Chapter 7).

In some countries bargaining skills have been improved through the creation of state mining companies whose primary concerns are with particular minerals. Such firms have been able, in many cases, to give financial rewards and prestige to their employees, thus attracting qualified people willing to devote themselves to obtaining the knowledge required for dealing with the foreign firms. These people have been retained and their experience has been captured for future negotiations.

In certain cases state enterprises have been able to take over actual negotiations with the foreign firm. These enterprises have acquired skills that enable the government to begin to exercise management control over its resources. The development of self-confidence and skill within the ranks of government has occasionally permitted the total displacement of the foreign firm in the control of mining operations.

Countries may also differ in their need to offer attractive terms to gain initial acceptance in the market. A country newly entering a particular industry may negotiate agreements that are less favorable to the host country than agreements for the same mineral in other countries. In some cases this is due to the inexperience of the government with the particular industry; in others it reflects a strategy on the part of the host country of gaining access to markets and of attracting firms to an unproven area.

Host countries not only have different bargaining strengths and skills, but they differ in their willingness to take risks. As noted earlier the host country's decision to accept foreign investment is usually influenced by a preference for income that is virtually certain now, as opposed to income that is uncertain in the future. Yet some countries, motivated by strong nationalistic sentiments or by rational calculations, have been willing to accept future uncertainties in place of accepting direct foreign investment on the company's terms. In Guinea, for example, exploitation of that country's rich bauxite deposits at Sangaredi was long delayed because of President Touré's preference to leave the bauxite in the ground until he could get foreign companies to agree to the conditions that Guinea wanted.[10]

Some countries have taken risks by nationalizing foreign investors with the prospects, in the short run at least, of gaining fewer benefits than the previous situation offered. In 1971 Chile completed its nationalization of the Anaconda and Kennecott copper holdings in favor of its own development and marketing of the resource in the face of an uncertain capacity for such development and marketing. Iraq, in mid-1972, nationalized the holdings of a consortium of Western oil companies, Iraq Petroleum Company, with only hopes that it could market its production in the Soviet Union and elsewhere.

Yet policies of delay in exploiting a country's resources or policies of total nationalization in the face of substantial uncertainty are the exceptions rather than the rule. This is so despite the widely held sentiment in developing countries that they should exercise sovereignty over the development of their natural resources.[11] Because of the need for foreign skills, foreign capital, and access to markets, host country sovereignty usually takes such forms as profit-sharing, production-sharing, equity-sharing, and participation in decisionmaking, rather than total ownership and control, if the economic costs and the uncertainties of national raw material development are too high.

RENEGOTIATION AND REVISION

In most cases, shifts in bargaining powers result in renegotiations of agreements. The patterns are, of course, blurred by the fact that negotiations are carried out by complex organizations. Governments are influenced by political factors to institute change even when bargaining positions have not shifted dramatically. Political pressures can force the government to demand more than its bargaining strength and economic interests warrant. In some cases restructured agreements satisfy political forces without serious economic consequences. But too often the firms feel unable to accept radical changes in the agreements, even though the economic costs may be small.

In spite of the difficulties, change does occur. Although most agreements are written to cover periods varying from 15 to 99 years, an agreement rarely remains unmodified for more than a few years.

The disappearance of some of the initial uncertainties is often the trigger for renegotiation. When the possibility of the existence of a particular resource is first brought to light in a country, the government is generally willing to accept virtually any terms to induce some company to develop the resource. At the outset the government may feel that any return is better than nothing.

At the same time the firm may see substantial risk associated with the investment. To make the expected outcome worthwhile, the firm insists on favorable
concession terms.

As soon as a commercially valuable mineral is developed, the psychology of
the government is altered. The company may begin to enjoy a high return on
its investment. The government—or at least the government's political opposition—may begin to feel that the resource is virtually being given away. The
stage is set for renegotiation, as the original risks are forgotten. Usually the old
terms are modified and the parties adopt new terms that are more favorable
to the government than those agreed to under conditions of relative uncertainty.

The moves to renegotiate the Bougainville Copper Agreement in Papua New
Guinea in 1973 and 1974 illustrate the pattern. The original agreement, signed
in 1967, looked reasonable enough at the time, given the uncertainties associated
with a low-grade copper deposit, located in difficult terrain, in an unproved
region, and with a questionable structure for world prices. By late 1973 the
situation looked very different in light of high world copper prices, lower costs
of production than were anticipated, and moves by other copper companies
into the region. The political pressures for renegotiation were substantial in
1973, but became overwhelming in 1974 when the financial returns of the
mine indicated profits of close to 100 percent of equity. Renegotiation had
become inevitable; at issue was only the extent of the changes to be made.

Concession arrangements are affected not only by changes in the particular
industry, political and bureaucratic changes within the host country, and the
reduction of uncertainty as commercial deposits are identified, but also by
developments in other countries. The inappropriateness of the terms of a particular agreement usually becomes apparent when they are compared with terms
negotiated in more recent agreements in other countries, or even the same
country. Even though the situations of the various arrangements may differ,
strong pressure for renegotiation or updating results.

In some instances the renegotiation process is a relatively friendly one; in
others it is not. In one case with which we are familiar, the host country's president simply called in the chief officers of the foreign mining operation and
insisted that the terms of the agreement be modified. The "renegotiations"
received little public attention, perhaps because the terms were so obviously
out of line with the norms in the industry. In other cases the negotiations also
have been reasonably smooth. In Chad, legislation was passed in 1964 "inviting"
foreign investors to take the first step in renegotiating their agreements.[12] In
Zambia the copper firms were invited in 1969 to submit proposals for the
takeover of 51 percent of their shares.[13] Changes were instituted in these cases
with relative ease.

There is, of course, a danger that the political pressures inside the host
country will lead it to demand so much that the foreign firm will be driven
away, even when this is not in the country's interest. If the foreign company

is driven out too early, the host country may lose access to technology, management skills, or capital. More important, it may lose access to foreign markets.

THE CASE OF COPPER

The changes in agreements covering copper production provide an illustration of some of the general principles that underlie the concessions process. The evolution of agreements in traditional copper-producing areas—Zaire, Zambia, and Chile—has followed the basic pattern of evolution that has characterized many other industries.

In the copper industry the need on the part of the host countries for the foreign firms has declined, resulting in a stronger bargaining position on the part of government. Before the 1950s most of the smelting and refining capacity for copper was in the hands of a small number of international firms. In recent years somewhat more open markets for copper have developed as the technology has become more widely available and as the Japanese have become major buyers, with few captive sources. The importance of the growth of new firms is shown in the following data. In 1947, at the peak of concentration, the top four copper firms accounted for 60 percent of the free world production; and the top eight firms accounted for 77 percent. By 1966 the top four firms accounted for 41 percent and the top eight for 64 percent.[14] These percentages will, apparently, continue to fall as new mines, which were in the planning stage in the early 1970s, begin to produce for new entrants to the industry. These new entrants will include state-owned enterprises, which are gradually becoming significant in the copper industry. State copper-producing firms in Chile and Iran provide two examples.

The early copper agreements in the traditional copper-producing areas generally relied heavily on royalty as the primary source of government revenue. Zambia, for example, until 1969 still required a royalty of 13.5 percent of the value of a ton of ore above k16, a floor that was not important after World War II. The value was based on the London Metal Exchange average at the time of production.

After 1966 Zambia imposed an export tax of 40 percent of the value of the ore above another base line. This tax was designed to capture a significant portion of the "windfall" that accrued from high copper prices. An income tax was imposed at the rate of 45 percent on profits after royalty and export tax. In 1969 Zambia dropped her royalty provisions entirely and relied solely on income tax arrangements, which worked out to a tax rate of approximately 73 percent, with some provision for relief for operations that had low rates of return.

By 1970 the host governments in the traditional copper-producing areas held significant shares of equity in the larger mining operations. Zaire had already nationalized Union Minière and as a result faced attempts on the part of the major companies to boycott its copper. Eventually, Union Minière received a management and sales contract for 25 years to handle the Congo properties. But the arrangements were not to return to the traditional concession format.

In 1969 Zambia took over 51 percent of the ownership of its major mines. The Roan Selection Trust, following the takeover, received a 10-year management and sales contract. Under this contract, Roan Selection Trust received 0.75 percent of gross sales proceeds, 2 percent of consolidated profits (after deduction of expenditures and some taxes) an engineering and service fee of 3 percent of certain costs of projects, and a fee of 15 percent of first-year salary for personnel recruited by the management.[15]

In Chile, another traditional supplier, the evolution of arrangements was similar. Initial agreements based on small royalties were altered to incorporate taxes. In 1969 Chile began the takeover of equity in two major firms, Kennecott and Anaconda; a process that was completed in 1971.[16]

In 1972, seeing an uncertain future in the region, Cerro took the initiative by offering to sell its mining properties in Peru to the Peruvian government. In 1973 Peru announced the takeover of Cerro's properties. Thus, a major transformation in the traditional copper-producing areas was completed.

By the late 1960s the technology of large scale mining and of beneficiation had become sufficiently developed that private firms were interested in copper ores of lower grade than had previously appeared attractive. The result was that new areas could be opened for copper mining, areas that had not appeared as economic sources before the development of the new technology. In fact, the future was even more uncertain in light of the possibility that deep-sea mining would open still more sources. The movement toward new areas and sources was led by firms from outside the traditional group of copper producers.

Freeport Sulphur (later Freeport Minerals Corporation) entered Indonesia's West Irian under a contract whose terms reflected the opening of a new, high-risk area. While copper properties were being taxed more heavily or being nationalized in the traditional producing areas, Freeport was granted, under a traditional concession, a three-year income tax holiday and a concessionary tax rate of 35 percent for seven more years in Indonesia. The company was not subject to any royalty charges or other taxes, although it agreed to a floor payment of 5 percent of net sales during the seven-year period of low taxes. In effect, it was subject to a royalty that was credited for tax purposes. For the remaining period, Freeport was to be subject to a 41.75 percent rate, with a floor of 10 percent of net sales.

During the same period, Rio Tinto Zinc entered Bougainville, a part of the Papua New Guinea territory administered by Australia. Its contract terms also reflected the patterns in a new area, anxious to attract firms and to gain access to established markets. The Bougainville agreement granted the firm a three-year tax holiday and a carry-forward of capital expenses that, according to some analysts, meant at least a seven-year period free of taxes. The initial tax rate of 25 percent was to rise gradually to 50 percent and remain there until the twenty-sixth year. After the twenty-sixth year it was to rise slowly to 66 percent. The income tax applied to 80 percent of the income. In addition, a 1.25 percent royalty was imposed.

The entry of Freeport Sulphur into Indonesia stimulated the interest of some traditional copper firms. Kennecott, for example, negotiated a concession in the same general area within three years of the Freeport concession. The terms granted by Indonesia to Kennecott were slightly less liberal than those granted to Freeport, but were far from being as restrictive as those that by this time governed in the traditional copper countries of Central Africa and South America. Kennecott did not receive a tax holiday, although it was to pay a concessionary rate of income tax at 35 percent for the first ten years, after which the rate would rise to 42 percent. It did receive a liberal investment tax credit and the right to some unusual deductions in the calculation of its taxable income. It was to be subject to a royalty of approximately 3.6 percent of sales. To the extent that the terms were tougher than those imposed on Freeport, they were probably due partly to the pressure that Kennecott was under to establish a foothold in this new region. The terms were also influenced by the increased sophistication of the Indonesian government in the art of negotiation.

At the same time that the Kennecott and Bougainville agreements were being negotiated, new concessions were being granted in areas adjacent to the traditional sources of copper in Latin America and Africa. These new African and Latin American agreements included provisions more in line with the recent contracts of the old producers (such as Kennecott) in those regions than with the new contracts of new producers (such as Freeport) in Southeast Asia. The Overseas Mineral Resources Development Company (OMRD) of Japan, for example, negotiated a concession in Ecuador in 1970 that gave the government terms much more favorable than those that characterized the agreements in the newly developing region of Southeast Asia. OMRD received no concessions on tax rates; the laws of general applicability were to apply. On the other hand, the state was to receive 55 percent of net profits before taxes. It agreed to royalties that ranged between 7.5 and 18.5 percent, depending on the quality of the ore. The government could take its royalty in kind, if it so desired.

These terms are very different from those that OMRD was requesting from Malaysia in 1971 for a copper project that it was considering in Sabah, in the new Southeast Asian belt. For this project OMRD was asking for tax holidays that would extend for a number of years, and insisting on other terms much more favorable to itself than it had accepted in Ecuador.

No doubt the terms that govern copper mining in Southeast Asia will change as the major firms make commitments and as new supply patterns are established. In fact, the rumblings of change were already being heard in Bougainville by 1973, where the old uncertainties had been forgotten in the heady atmosphere of the high current profits being generated by the mine. By 1974 those renegotiations had been completed. The new terms eliminated the exemption of 20 percent of the income from tax, the tax holidays, and much of the special provisions for writing off capital costs. Income tax would be imposed at a rate of 33 1/3 percent on profits, up to the point the firm earns a 15 percent return (after taxes) on capital. Beyond that, the marginal rate would rise to 70 percent.[17] Although renegotiation of the terms for many contracts in the copper belt on the Western Pacific is to be expected, terms in the region will probably lag behind those of the traditional copper belts for a number of years.

PROCESS AND CONTRACT

We have argued for a view of the concession as a process in which the bargaining powers and interests of the parties change over time. The change in these bargaining relationships may be due to changes in industry structure, the firm's position in the industry, the political, social, and economic aspirations of the host government, or the negotiating and administrative skills of both parties. In fact, we will conclude in the final chapter that the appropriate model for the future must also take into account the actions of third parties. Producing countries are banding together and consuming countries are taking a more active hand in negotiations.

No matter what the number of parties, the underlying factors affecting the contract appear to be changing in many industries. This fact has significant implications for the conceptualization of a concession agreement as a contractual undertaking. One must, perhaps, begin with the view that where there are substantial uncertainties at the outset concerning the quality of the resource, the prices to be received, and the costs to be incurred, it may be impossible in most instances to negotiate an agreement other than one that may, in retrospect, appear to "favor" the investor. Many of the uncertainties are typically resolved in the period of a few years. If the investor's worst fears turn out to have been justified, then the agreement may remain unchanged. If, on the other hand, the project proves to have a cost and price structure more favorable to the investor than was anticipated at the outset, the terms of the original agreement may turn out to be untenable.

In a world of changing bargaining positions and uncertainties, one feels uncomfortable talking about the "law" of concession arrangements. Whatever the law has been thought to be, the practice is clear: concession contracts have been constantly altered. Economic, political, and social factors have become more potent than legal factors in determining the viability and shape of concession arrangements. It is primarily to these factors, rather than to the legal document, that the businessman must turn if he is to grasp the likely nature of his relationship to his host government.

Finally, there are many examples of "renegotiations" in which changes have occurred more in form than in economic substance. These changes have responded to political and organizational needs of the host country, with little real cost to the foreign investor. In these cases the contract has not been desanctified but simply reshaped. This process is often misunderstood. The assumption of 51 percent equity interest by Zambia in two major copper companies in the late 1960s was widely viewed as a "partial expropriation." Yet close analysis reveals that the investors may have been left in about the same, or a somewhat better, financial position than before the change. The next chapter explores the relationship between form and substance of various concession arrangements.

NOTES

1. See "Declaration on the Establishment of a New Economic Order," Resolution adopted by the Sixth Special Session of the U.N. General Assembly (A/RES/3201 (S-VI), May 9, 1974).

2. See "Government Takes Tough Line on Mineral Development," *The Times* (London), August 17, 1974, special supplement, III.

3. Mira Wilkins, *The Maturing of Multinational Enterprise* (Cambridge: Harvard University Press, 1974), p. 107.

4. "Call for P.N.G. Control of Bougainville Copper," Press Release (Port Moresby), February 4, 1974.

5. In 1973 the U.N. Economic and Social Council recommended the establishment of a Revolving Fund to assist developing countries in natural resource exploration. See Economic and Social Council Resolution 1762 (LIV), of May 18, 1973, and U.N. General Assembly Resolution 3167 (XXVIII), December 17, 1973 reported in *International Legal Materials* 13 (January 1974): 236.

6. There are three tiers in the "balance": (1) bauxite production; (2) alumina production; and (3) aluminum production. (Alumina is the processed bauxite fed into an aluminum smelter.) For a description of Ghana's recent predicament in balancing bauxite production and aluminum production, see "Boom for Ghana's Bauxite?" *West Africa,* June 3, 1974, pp. 654–655.

7. "U.S. Studying Saudi Plan for Oil Investments Here," *New York Times,* October 3, 1972, p. 61.

8. Andrew Kamarck, *The Economics of African Development* (rev. ed.; New York: Praeger, 1971), p. 175.

9. Frederick T. Knickerbocker, *Oligopolistic Reaction and Multinational Enterprise* (Boston: Harvard Business School Division of Research, 1973).

10. See "Guineans Slowly Taking Steps to Develop the Nation's Wealth," *New York Times,* June 11, 1972, p. 4.

11. See U.N. General Assembly Resolution No. 1803 (XVII), December 14, 1962 and U.N. General Assembly Resolution No. 3171 (XXVIII), December 17, 1973, reported in *International Legal Materials,* Vol. 13 (January 1974): 238.

12. Chad, *Investment Code of the Republic of Chad* (Decree No. 156/PR), reprinted in *International Legal Materials* 3 (January 1964): 24.

13. Mark Bostock and Charles Harvey, eds., *Economic Independence and Zambian Copper: A Case Study of Foreign Investment* (New York: Praeger, 1972), pp. 145 ff.

14. Zuhayr Mikdashi, *Natural Resource Industries and the New Economic Order* (Ithaca: Cornell U. Press, forthcoming).

15. Mark Bostock and Charles Harvey, eds., op. cit., Appendix A, pp. 230–231.

16. For a valuable summary of the background of the takeover in Chile, see R. Mikesell, "Conflict and Accommodation in Chilean Copper" and Markos Mamalakis, "Contribution of Copper to Chilean Economic Development, 1920–67," in Raymond F. Mikesell, *Foreign Investment in the Petroleum and Mineral Industries* (Baltimore: The Johns Hopkins Press, 1971); in addition, see Theodore H. Moran, *Multinational Corporations and the Politics of Dependence: Copper in Chile* (Princeton, N.J.: Princeton University Press, 1974).

17. The actual agreement was much more complex than this typical summary. A tedious algebraic formula purported to take into account changes in capital and exchange rates. There were provisions for a transition year as well. See "Heads of Agreement for Variation of the Agreement of 6th June 1967 between the Government of Papua New Guinea and Bougainville Copper Limited," Port Moresby, 1974.

Chapter Two

The Agreements: Structures and Substance

Arrangements between foreign investors and host countries for the development of natural resources have carried many names: concession agreement; economic development agreement; service contract; work contract; joint venture contract; production-sharing agreement; and, most recently, participation agreement. Occasionally, within particular countries, the distinctions in terminology are significant in differentiating various forms of arrangements.[1] In other instances, varying terminologies relate to agreements of essentially the same nature. In still other cases the same terminology has been utilized in one country for agreements that are, in substance, quite different from each other.[2]

In many cases the choices of terminology and form reflect political considerations. A developing country may find more acceptable over the long run an agreement characterized as a work contract that provides—as the Indonesian Kennecott Copper Work Contract[3] did—that "all mineral resources contained in the territories of the Republic of Indonesia . . . are the national wealth of the Indonesian nation [and that] Kennecott shall be, and hereby is appointed, the sole contractor for the Government with respect to the Contract Area,"[4] than it would an agreement characterized as a concession agreement that provides—as the Liberian Gewerkschaft Exploration Concession Agreement[5] did— that "the Government . . . grants to the Concessionaire . . . the exclusive right and privilege to . . . exploit deposits of all kinds of ores. . . ."[6]

Aside from the possible implications for calculating compensation in the case of nationalization,[7] the differences between the Liberian agreement and the Indonesian contract are largely of terminology and of the point at which

A modified version of this chapter appeared in the *American Journal of International Law* 69 (July 1975): 560–590.

title to the resource passes to the investor. But choice of terminology may be crucial to a country's sense of sovereignty and control.

Contract provisions may differ substantially in terms of economic significance. The economic implications of agreements can be compared by projecting cash flows under alternative assumptions about the future and discounting these flows to a present value.[8] Yet the political and psychological issues are, in most cases, of overriding importance in the selection of a particular form of agreement.

Although the terminology is often confusing and inconsistent, it is possible to discern regularities in the various forms of arrangements that accord with a host country's bargaining power and negotiating skills, differences in the structures ·of various industries, and the interests of the particular company. Within certain countries and within certain industries, one can observe the influence of changes in relative bargaining powers. The pattern is frequently a shift from traditional concession agreements, in which the terms were primarily financial, to forms in which the government reserves to itself substantial participation in and control over the venture.

An examination of the major types of agreements provides a framework for understanding some of the complex technical and strategic problems faced by both parties, as well as some of the approaches commonly employed to achieve accommodation to the political and financial needs of the parties. For analytical convenience we have classified agreements under the following three rubrics: (1) the *traditional concession;* (2) the *modern concession;* and (3) *production-sharing, service,* and *work contracts.*

MINING CODES AND AD HOC AGREEMENTS

The terms governing the relationships between a foreign investor in minerals development and the government of a developing country are usually set forth in *ad hoc* arrangements. Although mineral-producing countries usually have general mining codes, foreign investment laws, and general income tax codes, these laws often allow government officials considerable latitude in shaping individual concession arrangements to fit the particular circumstances.

Many mining codes establish a general framework within which mineral contracts are negotiated. The 1971 Peruvian General Mining Law, for example, dealt with such basic problems as affirmation of state ownership of minerals, the granting of prospecting and exploration permits, the role of the state in mining operations, tax rates, the roles of various government agencies in granting and supervising concessions, and welfare and security of mine workers. The Law also set forth detailed provisions relating to such subjects as causes for lapsing or revocation of a concession and fines to be imposed for certain transgressions.[9] These matters are set forth at length in some individual agreements, but they seldom need special treatment. Their inclusion in a general mining code reduces the scope for bargaining, and standardization may make them easier for the host government to enforce. Moreover, their presence in the general laws tends to keep them from surfacing as terms to be modified if negotiations are reopened.

In petroleum, where governments have had considerable experience to draw upon and where many of the terms have become standard, less flexibility is evident in the negotiation of specific contracts than is typical of hard minerals. The Libyan Petroleum Law of 1955, for example, includes a standard form of concession that must be used for all oil concessionaires in the country. However, even for petroleum there are exceptions. The Indonesian Petroleum Law of 1960 (which governed oil contracts into the 1970s) nowhere specified the contents of petroleum contracts. Indeed, the production-sharing contract—the form of agreement used in Indonesia—was not mentioned in the 1960 law.

In general, *ad hoc* agreements for the exploitation of minerals in developing countries cover a wide range of issues, usually including such matters as taxation, import and export regulation, employment policy and conditions, management structure, exchange control, company and state rights and obligations, and infrastructure. Many concession agreements are an expression of virtually all the laws that will govern the company's operations in the country.

In the advanced countries one rarely finds comprehensive agreements of the type found in the developing nations. In the industrialized countries the mining firms are usually subject to the general laws of the land; only a few narrow issues may be handled on a company-by-company basis.[10] But there are significant reasons why most developing countries rely heavily on *ad hoc* arrangements: the special nature of the multinational company; the major role that the foreign extractive company typically plays in the general economic development of the country; and the legal tradition of the nation.

The multinational enterprise brings a bundle of problems that are usually inadequately covered by the legal system of the developing country. For example, transfer pricing among affiliated entities in different countries creates difficulties for tax and exchange control authorities. The income tax laws and exchange regulations in many developing countries were designed solely to govern locally-owned business operations; they simply do not contain the principles and regulations required to handle transactions among affiliated companies. Most host countries have not had the need or the resources to draft general comprehensive mining, income tax, and company laws appropriate for regulating the multinational enterprise. *Ad hoc* arrangements provide a way of handling the problems.

The importance of mining activities in many developing countries provides an additional incentive for *ad hoc* arrangements. The operation of the foreign extractive enterprise frequently occupies a major role in national budgetary planning. In Zambia 46 percent of gross domestic product in 1969 was attributable to a few large mining firms. In Liberia the income from four concession operations accounted for almost 65 percent of income tax revenue in 1968. In such a situation, general legislative approaches to govern the terms of mineral firms are not particularly attractive to government officials when a few agreements can be tailored directly to the circumstances. On the other hand, where the individual mine is relatively small, as in Bolivia, *ad hoc* agreements typically play a smaller role.

The legal traditions of many host countries do not favor comprehensive codes for mining. Rather, the tradition may be one of reliance on regulations and administrative decrees within a system in which general laws provide only broad guidelines. In some instances, the *ad hoc* concession agreement plays the role of a specific administrative regulation that elaborates a general law's policy directives.

It is not only the host government that may favor *ad hoc* agreements. Many foreign investors themselves seek such agreements to decrease the uncertainty of the investment. Unsure whether the political process in the host country is such that the general laws will develop in reasonable ways, investors turn to agreements whose terms will be fixed over a long time period. The result is that investors seek greater guarantees of stability in developing countries than they would dare hope for in similar projects in advanced countries. In the late 1960s, for example, Australian and British investors negotiated an *ad hoc* arrangement in the Australian territory of Papua New Guinea (for the Bougainville copper project) even though the general laws in Papua New Guinea were similar to those of Australia, in which they already had operations. Although the Bougainville agreement did provide certain important tax advantages not available under the general laws, one of its principal features was to freeze the general tax provisions in their status at the time the agreement was reached. As a result, a few years later the company was operating under a more favorable tax regime in Papua New Guinea than it faced in Australia. Both governments had changed their taxation of mining operations, but in Australia the company was subject to the changes, while in Papua New Guinea the *ad hoc* agreement froze the tax levies applicable to the project.

A few developing countries have tried to avoid *ad hoc* contracts, but their success has been limited. Faced with a major investment most countries, Bolivia included, usually revert to individual negotiations. The economic and political consequences are too important to be left to general laws that may not cover the situation adequately. Malaysia, like Bolivia, has long relied on general legislation to govern most of the conditions for small tin investments. When the prospects of a large copper development appeared in 1970, however, the government made sure that special negotiations were conducted, and that the federal government, not the state government (as in the case of tin), represented the nation.

Although there have been few successful efforts to abandon entirely arrangements that are tailored to a particular enterprise, in most countries the investor has been subject to general laws that govern a progressively wider area of activities. The host government may specify in its general legislation the tax regime, labor laws, and other terms to govern investment in a particular sector. This trend may be reinforced as foreign investors increasingly recognize that *ad hoc* arrangements do not provide the long-term guarantee that they purport to give. A few investors have begun to prefer general legislation to *ad hoc* contracts. The general legislation may, in practice, give more certainty than *ad hoc* contracts that purport to be binding for fifteen or more years, but which in reality are changed as bargaining powers shift. In fact, by 1975 in a few countries the only area of significant bargaining concerned equity participation. With most of the terms fixed by law, including tax provisions, participation in ownership becomes the principal vehicle for the parties to strike a bargain that reflects their relative bargaining powers.

THE TRADITIONAL CONCESSION

Agreements between foreign companies and host governments in the first half of the twentieth century were generally recorded in simple documents in which the concessionaire was given almost unrestricted rights in exploiting one or more natural resources. The concessionaire was typically granted extensive rights over a very large land area, often much larger than an investor could be expected to develop within a reasonable period.[11] The period of the contract was, however, seldom reasonable: in many the terms were to run for fifty or sixty years or more.[12]

Royalties as the Initial Basis for Calculating
Financial Obligations

The financial (and other) obligations imposed on investors in those early contracts were generally limited. Contracts negotiated from the turn of the century through the 1940s normally required the concessionaries to make payments based on the number of physical units of output or the value of output from particular mines. Although these royalty payments accounted for by far the greatest portion of government revenues from the concession, a nominal land tax was also usually imposed on the area under the concessionaire's control.[13]

Many of the earliest concession agreements called for royalties based on volume of output, rather than on value. Oil agreements illustrate the pattern. From 1900 to 1950 most oil concessions relied on the payment of royalties based on the tonnage of crude oil produced. A few attempts to collect income taxes were made early in the history of oil concessions, but they were abortive. The 1920 agreement between the Persian government and the Anglo-Persian Oil Company called for an income tax on the worldwide income of the enterprise, excluding only profits arising from transportation of the oil.[14] The experiment was premature and short-lived, and the contracting parties reverted to royalty arrangements. The Iraqi agreement with the Khanaqin Oil Company in 1926 provides a more typical example of an oil contract of that era. It called for payment of four gold shillings per ton of net crude oil produced and saved.[15] In another case the 1949 agreement between the Saudi Arabian Government and Getty Oil provided for a royalty of U.S. 55¢ per barrel.[16]

Iron ore, timber, and even plantation agreements in developing countries followed patterns similar to that of oil. The original (1945) agreement between the government of Liberia and the Liberian Mining Company, Ltd. (LMC) provided for a basic royalty of 5¢ per ton on all iron ore shipped.[17] Timber agreements, in the same pattern, normally called for a stumpage fee based on certain units of output.[18] And the United Fruit Company paid 1¢ per stem for bananas harvested in its fields.[19]

Many later agreements in such industries abandoned the fixed cash royalties in favor of royalties based on a percentage of the export price of the resource.[20] The LMC agreement in Liberia combined the fixed payment per unit of ore with a royalty that was based on the value of the ore. It provided that if, in any year, the average price of pig iron were to be more than 115 percent of the average price of pig iron for the prior ten years, an additional royalty was to be paid by the producing firm.[21] Similarly, timber and plantation arrangements have become more complex in many countries.[22]

Compared to income tax arrangements, profit-sharing contracts, and production-sharing agreements of more recent vintage, these early concession agreements have two distinct advantages for the host government. First, the royalty payment is a particularly easy type of levy to administer. To collect a tax based on units of output, the government need only have a physical count of the volume of production or shipments made by the concessionaire. Second, the royalty seems to guarantee a certain payment to the government for the depleted resources irrespective of the company's profits and the world market price for the resource. As long as there is production or sales, the government should receive revenue. This feature has its attractions to a government worried about the stability of its revenues.

In spite of the advantages of royalty arrangements, it was a rare concession agreement by the late 1960s that relied entirely on royalties as the source of payment to the host government. There were indeed some agreements, such as that governing Le Nickel in New Caledonia, which still depended on royalties in 1974. However, the major disadvantages of royalties led to a dramatic increase in the importance of other kinds of levies.

Increasing Importance of Income Taxation

By the 1950s the concept of taxation of concession income had gained general acceptance in the arrangements between oil companies and their host governments. The levy on income was implemented either through a direct income tax, frequently at a rate of 50 percent, or through a sharing-of-profits arranged in a way that made it roughly equivalent to an income tax.[23]

The shift from royalty to income tax in oil is well illustrated by the figures for Venezuela. Table 2-1 shows that the portion of government revenue accounted for by income tax increased dramatically, at the expense of royalties, during the post-World War II period. The same kind of evolution has occurred, although more slowly, in other extractive industries.

In oil, hard minerals, timber, and plantations, the shift from royalty to income tax has taken place in two ways. First, existing agreements have been amended, either to substitute income taxation for royalty payments or to supplement royalties with levies on income. Second, new agreements negotiated in the 1950s and later have incorporated income tax or profit-sharing principles as the primary source of government revenue.

The Liberian Mining Company (LMC) Agreement, one of our previous examples of a royalty-based agreement, illustrates the changes that have taken place. That arrangement has moved from one relying on royalty to one relying on income taxation as the source of government revenue. The original agreement, which provided for a fixed basic royalty and a supplementary royalty based on price, was changed by a 1952 collateral agreement, in which LMC agreed to the government's "participation in profits" after a certain point.[24] Participation was to begin when LMC had liquidated its debts and had brought its "recovery of investment" to $4 million, or by 1957, whichever came first. For the first five years from that date the government was to receive 25 percent of profits. During the next ten years it was to receive 35 percent of profits. Thereafter it was to receive 50 percent of profits.[25] The income tax was to supplement the royalty payments, which would continue. In 1965 the basic agreement was further amended to provide that the 50 percent par-

Table 2-1. Percentage of Venezuelan Government Revenues from Foreign Petroleum Firms that Came from Various Levies

Year	Royalty	Income Tax	Surface Tax	Customs	Other	Total
1938–1940	58.9%	0.0%	15.7%	21.7%	3.7%	100%
1941–1945	60.0	7.5	13.4	16.2	2.9	100
1946–1950	54.9	30.7	3.5	7.7	3.2	100
1951–1955	54.5	34.3	2.1	4.4	4.7	100
1956–1960	52.8	40.7	1.1	2.4	2.9	100
1961–1965	50.0	46.7	0.5	0.6	2.3	100

Source: K. Georg Gabriel, *The Gains to the Local Economy from the Foreign-Owned Primary Export Industry: The Case of Oil in Venezuela,* unpublished D.B.A. thesis, Harvard Business School, May 1967, p. 92.

ticipation rate would take effect as of January 1, 1965, and participation was to be in lieu of royalty payments.[26]

Although in most agreements income tax became the principal source of revenue, royalties by no means disappeared. Even with an income tax, royalties could serve the purpose of assuring the government of a minimum payment for the extraction of the resources when low prices led to little or no profits. For example, the structure of the Indonesian Kennecott agreement in West Irian in the early 1970s guaranteed that the government would receive a royalty of 3.6 percent on copper production, even if low prices were to lead to low taxable profits. Across the border in Papua New Guinea, the higher income tax rates of the Bougainville arrangement promised the government more when profits were high, but the low royalty rate could leave the government in an unfavorable position should profits turn out to be low.

In governments with federal systems, royalties have sometimes been retained as a payment to states or provinces, with the income tax going to the federal government.[a] In some cases a royalty that is progressive with the prices of the mineral has been designed to capture for the government a substantial portion of the windfall profits when prices are high. Malaya, and later Malaysia, for example, had complex royalties for tin that were designed for this purpose. In 1973 a similar royalty was being proposed in British Columbia to apply to all mining in that province.

The imposition of income taxes has resulted in a significant increase in the burden on the administrative capacity of host governments. To assess income tax, governments must be able to verify the sales prices of the resource and the calculation of deductions for expenses that are charged against gross income.[b] In many cases the transactions that led to the income or expenses have been with entities affiliated with the foreign investor. In those cases the firm might use prices other than those which would have resulted from transactions between non-related parties, or it might utilize other techniques to shift profits from one tax jurisdiction to another. The administrative machinery of many host countries would simply have been unable to deal with these problems in the first half of this century. Most governments were still struggling to obtain adequate administrative capability in the mid-1970s. The administrative problems that result from the shift to income taxes have been recognized repeatedly. In a study undertaken in the mid-1950s, for example, the difficulty in income tax administration was mentioned explicitly as a major reason for retaining the per-unit stumpage fee for timber concessions in Ghana.[27] In the early 1970s, one government consultant recommended royalties as the only tax for the proposed Asahan smelter in Sumatra, in recognition of the administrative problems Indonesia would have with an income tax on an operation primarily

---

[a]This is the case in Malaysia and Canada, for example.

[b]An exception to this is the situation where, as has been the case in petroleum, a posted price is used.

involving transactions among affiliated companies. In 1974 an official from Guyana claimed that Reynolds Aluminum had so set its transfer prices that it had never shown a profit on bauxite mined in that country. The tax on income had produced no revenue beyond a minimum sum that applied no matter what profits were reported.[28]

With the difficulties involved in the administration of income tax arrangements it is little wonder that many governments have been initially disappointed in their receipts from the tax. In one case we calculated that inability (or unwillingness) to administer properly the complex tax provisions of an agreement was costing the host government at least 35 percent of what seemed to be due under the terms of the arrangement.

The shift away from royalties to some form of income taxation has, however, been based on a realistic perception of the level of payments that the host government can collect under the two types of levy. One problem concerns the floor on payments that the royalty is supposed to provide. Although the per-unit royalty purports to guarantee the government a minimum level of income on its resources, in practice royalties have from time to time not been collected from companies that were not profitable. This has been the case for Zambian copper and for Malaysian tin, for example. Another difficulty has been in the level of revenue that could be collected. In practice, royalties have seldom represented a significant portion of actual company profits. It is clear that firms have been reluctant to take on heavy royalties. From the company's point of view, a commitment to a large royalty, particularly in the early years of an extractive operation, is potentially dangerous. At the outset the firm faces a great deal of uncertainty about whether it will be able to extract the natural resource profitably. The cost of the royalty represents to the firm an additional cost of extraction, one that will be incurred whether the project is profitable or not. On the other hand, a commitment to pay an income tax on profits if they do materialize appears less risky. If there are no profits, there is no obligation for the company to pay tax to the host government. Under a pure income tax arrangement the firm incurs significant obligations only if profits are high. With a desire to avoid risk, the foreign firms have usually been willing to agree to an income tax that, if the expected level of profits results, would be larger than any payments that would be agreeable under a royalty arrangement.

Although royalties had generally declined in importance by the early 1970s, the pace of decline was uneven. Indeed it was not certain that the days of royalty were numbered. In the case of oil, tax arrangements had reverted to something similar to royalty arrangements. The posted price had become the basis of calculation of profits in most agreements, and this price itself had become a subject of negotiation. In those countries where the expenses that could be deducted in calculating income tax were limited to a percentage of the value of the output, the income tax became, essentially, a large royalty if expenses exceeded the stated limit. In oil the effective royalty appeared to be short-lived. Late in 1973 the move was again in the other direction as oil producing countries began to tie the posted price to the market price plus an increment. By 1975 changes were placing the oil companies more in the position of service contractors than in the role of tax or royalty payers.

In an oligopolistic industry such as oil, large royalties could be tolerable for the companies. Periodic falls in price were hardly the threat that they represented in, say, copper, so profit levels seemed to be more predictable for the producing companies. Moreover, the form the effective royalty took enabled it to qualify as an income tax for tax credits in the home countries of the oil firms. Where profits are predictable—especially because of a tight oligopoly—and where the royalty could generate tax credits, the ease of administration provided by royalty arrangements could once again make them an attractive form of taxation.

Other Changes

The general shift from royalties to income taxation as the primary source of government revenue was probably the most significant change in the early development of concession agreements. But there were many other changes. The later agreements usually included a number of terms that were designed to bring benefits other than revenue to the host country.

The host government generally considered it important to introduce into the agreements, or into the general laws of the country, provisions that were designed to promote linkages between the extractive operation and the rest of the economy. As host countries perceived the possibilities of using the foreign firm more fully to promote local development, they sought ways to influence the actions of the firm.

Requirements that a project purchase goods of local manufacture and provisions that the company must hire and train local citizens were incorporated in a large number of arrangements. Clauses from this kind of agreement required the foreign company to guarantee access for local users to such infrastructure as roads, railroads, and communications systems. Provisions were made for the concessionaire to build and operate schools, hospitals, and other services for the company's local workers. The foreign firm was sometimes encouraged or required to contribute funds and talent to local community development or to educational, agricultural, or technical institutions.

At the same time, rudiments of general labor and mining codes appeared, either in the agreements or in the general laws of the host country. *Ad hoc* agreements or the mining laws would specify such matters as the minimum grades of ore that must be mined and the quality of timber that must be harvested. Safety and pollution standards were introduced, though frequently in vague language and with little provision for enforcement.

The terms of agreements, furthermore, typically gave some attention to the rights of third parties. These included, for example, the rights of local residents to payment for land that was taken for the concession, and to access to traditional timber sources, agricultural land, water sources, and sacred sites.

Advantages of the Traditional Concession

With modifications in taxation and linkage provisions, the traditional form of concession agreement has survived into the 1970s in many countries and for many industries. The original Bougainville agreement and some of the concessions for hard minerals negotiated in Indonesia in the late 1960s were, for example, similar in format and substance to hard mineral agreements negotiated elsewhere in the 1940s and 1950s.

There is much to be said for the traditional form of concession. The agreements are often less complicated and may therefore be easier to administer than some of the newer forms of agreement. The income tax provisions, if well-conceived and well-drafted, can be relatively straightforward. A country with a weak income tax administration or without a sophisticated governmental body to police an agreement might well prefer a traditional agreement, which raises minimal administrative problems, to one that is so complex that the governmental machinery simply cannot cope with its administration. Government income might well be higher when complex, though purportedly more favorable, financial arrangements are avoided.[29]

Nevertheless, many developing countries have been under pressure to break away from the traditional form of agreement. The pressure has usually been: (1) for increased government participation in the ownership of the enterprise; and (2) for an increased governmental role in the management of the extractive operation. The result has been agreements that differ significantly in structure from the traditional concession arrangements. In most cases they have been more complex.

THE MODERN CONCESSION

Equity-Sharing

In the late 1960s and early 1970s there was a rapid increase in the number of agreements that provided for some local participation in the ownership of the extracting firm. Major participation has usually meant ownership of shares by the host government. The most publicized cases of participation were in petroleum. In the major oil-producing nations, negotiations in the early 1970s led to agreements under which government participation in a number of operating companies was scheduled to reach 51 percent by 1983. This timetable has already been accelerated in a number of countries. Although public awareness of participation was created by oil in the 1970s, the trend had started earlier and was not limited to petroleum.

Equity-sharing, or "participation," may or may not bring the government an effective voice in management decisions within the operating company, and may or may not mean that the government plays an active role in other activities leading to the ultimate disposal of the resource. The concept of participation as it has been developed in the oil industry has been characterized as "pseudo-participation," since it does not assume that the host country produces, refines, or sells the oil. Rather, participation was criticized by one observer simply as "an ingenious way of further increasing the tax per barrel without touching either posted prices or nominal tax rates."[30] But ownership itself has political appeal to governments, even when actual participation in management may be minimal. Many mechanisms have been devised to bring about political benefits of joint ownership.

One form of equity-sharing agreement is that in which the government obtains equity interest without a financial contribution, but in exchange for all or part of its right to levy an income tax. The economic advantages to the host country of such an arrangement are not always self-evident. Some government negotiators have believed that an exchange of the right to impose, say, a 50 percent income tax for 50 percent of the equity is an even exchange. It often is not. In general, holding 50 percent of the equity is, in purely financial terms, less attractive to the government than is an income tax at a 50 percent rate. Under the ownership arrangement the government receives half the dividend payments. But half the dividend payments is usually less than half of the taxable profits of an enterprise. Dividends come out of the funds that remain after the repayment of principal on debt and after the provision of funds out of profits for reinvestment in the ongoing operation. Under a normal equity-sharing arrangement, the government shares in capital expenditures; under a tax arrangement, the government takes its funds before the deduction of such expenditures. In rare cases, however, net cash flow from which dividends are paid may be greater than taxable profits.

As an illustration of the problem, consider the Liberian American Company (LAMCO) agreement of 1960 in Liberia. As a co-owner of the Swedish interest in the LAMCO-Bethlehem Steel joint venture, the government was to receive, as dividend payments, half of the annual dividends accruing from the Swedish interest.[31] The dividends were to be in lieu of royalties and income tax. Because of the low ratio of equity to loan capital, a substantial amount of the funds generated (estimated to be about $15 million a year for the first ten years of production)[32] was to go to the repayment of debt and interest.[33] While under a normal taxing arrangement the government would receive, through taxes, a portion of the profits calculated before the repayment of debt, under the equity-sharing arrangement the government shared in "profits" calculated after repayment of debt was deducted. Although there could have been a higher rate of participation that would have been equivalent, over time, to the surrendered taxes, the equity-sharing arrangement at 50-50 did not benefit the government to the extent that taxes at 50 percent would have.

Actually, the LAMCO arrangements were even less favorable to the government than has been suggested. Two other factors affected the "profits" in which the government was to share: the Export-Import Bank, as a condition of its loan, required that $25 million in profits be set aside by 1970 in a special reserve; and there were to be deductions from gross profit for "equipment replacement" (at a rate of about 30¢ per ton) in addition to what was to be allowed for depreciation. These items were to be deducted from the company "profits" in which the government was to share. Under the usual taxing arrangement, these items would not have been deductible in the calculation of net taxable income. The result was that the Liberian government paid for a substantial part of the company's capital facilities out of forgone dividends.

Reinvestment of profits by the mining enterprise may, of course, mean larger payments out of earnings sometime in the future. But if reinvestment promises adequate returns, the foreign company would probably provide all of the funds, in the absence of government participation, leaving the government with its increased future revenues from taxes in any case.

Clearly the exchange of some rights to tax for equity may make political and economic sense. In fact, that exchange is explicit in many of the equity-sharing agreements, even where some income tax remains. Much more unusual is the case where the government has paid for its share of equity at the price paid by other stockholders and, at the same time, has given up its right to tax profits. The Liberian-National Iron Ore Company Agreement of 1958 may be a unique example.[34] The financial consequences of this agreement were so disadvantageous to the government that the most charitable interpretation must be that the issue was not clearly understood by government negotiators.

A common pattern in more recent equity-sharing agreements has been for the government to buy shares of equity and to retain all its rights to tax corporate profits. In the vast majority of cases the government contribution has been made only after the existence of a commercially viable source has been proved, that is, after a significant portion of the uncertainty has been eliminated. Two agreements, (1) the 1970 nickel contract between the Government of Colombia and Chevron Petroleum Company and the Hanna Mining Company and (2) the 1967 Bougainville Copper Agreement provide examples of this type of arrangement.[35] The Colombian government, through its wholly-owned Instituto de Fomento Industrial (IFI), entered into a joint venture with the Hanna Mining Company. The government retained the right to tax both the joint venture and any profits accruing to Hanna Mining from its Colombian operations. Similarly, Papua New Guinea bought equity in the Bougainville mine while imposing a gradually rising rate of income tax.

To share in ownership the host government may obtain an interest in a contractual joint venture, rather than holding shares in an incorporated entity. In 1965 the National Iranian Oil Company, for example, provided 50 percent of the capital in a partnership for offshore oil, with the other half invested by a consortium of foreign firms. In this arrangement the government retained its right to tax.

When a shift is made in a particular project from a traditional arrangement to one that provides for sharing of ownership, the steps may be complex and confusing. An illustration is the Chilean government's 1969 purchase of shares in Kennecott's subsidiary. In the change, the government acquired 51 percent of the shares in the copper mining operation, but the taxing arrangements were revised considerably at the same time. In fact, the result of the combined changes appeared to be that the burden on the company of taxation and dividends paid to the government remained approximately the same after the new arrangement as they were before.[36]

The Zambian government's takeover of 51 percent of the shares in its copper operations in 1969 had much in common with the Chilean change. Shares were purchased on the basis of book value and paid for with 5 percent government bonds. At the same time there was a major revision of the tax arrangement, thought by some observers to favor the foreign companies.[37]

There are numerous technical difficulties that should be dealt with in the negotiation of equity-sharing arrangements. Two important ones relate to the rights of one partner to purchase shares offered by another, and the method by which any expansion of the project will be financed. In Zambia the copper agreements assured the government of rights to acquire shares that a minority shareholder wished to sell. In that agreement, funds for expansion were to be provided *pro rata* by all equity holders.

There are many variations on the equity-sharing theme. An interesting arrangement between the Libyan National Oil Company and Shell Exploration (Libya) Ltd. combined some of the features of ownership-sharing with those of production-sharing. That agreement provided for a changing division of interest in the project. The national company's share began at 25 percent and remained at that level until production reached 260,000 barrels per day; it was to increase to 50 percent when output reached 500,000 barrels per day. Exploration expenses were to be borne by Shell, which also advanced the state company's share of capital for development and funds needed for operating expenses. The state company was to reimburse Shell for these advances out of the state company's share of production.[38]

Arrangements that allow workers rights of participation illustrate some variations on the equity-sharing theme. The Peruvian General Mining Law of 1971 provided that mining companies were to deduct, free of taxes, 10 percent of their net income: 4 percent as "liquid participation" for Peruvian workers and 6 percent for "property participation" by Peruvian workers.[39] The 4 percent was to go to a workers' cooperative and the 6 percent was to be invested as shares in the company held by the workers. Once the workers had shares, they would be guaranteed one representative on the board of directors. Workers' representation on the board thereafter was to be in proportion to equity ownership.

Still rare in the mid-1970s was direct equity-sharing between governments, although state companies from developed countries had fairly frequently participated in the exploitation of a developing country's minerals. In early 1973 Guinea had under consideration the creation of two mixed companies to develop the iron ore deposits of Mount Nimba and Mount Simandou near the Liberian frontier. The two companies were to include capital from Guinea, Liberia, Algeria, Nigeria, and Zaire, as well as from companies from Japan, Yugoslavia, and Spain. One motivating factor for including Liberia was to link the Guinea operation to the 250-km railway running from the LAMCO iron ore operation on the Liberian side of Mt. Nimba to a Liberian port.[40] Nigeria decided in 1974 to take a 5 percent interest in two iron ore companies in Guinea, with an apparent view to establishing a Nigerian iron and steel industry, which would stimulate demand for abundant Nigerian coking coal.[41]

While a general trend toward some variant of increased government participation in the equity of mining enterprises was evident in the early 1970s, some countries have had second thoughts as they approached the issue, especially as the risks became apparent. The government of Sierra Leone had, in 1969, stated its intentions of taking a 51 percent share in four major mining companies operating there. Interest in equity participation was apparently inspired by events in Zambia, where the government had taken shares in copper operations. In 1973, however, the Sierra Leone government, claiming that it did not have sufficient liquid assets, gave up plans to take an equity interest in one of the companies, Sierra Leone Development Company. The prospects for high profits were dim. Although the company was apparently willing to sell shares below book value, the equity participation plan, which was beginning to appear rather risky, was replaced with an agreement providing for higher taxes and for government representation on the board of directors.[42]

The success of governments in Latin America and Central Africa in obtaining equity in copper operations influenced still other countries. In 1972 Papua New Guinea passed a resolution in its House of Assembly announcing its goal of substantial equity participation in mining operations in the country. When it was faced with a renegotiation of the Bougainville arrangements in 1974, however, the government was confronted with conflicting advice from the plethora of advisors it had called upon. Ultimately it ignored the calls for more ownership and simply increased the taxes.

In spite of its complexities, equity participation will almost certainly continue to grow in importance. Some countries seem to view ownership itself as an objective. In countries where taxes are fixed by the general laws, shared ownership provides a way of rearranging the financial benefits on an *ad hoc* basis to reflect bargaining powers.

Management Control

Governments often acquire equity for other than purely financial reasons, or for the satisfaction that ownership itself provides. It is often assumed that more ownership gives more control. Increased control over the operations of the foreign firm, either real or imaginary, promises political benefits in addition to the possible financial ones.[43] The extent of the government's share of control may be in proportion to its share of equity ownership. As we have indicated, however, in many instances, it is not.

One device for dissociating equity ownership from control is the assignment of different classes of shares to the different parties. One class of shares may have no voting rights. In some cases holders of a particular class of shares may be empowered to appoint a certain number of members of the board of directors, and those of another class may be entitled to another number, regardless of the claims on the assets of the enterprise represented by the shares. The 1960 LAMCO agreement in Liberia is one example of this kind of arrangement. Although each shareholder had 50 percent of the equity, the holder of Class A shares, the government of Liberia, could appoint only five members of the board of directors. The holders of Class B shares could appoint six.

The arrangements for control do not, of course, always favor the foreign firm. In a given situation a government may have sufficient bargaining power to insist on a voice in management beyond that represented by its stockholdings. In some cases a government's class of shares may carry certain rights, but more commonly the agreement itself simply specifies the right of the government to name a certain portion, say 50 percent, of the directors on the operation's board. Moreover, it has not been uncommon in modern concessions for the government to have a veto right over certain kinds of decisions, regardless of the size of its shareholdings. A common mechanism for granting the veto has been a requirement that a unanimous vote of the board of directors be obtained before certain steps can be taken by the management. The presence of at least one government-appointed director can enable the government to block a decision.

Most host governments have chosen not to become involved in the day-to-day operations of the firm. To make sure that decisions of importance reach the board, however, some governments have insisted that agreements require a general operating plan to be submitted by the line management for approval by the board. The agreement spells out the contents of the operating plan: usually production volumes, major investments, sales plans, operating budgets, and employment plans. The line management is required to operate within this plan, or to seek approval from the board for any departures. In such cases the government and the company are usually pleased to keep the government out of day-to-day operations, and yet the government is assured that it can review important decisions.

Perhaps the two central problems faced by a government in structuring its representation on a board of directors of an extractive operation have been: (1) defining those issues in which it is vitally concerned; and (2) assuring that its representatives on the board have the necessary technical data to make intelligent decisions on matters before the board. The Colombian nickel agreement with Chevron and Hanna Mining Company, mentioned above, illustrates one approach to the solution of these problems.

During the negotiations with the foreign company, the Colombian government made a careful appraisal to determine which decision areas were of special concern to the government in its role both as a minority partner in the venture and as a sovereign power. It determined that there were many areas in which the interests of the foreign firm and the government would probably coincide. Each party would be interested, for example, in purchasing goods, services, technical assistance, and know-how at minimum prices, so long as the suppliers were not parties affiliated to the foreign investor. The Colombian government would have little need for veto power over such matters. On the other hand, the government was able to define certain classes of decisions in which the interests of the majority and minority parties to the joint venture might diverge, or in which national interests might differ from those of the enterprise. These classes of decision included:

1. The purchase or sale of goods, services, technical assistance, or know-how from or to a partner or an affiliate of the major shareholder.
2. The appointment of a management group and the terms of a management contract.
3. The approval of the annual exploration, development, investment, production, and budget plans to govern operations under the management contract.
4. The approval of purchases by the operator that represent expenditures over certain amounts.
5. The geographical location of facilities.
6. The appointment of an auditor for the books of the joint venture and the approval of financial statements.
7. The contents of any annual reports of the joint venture operations.
8. The mortgaging of any assests of the joint venture.
9. The purchase or sale of goods, services, etc., to or from nations unfriendly to Colombia.
10. The use of technology harmful to the environment.

For decisons of these types, government consent was required.

After spelling out the areas of concern, government negotiators were worried that their representatives would not be sufficiently well-informed to make intelligent decisions in all these matters. To help overcome these difficulties, the government made provision in the agreement for the creation of a technical committee, composed primarily of Colombians, whose main task would be to assure: (a) that adequate training of Colombians would take place; (b) that the government would be apprised of any past or future decisions by the operator that would affect its interests; and (c) that technical information and analysis would be provided to the government representatives on the board of directors so that they would have an adequate basis for participation on the board.

This approach has its parallel in the United States, where the idea of providing and financing an autonomous staff of technical specialists to assist outside directors in making decisions has been put forward. The proposal has come as a response to the increasing recognition that outside board members have rarely been equipped to make complex management decisions or to exercise effective control over day-to-day management.[44] Such a committee promises possible help.

In the Colombian case, the government was the holder of a minority interest. Under the increasingly common arrangements whereby the host government owns the majority of shares, the problems can be reversed. The task is then to provide protection for the foreign company as the minority stockholder.

In Zambia, where the government held 51 percent of the shares in a particular copper concession, the private interests were granted the right to veto expansion plans or appropriations for capital, exploration, or prospecting expenditures. An agreement in Sierra Leone provides another example of minority interests in the hands of the foreign firm. Under a renegotiated agreement with the Sierra Leone Selection Trust Ltd. (SLST),[45] a new company was formed, with the capital held 51 percent by the government and 49 percent by SLST. The board of the new company was to consist of eleven directors, of whom six (including the chairman) would be appointed by the government. All the operating assets of the old company were to be acquired by the new joint company, which would carry on the diamond mining. The government agreed to pay for its proportion of the fixed assets of the business by issuing negotiable bonds and to pay for its share of the net current assets in cash. The joint company was to be taxed on its profits at a rate of 70 percent. The foreign firm was to appoint the first managers to carry on the day-to-day operations of the company.

The agreement had provisions for the protection of the foreign firm, as minority shareholder, as well as guarantees for the government. For the security of the private firm, an affirmative vote of three-fourths of all the directors was required for:

1. The termination of operations of the joint company or the sale or transfer of the assets or rights of the joint company.

2. The issue of additional shares, the borrowing of funds, the creation of charges, the making of loans, or the giving of guarantees.
3. The appointment or removal of the auditors of the joint company.
4. Any purchase or sale of any product or asset or any other transaction carried out otherwise than on the best commercial terms reasonably available or in the normal commercial activities of the joint company.
5. Any restriction on the effective implementation of agreements with the government.
6. The expenditure by the joint company of any funds or the making of any commitments in respect of any new mining operation or facility, or the making of any expenditure, considered by at least three directors to be outside the ordinary course of business.
7. The appointment of any committee, board, or attorney whose powers included the doing of certain acts.

Many government officials think that equity-sharing arrangements, such as the Colombian and Sierra Leone cases, can help in reducing some of the political problems associated with foreign activities in the minerals field. The promise, and sometimes practice, of increased control in the hands of the government at least provides politically useful evidence that the government is concerned about national sovereignty. Participation in management, where it actually occurs, may provide experience that hastens the day when the host country is able to operate its mines without the direct involvement of foreign firms.

Management Contracts

Under equity-sharing arrangements or in a situation where the foreign company's shares have been nationalized, the government may want to return the foreign firm to the day-to-day management of the operating company's activities. The usual device for this is the management contract.

Zambia provides an example of the use of a management contract under shared ownership. Part of the terms of the 1969 agreement between the government of Zambia and Roan Selection Trust (RST), under which the government was to acquire 51 percent equity interest in RST's subsidiary operating in Zambia, included provision for separate management and consultancy contracts.[46] RST was to provide: (1) technical services (including preparing progress reports, long-term plan reports, capital expenditure estimates, advice on operating problems); (2) general services (including advice on preparation of company reports and financial statements, development and processing of minerals); and (3) specialized services (including engineering consultancy services, staff, recruitment).

Under the management contract RST was to be remunerated in the amount of 0.75 percent of the state operating company's gross sales proceeds. In addition it would receive 2 percent of the operating company's consolidated profits after certain deductions. RST would also receive an engineering fee of 3 percent of specified construction costs of projects and a recruiting fee of 15 percent of the total emoluments payable to expatriate employees during their first year.

Under a separate sales and marketing contract RST was to receive 0.75 percent of the gross sales proceeds of all sales of copper metal throughout the world, and 2.5 percent on cobalt sales.

Copper mining in the Congo illustrates the possibilities for using management contracts after a complete nationalization. In 1967 the Congo (now Zaire) government took over the Belgian-owned Union Minière du Haut Katanga, without compensation. In 1969, however, the government and the Belgian firm reached agreement on compensation and on an arrangement under which the company would provide management assistance, on a fee basis.

No standard terms have developed for management contracts. In some, remuneration has been based on sales volume and expenses incurred. Others have turned to a share of profits, with a hope that the managing firm would have an incentive to increase efficiency. Whatever the basis of compensation, the interest of foreign firms in management contracts has generally been limited, unless they have some equity ownership or another form of access to a significant portion of profits. In most cases where management contracts have been successful, the foreign firm has had a clear and strong interest in the success of the operation. Where the firm's downstream operations depend on inputs from the project it is managing, the conditions may be met.[47] In any case, experience suggests that the host government can face tough administrative problems even with management contracts. There have been numerous cases, for example, where the managing enterprise has siphoned profits out of the project managed under contract through purchases from affiliates of materials at prices far above those that would be available elsewhere.

PRODUCTION-SHARING, SERVICE, AND WORK CONTRACTS

Some agreements have gone beyond the modern concession format in which the foreign firm holds equity in the facilities. Under some arrangements the government simply purchases the services of a foreign enterprise that has no ownership interest in the producing company. Service contracts, work contracts, and production-sharing arrangements provide examples of agreements that in varying degrees reflect this structure.

Some of the most confusing terminology surrounds these three types of agreement. In the early 1970s such arrangements were still, as one commentator observed earlier with regard to service contracts, "too new and too few to have developed any very pronounced standardization in name, form, or substance."[48]

In theory, under all three arrangements the foreign firm is a "contractor," not a concession holder or partner. The investor is a "hired technician" rather than the "operator of a subsoil interest." In practice the line between the conventional concession contract on the one hand and a service, work, or production-sharing contract on the other has been less than distinct. And the boundaries dividing service contracts, work contracts, and production-sharing agreements from each other have often been very blurred indeed.

Service and Work Contracts

Perhaps the most basic content of service and work contracts is illustrated by mineral agreements in Indonesia, negotiated between 1966 and 1973, for copper, nickel, and tin operations. Indonesia adopted the terminology of "work contract" for these arrangements. The essential feature of these contracts was that the title to the ore remained with the government until it was extracted. In other respects, however, the Indonesian work contracts were quite similar to the traditional concession, and quite dissimilar to the service contracts of the Middle East. For example, the Indonesian contractor simply paid a corporate income tax, although sometimes at special rates, on his profits from the sale of the ore.[49] And the ownership of the mining facilities was unambiguously vested in the hands of the foreign firm.

Clearly, more has usually been implied in the terminology of service and work contracts than was evident in the case of the Indonesian agreements for hard minerals. Passing of title is usually, in practice, not much more than a legal nicety.[50] In fact, if no more is meant, many of the traditional concessions in Hispanic law countries would technically qualify, since according to the legal tradition the title to ore bodies resides automatically in the state, although many concession documents in those countries have carefully skirted the issue of title. ·

The use of the terms service or work contracts usually implies a rather different relationship from that which is understood under typical concession agreements. The foreign firm is considered to be working as a contractor, in some sense, for the host government. The foreigner's services may be paid for in cash or kind. His remuneration could be based on an annual fixed fee, but he generally receives reimbursement for actual costs plus a payment based on profits.

The 1966 agreement between the National Iranian Oil Company (NIOC) and the French state agency, Enterprise de Réchèrches et d'Activités Petrolières (ERAP) and ERAP's subsidiary, Société Francaises de Petroles d'Iran (SOFIRAN), provides a typical model of what is usually understood as a service or work contract. The agreement avoided words of direct grant and described ERAP and SOFIRAN as contractors. ERAP agreed to provide the risk capital for the exploration, and its subsidiary agreed to provide the technical know-how and services and to serve as general contractor. The oil produced was to belong to NIOC, an essential point of the agreement, but sale to ERAP of a percentage of the oil produced was guaranteed at an agreed price. ERAP also agreed to act as a broker and to sell certain quantities of crude oil on behalf of NIOC on the world market. Funds advanced by ERAP for exploration and development were to be repaid after oil was produced in commercial quantities.[51]

As in the ERAP case, most arrangements have called for the foreign firm to bear the risk of exploration. Some agreements have treated development expenditures as an interest-bearing loan from the foreign firm to the government, which could be repaid in cash or kind. In other arrangements the company would bear these expenditures entirely on its own account. The only commitment to the company would be that, as contractor, it was guaranteed a certain amount of the production to cover costs and profits.

Arrangements in Bolivia were similar to the NIOC-ERAP agreement, but the terminology was rather different. Under the 1972 Bolivian general law relating to hydrocarbons, Yacimientos Petroliferos Fiscales Bolivianos (YPFB), the Bolivian state oil enterprise, was authorized to enter into "operation contracts."[52] Under these agreements, the contractor would initially bear all the costs and risks of exploration and exploitation, but would eventually be compensated for expenses incurred during the exploitation phase should oil be found. All hydrocarbons produced by the operator were to be delivered to YPFB. YPFB retained, at wellhead prices, the volumes necessary for paying national and departmental taxes. Part of the balance was retained by YPFB and a portion was to be delivered to the contractor.

The 1972 Bolivian law made provision for "petroleum service contracts" as well as "operation contracts." These petroleum service contracts were of a very special nature: they could be entered into by either YPFB or an operation contractor to engage a third party to perform a specialized task such as marketing, transport, or refining.

Venezuela also has negotiated agreements that are labelled service contracts, but with a rather different meaning from Bolivia's petroleum service contracts. In Venezuela a service contract for oil in South Lake Maracaibo between Corporacion Venezuela de Petroleo and Shell provides an example. Under this arrangement the financing was to be provided by Shell, the contractor. After a three-year period, a formula came into operation requiring the contractor to surrender a part of the contract area that is likely to have oil. During the operating period, the contractor would retain 90 percent of the oil, with the remainder going to the state corporation. Shell would pay to the government a royalty of 16.6 percent and an income tax of 60 percent, based on a kind of posted price. The state firm would receive 5 percent of the royalty going to the government, and a portion of Shell's after-tax profit, varying from 0 to 55 percent when the net profits were more than 50¢ per barrel.[53]

As with equity-sharing arrangements, the amount of supervision exercised by the government, or a state enterprise, over a contractor has varied from case to case. In many situations government control has been more theoretical than actual. In other cases it has been very real. The problems facing the government that has granted a service contract are akin to those faced by government directors on the board of a venture in which the government shares equity ownership. Without assistance, perhaps from a technical committee of the type attempted in the Colombia-Hanna-Chevron agreement mentioned above, government representation may generate little influence over decisionmaking.

Actual agreements have differed with regard to the mechanism through which the government is to participate in management. The 1972 Bolivian general law relating to hydrocarbons provided, in the case of an operation contract, for a control committee composed of representatives of YPFB. That committee was to approve all budgets, programs of work, and methods of operation, as well as to perform audits, among other things. In the Venezuelan agreement with Shell, there were joint operating committees. In addition, the state firm could exercise influence by taking up an option to purchase 20 percent of the equity in the contracting firm.

Production-Sharing Agreements

Along with service contracts, production-sharing agreements have become popular. The term production-sharing agreement could, perhaps, be reserved for arrangements whereby the foreign firm and the government share the output of the operation in predetermined proportions. In practice the term has been applied to almost any kind of arrangement in which there is at least an option that the firm and the government receive their benefits in kind rather than in cash. The distinction between service contracts and production-sharing contracts had become one of small technicalities as they had evolved by 1975.

Perhaps the purest examples of production-sharing agreements were the so-called co-production agreements that had been negotiated for manufacturing by Western firms in the Communist countries of Eastern Europe. Typically, the Western firm provided licenses, machinery, and technical assistance. It agreed to accept a certain amount of the product of the firm in payment.

For raw materials in the developing countries, the agreements have generally been more complex, partly as a result of the fact that the foreign investor has contributed more than simply technical know-how and partly because of the greater risk usually involved. A number of petroleum agreements negotiated in Indonesia illustrate production-sharing arrangements for raw materials. These arrangements are of two distinct types: (1) those reached under the Sukarno regime between 1960 and 1965; and (2) those that emerged in the early Suharto period.

In the years 1960–65, most foreign-owned enterprises in Indonesia were taken over by the government. At the same time, however, the government negotiated a number of production-sharing agreements, primarily with the Japanese.[54] Production-sharing was characterized "as the preferred form of foreign investment."[55] The basic theory behind these agreements was that they called for "redeemable fixed interest loans"[56] by the foreign company to the government. The loan would be repaid by the government within a stipulated time in the form of an agreed percentage of the product of the project. Under these arrangements the foreign investor was generally regarded as a creditor, rather than as a partner or contractor, even though he was responsible for certain services. Principal, interest, and remuneration for technical and marketing cooperation were to be paid to the firm only with a percentage of the annual product valued at world prices. The Indonesians negotiated such production-sharing agreements for timber, oil, nickel, and a number of other commodities.

The change of government in 1965 brought with it corresponding changes in the form of production-sharing contracts. The new production-sharing agreements bore only superficial resemblance to the production-sharing agreements of the 1960–65 period or to traditional concession contracts. These contracts were negotiated only for petroleum exploration and development; the government adopted different forms of contract for other minerals and for timber.

By early 1971 some thirty-six foreign companies had negotiated the new style agreements with Pertamina, the state oil company. These agreements were entered into by small and medium-sized firms, as well as by such large international enterprises as Shell, Compagnie Française de Petroles, Gulf, BP, and Mobil.[57]

Under these arrangements the foreign companies were "contractors" to Pertamina. Although the terms of the various oil contracts varied in some particulars, the production-sharing contract between P.N. Pertambangan Minjak Nasional (Pertamina) and Phillips Petroleum Company (1968) may be considered typical of the genre. Under the terms of the agreement, Pertamina was responsible for the management of the operations. Phillips was made responsible to Pertamina for the execution of operations and provided all financial and technical assistance required for the operations. Phillips carried the risk of operating costs (which included the costs of exploration and development), and was required to market all of the crude oil produced, if Pertamina so required.

The two key elements of the agreement that distinguish it from the simple service contract are that (1) Phillips was entitled to recover, in the form of oil, operating costs up to an amount equal to 40 percent per calendar year of crude oil produced; and that (2) of the balance of oil, Pertamina took 65 percent and Phillips received 35 percent. While it was provided that "Phillips shall be subject to the income tax laws of the Republic of Indonesia and shall comply with the requirements of such laws," Pertamina undertook to pay such taxes on behalf of Phillips. Title to Phillips' portion of oil (including the portion to be sold to recover operating costs) passed to Phillips at the point of export. Title to equipment purchased (not leased) by Phillips was vested in Pertamina when the equipment was landed in Indonesia.

Two important pricing provisions were included in the contract. All sales to third parties were to be valued at net realized prices f.o.b. field terminal received by Phillips unless Pertamina found a more favorable market, in which case this market price was to be used. Sales to affiliates were to be valued by using "the weighted average per unit net price f.o.b. field terminal received by Phillips for sales to Third Parties during the preceding three (3) calendar months."[58] Any commissions paid to affiliates in connection with sales to third parties were not to exceed the "customary and prevailing rate."

The pricing provisions gave important protection to the government against the firm's underpricing of oil sold to affiliates. In addition, the fact that Pertamina had the option of taking its share in oil rather than money provided further protection. If the government was not satisfied with the price of sales to affiliates (or to nonaffiliates), it could take payment in crude oil and attempt to sell it to a higher bidder.

In a production-sharing arrangement such as the Pertamina-Phillips Petroleum agreement, the host government must be concerned not only with sales to affiliates. The costs of operations, although limited to 40 percent, must be calculated to determine the amount of oil that goes to each party. The problem was rather more than in the earlier agreements, which provided only for the repayment of predetermined "debt." Slippage in the amount of income accruing to the government could occur in the calculation of these "operating costs" incurred by the company under post-1965 agreements. Such deductions must be given the quality of scrutiny that would be given by a government tax office to deductions from gross income in a traditional concession agreement.

Several production-sharing agreements negotiated in Indonesia after the Phillips Petroleum contract added a new provision requiring the contractor to offer a stated percentage of his "contractual rights and obligations" to an Indonesian participant as soon as commercial sales were made.[59] Depending on the particular contract, the local participants could be either individuals, corporations, or state entities. Typically, the portion required to be offered to Indonesian participants was either 5 or 10 percent.

It is not surprising that most of the production-sharing agreements have been in the oil industry. For the arrangements to be of significant benefit to the host country, the government must be able to sell domestically or on foreign markets a share of the output of the extractive operation. This has been possible for oil, as was effectively demonstrated in 1973, as oil producing countries made the most of their "participation oil." For many other minerals, sales of large quantities on spot markets can not be arranged easily. In many industries the government must depend on the foreign firm to sell to affiliates and to arrange long-term sales contracts with other firms in the industry. In fact, even oil agreements usually make some provision for the company to take the government's share of the oil. At times the cost to the company can be high. In August 1973, Occidental had to buy back Libya's share at $4.90 per barrel, a price that appeared at the time to be high — 32¢ above the posted price.[60] Soon thereafter, the price structure had changed in such a way that most producing countries were selling, on the open market, some of the participation oil that had previously been sold through the companies' marketing channels.

There have been signs that the changes in structure of other minerals industries may increase the attractiveness of production-sharing in those industries. The nationalizations of copper operations in the late 1960s and early 1970s have shown that host countries can sell their own copper.[61] With more open markets the production-sharing model may have something to offer governments. For example, the 1970 OMRD Ecuadorian copper agreement called for the government to take its royalty payments in the form of ore, if it so chose.[62] Some other industries show similar possibilities. A 1974 agreement between Niger, Continental Oil Company, and the French Atomic Energy Commission (CEA) gives the government the right to market its share of uranium produced.[63]

THE FUTURE OF THE NEW STRUCTURES FOR AGREEMENTS

The 1960s brought major innovations in the structure of mineral agreements. Most important, the new structures have broken the tight link between ownership, control, and financial risks and benefits that was inherent in the traditional concession. Arrangements have been negotiated that have repackaged these elements in ways not feasible under the old structures. Because ownership and control have become important political symbols in most developing countries, new contractual forms have been created to allow greater freedom in allocating ownership, control, and financial risks and benefits in ways that satisfy both the economic and new political imperatives. Where a foreign firm is considered important for its financial, technological, or marketing contributions, the new structures permit the negotiation of agreements that grant control and financial arrangements reflecting the bargaining powers of the parties. Ownership can be allocated in a way that makes the presence of the foreign firm politically acceptable in the host country.[64]

In some cases ownership has had symbolic or real meaning for the foreign firm as well as for the host government. In many cases extractive firms have resisted arrangements that would leave them with less nominal ownership than that to which they have become accustomed, even though the financial and control aspects of the proposed agreements might be perfectly satisfactory. In other cases the problems facing the private managers considering innovative arrangements have been real. They have worried about how to explain the new structures to shareholders, how to set up insurance against expropriation and other risks on assets they do not own, or how to raise loans on property to which they do not have title. Usually, however, resistance from management seems to have been based less on economic and legal grounds than on the symbolic meaning of ownership.

Managers have increasingly recognized that financial benefits—their principal objective—need not be completely linked with control. And control need not be linked at all with ownership.

The new forms of agreement will almost certainly spread to a number of industries where they have not been common. In some instances the new arrangements will not generate significant shifts in the allocation of financial benefits. But in industries in which bargaining powers continue to shift in favor of the host country, and where host country negotiating skills are sufficient, the changes will be more than political. There will be real changes in who controls the operations and who receives the financial benefits from the projects.

It appears that many of the innovations for minerals typically governed by traditional arrangements come from firms that have had experience in other industries. Petroleum firms, in their efforts to diversify, are expressing a willingness to transfer the structures of petroleum agreements to hard mineral operations such as copper. They have learned that some of the ways of repackaging ownership, control, and financial claims are feasible and acceptable to management. The concept of ownership has lost some of its significance for managers of companies that have had experience with arrangements in which the company has had sufficient control over critical decisions and has received attractive financial benefits with little direct claim to ownership.

Yet while the new forms of agreement have provided ways of sharing symbolic power and economic benefits in ways that the traditional concession could not, they have not eliminated the complex technical problems relating to the allocation of financial benefits and financial risks. The technical issues remain no matter what the structure of the agreement.

NOTES

1. In Indonesia the "work contracts" for the development of hard minerals are quite different from the "production-sharing contracts" for the development of oil. Compare, e.g., *Contract of Work between the Republic of Indonesia and P.T. Kennecott Indonesia* (November 1, 1969), (for the development of copper) and *Production-Sharing Contract between P.N. Pertamina and Phillips Petroleum Company* (1968). Unless otherwise indicated, specific contracts are in the personal files of the authors.

2. In the early 1960s in Indonesia a number of "work contracts" for the exploration and exploitation of oil were negotiated. They were essentially profit-sharing arrangements. See, e.g., *Contract of Work between P.N. Pertambangan Minjak Nasional and P.T. Stanvac Indonesia* (1963), reproduced in *International Legal Materials* 3 (March 1964): 243. The recent hard mineral "work contracts" provide for the imposition of a normal corporate income tax. See *Contract of Work between Republic of Indonesia and P.T. Kennecott Indonesia* (November 1, 1969).

3. *Contract of Work between Republic of Indonesia and P.T. Kennecott Indonesia* (November 1, 1969).

4. Ibid., Preamble and Article 1(a).

5. *Concession Agreement between the Republic of Liberia and the Gewerkschaft Exploration Company, Dusseldorf, West Germany* (1958), in Chapter 33 of the *Acts Approved by the Legislature of the Government of the Republic of Liberia,* 1958–59 Session.

6. Ibid., Article 1.

7. The implications may, of course, be very important. On this issue, see Richard Lillich, ed., *The Valuation of Nationalized Property in International Law,* (Charlottesville: University of Virginia Press, 1973), Vol. II, pp. 78, 111–12.

8. This has been done by us for host governments and by others in unpublished materials. See Eldon G. Warner, "Mixed International Joint Ventures in the Exploration, Development, and Production of Petroleum," unpublished M.S. thesis, Sloan School of M.I.T., June 1972; W.T. Levy Consultants Corp., N.Y., "A Comparative Evaluation of Major Concessionary Arrangements Now in Effect," cited in Warner, pp. 40, 60. See also Thomas R. Stauffer, "Economics of Petroleum Taxation in the Eastern Hemisphere," paper delivered at an OPEC seminar on International Oil and Energy Policies of the Producing and Consuming Countries (Vienna, June 30–July 5, 1969).

9. Peru, *General Mining Law; Decree Law No. 18880* (Lima: Ministry of Economics and Finance, Office of Public Relations, 1971). A number of countries legislated new mining codes in the first half of the 1970s. See, e.g., Ecuador, "Mining Development Law (Supreme Decree 101 of January 24, 1974)", U.S. Department of Interior, Bureau of Mines, *Mineral Trade Notes* 71 (April 1974): 7; Saudi Arabia, "Mining Code," *Mineral Trade Notes* 70 (June 1973): 20; "Sudan Mines and Quarries Act, 1972," *Mineral Trade Notes* 70 (May 1973): 15.

For general guidance on the drafting of mining legislation, see U.N., ECAFE, *Proceedings of the Seminar on Mining Legislation and Administration* (Mineral Resource Development Series, No. 34), 1969 (E/CN.11/919); and U.N., ECAFE, *Proceedings of the Seminar on Petroleum Legislation with Particular Reference to Offshore Operations* (Mineral Resource Development Series, No. 40), 1969 (E/CN.11/1052).

10. For details, see *The Exploration and Exploitation of Crude Oil and Natural Gas in the OECD Area Including the Continental Shelf: Mining and Fiscal Legislation* (Paris: OECD, 1973).

11. In describing a 1906 concession grant by the Congo Comité Special du Katanga to the Union Minière du Haut-Katanga, two commentators write that "the Company's rights were so extensive as to partake of quasigovernmental powers akin to those accorded the great trading companies of an earlier concession era." J. Gillis Wetter and Stephen M. Schwebel, "Some Little Known Cases on Concessions," *The British Yearbook of International Law,* Vol. XL (1964), p. 193. Fifty years ago the United Fruit Company owned or leased about 5,000 square miles of tropical lands, using only about 10 percent productively at the time. John M. Fox, "United Fruit and Latin America," *The Harvard Review* (Fall 1968): 32–33.

12. The lease given to the Firestone Company by the Liberian government in 1926 was to run for 99 years and covered one million acres of land. See Wayne Chatfield Taylor, *The Firestone Operations in Liberia* (Washington: National Planning Association, 1956), p. xi.

 13. See the various land taxes listed in Ghana, *Report of the Commission of Enquiry into Concessions* (Accra-Tema: Ministry of Information, 1961), pp. 32–79.

14. Henry Cattan, *The Evolution of Oil Concessions in the Middle East and North Africa* (Dobbs Ferry: published for the Parker School of Foreign and Comparative Law by Oceana Publications, 1967), p. 8.

15. Ibid., p. 33.

16. Ibid., p. 34.

17. *Concession Agreement between the Government of Liberia and Liberian Mining Company, Ltd.* (August 27, 1945), Article 9(a); Approved by an Act of the Legislature, January 22, 1946 (hereafter cited as *LMC Concession Agreement: Liberia*).

18. See Ghana, *Report of the Commission of Enquiry into Concessions* (Accra-Tema: Ministry of Information, 1961), p. 32 ff.

19. Mira Wilkins, *The Maturing of Multinational Enterprise* (Cambridge: Harvard University Press, 1974), p. 127.

20. The Ghana Commission of Enquiry into Concessions concluded in 1961 that "all mineral and timber royalties should [henceforth] be required by law to be computed on a percentage of the sales price. . . ." Ghana, op. cit., p. 10.

21. *LMC Concession Agreement: Liberia.*

22. For an example of a stumpage fee adjusted in accordance with the wholesale price of standard newsprint, see the *Agreement between the Province of Newfoundland and Newfoundland Pulp and Chemical Co., Ltd.* (July 5, 1960), Sec. 14.

23. See Cattan, op. cit., p. 44.

24. *LMC Concession Agreement: Liberia.*

25. See *Collateral Agreement* of March 12, 1952, approved by an Act of the Legislature, March 10, 1953.

26. *Amendatory and Tax Agreement dated as of January 1, 1965, between the Government of the Republic of Liberia and Liberian Mining Co., Ltd.,* Clause 1.

27. Ghana, *Report of the Commission of Enquiry into Concessions* (Accra-Tema: Ministry of Information, 1961), p. 10.

28. Private interview.

29. See William Wedderspoon, "Simplifying Taxes in East Africa," *Finance and Development* 6 (March 1969): 51.

30. Morris Adelman, "Is the Oil Shortage Real?" *Foreign Policy* 9 (Winter 1972–73): 84.

31. "Joint Venture Agreement between the Liberian American Mining Co. and Bethlehem Steel" (April 28, 1960), Chapter LXV of *Acts Passed by the Legislature of the Republic of Liberia During the Session 1959–1960* (Monrovia: Government Printing Office, 1960). For a detailed discussion of the finan-

cial structure of the LAMCO Joint Venture see Robert W. Clower et al., *Growth without Development: An Economic Survey of Liberia* (Evanston: Northwestern University Press, 1966), pp. 210 ff.

32. Clower, op. cit., p. 219.

33. Analysis suggests that much of the loan capital might better have been characterized as equity rather than debt. In such a case "interest" payments would be treated as "dividend" payments and would not be deductible from gross income for tax purposes. This problem is discussed in detail in Chapter 3.

34. *Concession Agreement between the Government of the Republic of Liberia and the National Iron Ore Company, Ltd.* (March 13, 1958), Article 7: "Since the Government presently owns, or has the right to acquire, one-half of the shares of the Concessionaire to be issued, the Government forever waives all royalty. . . . In lieu of all other Liberian taxes . . . the Concessionaire shall pay an exploitation tax and a surface tax." In commenting on the NIOC arrangement, an economic survey team has observed that "The government's equity participation in the National Iron Ore Company is extremely costly. It has invested $5 million as a stockholder, just half of the total equity capital. As a 50 percent stockholder, it will get 50 percent of net (distributed) profits, *the other shareholders paying zero income taxes on their 50 percent of net profits.* Clower et al., loc. cit.

35. Agreement between Instituto de Fomento Industrial and Compania de Niquel Colombiano, S.A. (July 1970). See "Colombia Mine Accord Regarded as Pace-Setter," *New York Times,* August 15, 1970, p. 31. The Bougainville agreement was ratified in 1967. See Territory of Papua and New Guinea, *Mining (Bougainville Copper Agreement) Ordinance 1967.* The Agreement was amended in 1974 (See *Mining (Bougainville Copper Agreement) (Amendment) Bill 1974.*)

36. Private interviews.

37. Charles Harvey, "Tax Reform in the Mining Industry," in Mark Bostock and Charles Harvey, eds., *Economic Independence and Zambian Copper: A Case Study of Foreign Investment* (New York: Praeger, 1972), p. 131.

38. OECD, *Oil: The Present Situation and Future Prospects* (Paris: OECD, 1973), p. 91.

39. Peru, *General Mining Law; Decree Law No. 18880* (Lima: Ministry of Economics and Finance, Office of Public Relations, 1971), Art. 281 ff.

40. "Sekou Touré's Iron Mountains," *West Africa,* February 19, 1973, p. 239. But see "Big Bauxite Mine Begins," *West Africa,* March 26, 1973, p. 421.

41. "Interest in Nigerian Coal Grows," *West Africa,* May 6, 1974, p. 535.

42. "Opting Out of Iron Ore," *West Africa,* March 5, 1973, p. 303; and *West Africa,* April 30, 1973, p. 577.

43. It has been suggested that despite the management control provisions in the production-sharing oil agreements, Indonesia's highly touted state oil company, Pertamina, actually exercises little real management control over foreign operations. Robert Fabrikant, *Oil Discovery and Technical Change in Southeast Asia–Legal Aspects of Production-Sharing Contracts in the Indonesian Petroleum Industry* (Singapore: Institute of Southeast Asian Studies, 1973), pp. 21 ff.

44. Arthur J. Goldberg, "Debate On Outside Directors," *New York Times,* October 29, 1972, sec. 3, p. 1. See also Louis Levy, "How An Audit Committee Can Help," *New York Times,* December 3, 1972, sec. 3, p. 16. See also Robert Townsend, "Let's Install Public Directors," *Business and Society Review,* Number 1 (Spring 1972), pp. 69–70.

45. For a full statement of the terms of the new agreement, see Consolidated African Selection Trust Ltd., "Report to Members on Agreement with the Government of Sierra Leone," September 11, 1970.

46. These contracts are described in some detail in Mark Bostock and Charles Harvey, eds., *Economic Independence and Zambian Copper: A Case Study of Foreign Investment* (New York: Praeger, 1972), p. 229.

47. For a discussion of management contracts, see Peter P. Gabriel, *The International Transfer of Corporate Skills: Management Contracts in Less Developed Countries* (Boston: Harvard Business School Division of Research, 1967).

48. Ewell E. Murphy, Jr., "Oil Operations in Latin America: The Scope for Private Investment," *The International Lawyer* 2 (1968): 471.

49. See, for example, *Contract of Work between Indonesia and Freeport Indonesia, Inc.* (April 7, 1967), Art. 5. The tax legislation implemented by Canada in 1973 produced different tax rates for mining and processing operations (49 percent and 40 percent, respectively).

50. But see note 7, above.

51. Henry Cattan, "Present Trends in Middle Eastern Oil Concessions and Agreements," in Virgina S. Cameron, ed., *Private Investors Abroad—Problems and Solutions in International Business in 1969* (New York: M. Bender, 1969), pp. 140 ff.; and OECD, *Oil: The Present Situation and Future Prospects* (Paris: OECD, 1973), p. 92.

52. "Bolivia: General Laws of Hydrocarbons," *Mineral Trade Notes,* 69 (November 1972): 14ff.

53. OECD Oil: *The Present Situation and Future Prospects* (Paris: OECD, 1973), p. 92.

54. For a full discussion of the agreements negotiated during this period, see Joyce Gibson, "Production-Sharing," *Bulletin of Indonesian Economic Studies* 2 (February 1966): 52 ff. (Part I), and ibid. 4 (June 1966): 75 ff. (Part II).

55. Ibid., Part I, p. 52.

56. Ibid., Part I, pp. 52–54.

57. Alex Hunter, "Oil Developments," *Bulletin of Indonesian Economic Studies* 7 (March 1971): 98. For a thoughtful analysis of post-Sukarno production-sharing contracts, see Robert Fabrikant, *Oil Discovery and Technical Change in Southeast Asia—Legal Aspects of Production-Sharing Contracts in the Indonesian Petroleum Industry* (Singapore: Institute of Southeast Asian Studies, 1973).

58. "Affiliate" is defined in Section I, subsection 1.2.14. It is noteworthy that the earlier *Production-Sharing Contract between P.N. Pertambangan Minjak Nasional and Kyushu Oil Co., Ltd.* (1966) makes no reference to affiliates.

59. See the Arco contract of August 9, 1971 and the Indonesian Offshore contract of March 3, 1972, for example. Both are reproduced in Robert Fab-

rikant, *Oil Discovery and Technical Change in Southeast Asia—The Indonesian Petroleum Industry: Miscellaneous Source Material* (Singapore: Institute of Southeast Asian Studies, 1973).

60. William D. Smith, "Libya Intensifies Oil Restrictions," *New York Times,* August 14, 1973, p. 43.

61. See Raymond Vernon, *Sovereignty at Bay: The Multinational Spread of U.S. Enterprise* (New York: Basic Books, 1971), pp. 41–43. The ability of Chile to sell copper was, of course, subject to attempts by the companies whose properties were nationalized to block sales of Chilean copper shipments through court action.

62. In mid-1973 Ecuador signed a new agreement with Texas-Gulf Consortium providing for the right of Ecuador to purchase up to 51 percent of the company's total production for her own merchandising. See "New Oil Contract Signed by Ecuador and Consortium," *New York Times,* August 8, 1973, p. 47.

63. "Uranium - Niger," *Mineral Trade Notes* 71 (May 1974): 12.

64. For a strong argument in favor of wide use of service and management contracts, see Theodore H. Moran, "The Impact of U.S. Direct Investment on Latin-American Relations," prepared for the Commission on U.S.-Latin American Relations, Washington, June 1974. An interesting study of minerals investment in Australia found a strong relationship between the benefits to Australia and the kinds of variables discussed in the first chapter of this book. However, ownership appeared to be unrelated to the determinants of bargaining power. Apparently, Australia had not attached great significance to equity holdings, but had concentrated on the economic returns. See Robert Bruce McKern, *Multinational Enterprise and Natural Resources: A Study of Foreign Direct Investment in the Australian Minerals Industry,* unpublished doctoral dissertation, Harvard Business School, February 1972.

Chapter Three

Financial Provisions

At the heart of all negotiations of concession agreements is the problem of allocating the financial benefits and risks between the parties. Whether government income is based on royalties, income taxation, equity-sharing, production-sharing, or some other technique to apportion the revenue of the operating company, the allocation of these benefits and risks is seldom a simple matter.

There are numerous pitfalls that the parties to a negotiation may encounter in their attempts to allocate the income of a concession. The possibilities for ambiguities in the contract and for misunderstandings on one side or the other are manifold. Although these problems are presented in this chapter primarily in terms of the two most usual devices for sharing income—royalties and income taxation—the various warnings we raise in connection with these two revenue-sharing techniques are also generally applicable to equity-sharing and production-sharing arrangements, and other methods of allocating income that are growing in popularity.

The effective tax rate and the allocation of risks are two problems basic to concession negotiations. We refer here primarily to risks that profits, grade of mineral, and costs of production may differ from original forecasts. Choices between royalties and income taxes as the basic source of host country revenue will, to some extent, reflect concerns about risk allocation.

The major sources of ambiguities and misunderstandings concerning financial allocations have generally involved prices to be used in the determination of gross revenue, the calculation of depreciation, amortization, and depletion allowances, and the deductions to be allowed for payments to affiliated enterprises for purchases of goods and services and for interest on debt.

Clearly, many of the financial issues are so complex that we cannot, in the space of this chapter, do full justice to them. Our goal is simply to draw attention to the primary problems and to suggest some of the possible responses and approaches to resolving them. In many instances, once the parties are alerted to the possibility of a problem, they will want to turn to some of the highly specialized literature. The references in the notes section at the end of this chapter will, in many cases, provide useful starting points.

In Chapter 1 we argue that an examination of relative bargaining powers is a useful way of gaining an understanding of how the benefits of a particular project are likely to be allocated. It is tempting, but misleading, to look for the results of bargaining simply in the royalty rates, the tax rate, or the division of gains spelled out in profit-sharing or other formulas. Generally, the financial flows are sufficiently complex that rates alone seldom reflect the full picture of how benefits and risks are borne by the parties. Other factors are involved.

One factor is the determination of who bears the initial costs and risks of exploration. Where the foreign investor carries these costs and risks, it is possible that this fact is reflected in the tax rate, particularly where there are not separate exploration and exploitation contracts. The 1967 Indonesia Freeport Sulphur Copper Agreement is one example of this. The low tax rate in that agreement is said to have been a function, in part, of the high risk carried by the company in exploring and developing a resource in a geologically uncertain region.

The risk is not always so high nor is it necessarily borne by the company. Often, the deposits are well known. In some cases the government has undertaken some of the exploration. In the early 1970s some initial exploration was being conducted by the United Nations Development Programme on behalf of developing countries.

The source of finance for infrastructure may also be a significant factor. If the host government finances capital expenditures for infrastructure necessary to the project, as is becoming more common, the company's expenses will be accordingly decreased. The International Bank for Reconstruction and Development (the World Bank) has become one important source of finance for infrastructure that in earlier days would have been financed by the foreign investor. Funds from the World Bank Group have been used, for example, to finance the Shashi power, water, railway, and township project in connection with the Botswana Roan Selection Trust nickel and copper operation; the Boké railway, port, and township project in connection with the international aluminum consortium operation in Guinea; and the REFFSA Minas Gerais-Sepatiba Bay railway link in Brazil serving the MRB iron ore mine. In each of these cases the loan was made to the host government or one of its agencies.[1]

The effects of the various financial flows on government and company income can be captured in the calculation of discounted cash flows. Although such calculations are practically routine for private investors, they are all too rare on the part of host governments.[2] Where governments have attempted to estimate the cash flows that would accrue to them under alternative arrangements and in the light of alternative assumptions about future prices for raw materials and costs of production, the exercise has usually had its rewards in terms of better understanding of financial issues and higher financial rewards. Such calculations do not, of course, take account of social benefits and costs. Trade-offs between such benefits and costs on the one hand and financial benefits and costs on the other may be very significant. It may be possible in many cases for the government to approximate the costs of social objectives, in financial terms. If this is so, the trade-offs between social and financial benefits and costs can be made much more intelligently.

ROYALTIES

As pointed out earlier, a number of years ago royalties were the primary source of revenue for the majority of concession arrangements. By the early 1970s they played only a minor role in most agreements. But there were still a number of arrangements in which they remained an important source of government revenue. And in many agreements they still served the role of placing on the company a part of the risk of high costs or low prices for the mineral.

The royalty payment required in a specific agreement may be based on a physical unit of production or shipment or on the value of the production or shipment. The rate may be constant for a particular mineral or it may vary with the quality or price of the ore. The royalty may be deductible for corporate income tax purposes, it may be credited against such taxes, or it may be neither deductible nor creditable. If based on value, the royalty may be based on actual realized prices or on a reference, or "posted," price. The royalty may be taken in cash or kind.

Royalties based on physical units of production[3] have been the easiest to administer since they do not involve price determination. They have tended, however, to decrease in "real" value in the face of inflation over the life of a concession agreement. To minimize the erosion of value and to capture for the government some of the increased profits when prices of the raw materials rise, many agreements have abandoned the physical unit basis in favor of a royalty based on value.[4] The reference is ordinarily the sales price of the ore or a published price of the ore.

In spite of the advantages, the problems of administering a royalty based on sales price may be considerable. Many mining ventures sell much of their output to affiliated customers. The price at which such a transfer takes place within the enterprise is likely to reflect tax, tariff, or management control problems. And there may be no open-market price that can be used for purposes of adjusting the "transfer price." In an effort to avoid the pricing problem, some royalties have been based on a downstream product. Such a price may be used when it is observed to vary roughly with the value of the ore.

Jamaica provides examples of royalties based on volume and on a downstream product. In its efforts to increase concession income, the Jamaican government, in 1974, announced plans to base new royalty payments for bauxite on the price of aluminum ingots (a downstream product) rather than the tonnage of bauxite extracted as provided for up to that time.[5] Jamaica's move was followed by a similar step in Guyana.

The treatment accorded royalties in the calculation of income tax liability is usually critical to revenue allocation. In cases where royalties are credited against income taxes, the royalties are counted as a payment toward income taxes. In these instances the royalty serves essentially to assure that the government receives a minimum tax payment based on production volume, no matter what happens to costs and prices. Some agreements have a provision that requires the company to make a minimum annual payment no matter what level of production is attained. The royalty is primarily a device for allocating risks. An arrangement equivalent to a credited royalty was provided for in the 1967 Indonesian Freeport Sulphur Copper Agreement which called for a base tax payment of 5 percent of sales, increasing in later years to 14 percent.

In cases where the royalty is not credited, royalties have usually been treated as deductible expenses for the calculation of income taxes. In such arrangements the royalty has served to raise the total financial flows to the government above what they would be under the credit system, in addition to serving as a floor on company payments, guaranteeing the government revenue when profits are low or when profits disappear.

There is a third alternative, under which the royalty income is supplemental to taxation income. The royalty in this case generates neither a credit nor a deduction for income tax purposes. This was the proposal presented in Canada in 1974, to be accompanied by a standard abatement in the income tax rate.

The importance of how royalties are handled is apparent from a simple illustration: take a mining company that exports 5 million tons of ore at $6 a ton with production costs of $4 a ton. Let the agreement call for a royalty of 50¢ a ton and an income tax of 50 percent.

1. If the royalty is not deducted as a cost of business (expensed), and not credited against income tax, the income will be allocated as follows:

Gross receipts	$30,000,000
Costs	20,000,000
Net profits	10,000,000
Income tax 50%	5,000,000
Royalty 50¢	2,500,000
Government share	7,500,000
Company share	2,500,000

2. If the royalty is deducted as a cost of business, but not credited against income tax, the following allocation of income results:

Gross receipts	$30,000,000
Costs	20,000,000
Royalty 50¢	2,500,000

Net profits	7,500,000
Income tax 50%	3,750,000
Royalty 50¢	2,500,000
Government share	6,250,000
Company share	3,750,000

3. If the royalty is not deducted as a cost of business but is instead credited against income tax, the income allocation takes the following form:

Gross receipts	$30,000,000
Costs	20,000,000
Net profits	10,000,000
Tentative income tax 50%	5,000,000
Credit for royalty 50¢	- 2,500,000
Net income tax	2,500,000
Government share (royalty	
plus income tax)	5,000,000
Company share	5,000,000

The question of whether royalties are to be credited or "expensed" became a major issue in the oil industry in the early 1960s; and in 1964 agreement was reached between most of the OPEC countries and the oil companies to the effect that, in the future, royalty payments would be expensed rather than credited in the calculation of income taxes.[6] The effect was an increase in the tax burden imposed on the companies. Although the expensing of royalties has become the general pattern in petroleum, the practice in other industries had not become uniform by the mid-1970s.

Not only has there been little standardization in the methods of levying royalties, but there also appear to be only limited standards for appropriate levels of royalties, even within particular industries. Part of the difficulty, of course, has been in the complexity of tax arrangements. Since royalties have been combined with income tax in most agreements, and since there are alternative ways of handling royalties vis-à-vis income taxes, a nominal rate in one agreement may generate a tax burden very different from the same rate in a different agreement.

Copper again provides an example of variations of rates among different agreements. Freeport Sulphur in Indonesia paid no conventional royalty under its 1967 agreement. Kennecott, in the same region, was to pay a royalty of 3.6 percent, based on the value of sales. Papua New Guinea, nearby, was to collect 1.25 percent of value from copper out of Bougainville. In Zambia before 1969 royalties were 13.5 percent of the value of ore over a certain base line. Royalties increased progressively to 40 percent on an increment of value.

Rates are not always specified. Formulas are occasionally used. The 1974

Mining Development Law of Ecuador provided, for example, that royalties on metal ores were to be computed by dividing the gross profits by the "updated investment." The result would be the percentage to be collected from gross profits in the form of royalty. The percentage was not to exceed 16 percent. The updated investment was to be the sum of the net amount of capital assets subject to depreciation at a particular date (apparently the beginning of exploitation activities), the operating capital required for carrying on work for two months, and the expenses incurred in the exploration and preliminary production stages. At the same time, royalties on nonmetal ores were more conventional, to be 4 percent of the value of production.[7]

Royalty rates have sometimes reflected the quality of the ore. Some countries have offered lower royalty rates for low-grade ores to compensate for the higher costs of extraction and to encourage firms not to ignore the low-grade ores. Ecuador, for example, in its agreement with OMRD of Japan, specified a table of royalties that varied with the grade of the copper ore. Although there are apparently no relevant data on the behavior of mining companies, a high royalty, it is thought, discourages the extraction of marginal ores. Often low-grade ores can be profitably extracted only at the time of extraction of the higher-grade ores. In a similar manner, royalties can discourage moving into additional stages of ore beneficiation.

Occasionally the problem is one of encouraging the development of a generally low-grade field. In late 1972 it was argued by Nigerian tin miners that, because of the high rate of royalties, only the highest yielding fields—those yielding over 0.75 pounds of tin metal per cubic yard—could be mined economically. A reduction in royalties was urged to encourage operators to begin extracting the generally untouched extensive low-grade ore fields on the Jos Plateau.[8]

Finally, it should be noted that the imposition and handling of royalties has had, in some cases, important ramifications for taxes imposed on the company in its home country, as well as in the country in which the mining was being done. Taxes paid by their firms abroad have been handled differently by various advanced countries. Either through unilateral legislation or through double taxation agreements, the tax systems of advanced countries take into account the need for their firms operating abroad to pay foreign taxes. Many allow a credit for taxes paid abroad as if they had been paid in the home country. Thus an income tax at a 25 percent rate paid in a developing country would count as a credit toward the tax bill on that income in the home country. In general, however, credits have been limited to payments of taxes that qualified as income taxes. Royalties might not count as an income tax, since the tax base is not income.[9] Thus, a firm may receive a full credit for income taxes paid in the developing country, but receive only a deduction for royalties paid there. Obviously such companies have favored income tax arrangements in preference to equivalent royalty arrangements where the royalties have not given rise to tax credits.

In some cases proper structure of the tax may not be enough; the label itself may be an important factor. In the United States two types of foreign taxes are creditable: income taxes and taxes paid in lieu of income taxes. In either case a foreign levy must not only meet the test of being based on income (as understood in United States tax law) but must also meet the test of being a tax rather than some other type of payment. In some cases, payments denominated income taxes have qualified while similar levies denominated royalties have not.[10]

INCOME TAXES

Although the central administrative problem of many royalty arrangements is the determination of appropriate prices on which to base the calculation, income taxation presents problems not only of determining sales prices (or calculating gross income), but also of determining appropriate deductions to arrive at net income. In fact, many of the issues concerning deductions result from the fact that goods and services are purchased from firms affiliated with the foreign investor.

The inadequacies of the general tax laws and administration in many developing countries have usually caused a considerable burden to be put on the concession agreement. Many arrangements have required detailed tax provisions in the *ad hoc* agreements.[11] The importance of the general tax laws is illustrated by a comparison of the Australian and Canadian concession contracts with those of the less-developed countries. Canadian timber agreements and Australian iron ore agreements, for example, have said nothing about the income tax.[12] The long history of international firms in Australia and Canada has led to general tax laws, supplemented by general tax provisions relating to extractive industries, that deal with the particular problems caused by the operations of the foreign firm. In these countries it has been satisfactory to submit the foreign extractive enterprises to laws of general application for income tax matters.

In contrast, in such countries as Liberia, Ethiopia, Indonesia, and Malaysia, special tax provisions have been negotiated, on a case-by-case basis, in the concession arrangements themselves.

The incorporation of elements of tax laws into *ad hoc* agreements raises a number of technical problems. We have selected for discussion those that have proved to be of special importance in negotiations with foreign extractive enterprises; the discussion is not intended to be a general treatment of all the problems of corporate income taxation.[13]

Gross Income
Issues concerning the calculation of gross income have arisen frequently in negotiations. Two key problems have involved the sources of income that will be taxed and the prices that would govern the sales of the enterprise.

A few agreements have attempted to subject to the tax regime of the host country not only the income of the operating company but also part of the worldwide income of the corporate system with which the operating company was associated. We have mentioned the early agreement in Persia with Anglo-Persian Oil Company, in which the Persian government claimed a right to share in the profits of all companies "dealing with oil extracted under the concession, whether or not such companies operated in Persia."[14]

For practical administrative reasons, these early attempts to reach the worldwide income of a network of extractive companies were unsuccessful. More recently, and more typically, only revenue earned by the local partnership or the locally incorporated company has been subject to tax under the mineral agreements in developing countries. Although in some cases the worldwide income of a local subsidiary has been subject to tax in the developing country, generally tax is limited to income derived from local operations. The 1955 Libyan Petroleum Law provided, for example, that the host country shall impose a tax on income "resulting to the concession holder from his operations in Libya." This was defined to include, in relation to crude oil exported by the concession holder, total gross receipts realized from exports. Exactly what is to be included in income "resulting from [local] operations" has not, however, been self-evident. United States income tax law, for example, has provided a number of rules that have been elaborated by specific regulations for determining whether income "shall be treated," for tax purposes, as income from sources within the United States.[15] Some of these rules have become very complex.

In some cases the question of defining what income is a result of local operations has been handled by treaty. Agreements for the avoidance of double taxation have provided that, with regard to income derived from the sale of goods purchased, manufactured, or produced in one country and sold in another by a single entity, the source of the profits should be allocated in a specified way between the two countries involved. For example, a treaty between India and Ceylon provided that half the income from goods manufactured by, or on behalf of, a person in one country and sold by him in the other country through a branch or regular agency would be subject to tax in each country. Profits on the sale of metal ores, minerals, mineral oils, and forest products extracted by a firm in one of the countries (the firm having no branch in the other country) and sold to a purchaser in the other without further processing were to be taxed solely by the country in which minerals or timber were extracted. If the minerals or timber were sold in the other country through a branch or regular agency in the second country, 75 percent of the income was to be taxed by the first country and 25 percent by the second.[16]

Once the basic source rules are established, many host countries have found it necessary to deal with the problem of allocation of income between two separate operations within the local company. The problem arises, for example, when agreements make special provision for the exclusion or special treatment of income from processing facilities. Under the 1958 "Brokopondo" agreement between Alcoa and Surinam, Alcoa was to pay a 35 percent rate of tax on its bauxite operations and a 30 percent rate of tax on its alumina operation.[17] In some cases a tax holiday may be granted for income from refining or other processing to encourage the establishment of facilities in the country. In such situations the agreement must provide formulas for the allocation of revenue between the extractive and processing operations, even though they may be undertaken by the same company. More typically the problem of allocation arises for two or more companies that are affiliated but subject to different tax rates in the same or in different tax jurisdictions.

The allocation problem has been made particularly complex by some concession agreements that have made special provision for the exclusion or special treatment of income from related services provided by other companies. For example, the Liberian LAMCO agreement, previously described, granted tax holidays to contracting firms that provided services to the basic iron ore mining operations. Such exclusion of income of contracting firms can generate significant problems for host governments. The most important, perhaps, have arisen because mining firms have set up their own contracting enterprises and priced their services in such a way that income has been shifted to the affiliated enterprises, out of the reach of the tax regime. To avoid such maneuvers, either the affiliated enterprises must be denied tax exemption or the government must be prepared to police many complex transactions. In fact, the difficulties in reallocating income suggest that provisions calling for the different handling of income within a company or between affiliated companies should probably be avoided, unless an overwhelmingly convincing case can be made that the benefits exceed the administrative costs.

The most common and most difficult problem in determining gross income is the determination of the price to govern sales of the product of the operations. In some cases actual realized prices have been used; in other cases a formula price has been utilized as a basis for calculating gross income.

If the industry is one in which the product that leaves the developing country is sold on an open market, there is usually no difficulty. In most cases, that open market price is the one that has been used in the calculation of gross income. In such an industry, if the company sells the product to affiliates at a price different from the market price—that is, at a "non-arm's length" price—the price to rule for tax purposes is, according to most agreements, that which would have ruled on the free market if the free market price is higher than the recorded transfer price. Petroleum has been an exception to the general rule. Many oil agreements have required that the taxes be calculated on the basis of an artificial "posted price," even for sales on the open market.[18] By late 1973 the Middle Eastern producers were maintaining this posted price at a fixed percentage above the market price.

The more difficult cases arise in the large number of extractive industries in which a meaningful quoted market price does not exist. In these cases agreements have generally spelled out the details of how, for tax purposes, a price would be calculated for sales of the extractive operations. Where sales are to unaffiliated parties, the actual realized prices have usually governed. If sales are to affiliated parties, as they frequently have been in such industries, some adequate yardstick of value must be specified in some detail.

Without supervision the prices that are recorded for transactions with affiliates may reflect the investor's objectives only. The investor may be motivated to set prices in such a way that they shift recorded profits from one tax jurisdiction to another in order to reduce taxes, to provide management incentives, to avoid exchange controls, or to avoid accumulation of profits where they have to be shared with local equity-holders.

The problem of transactions among affiliates is not unique to international business, although it is with these that the tax authorities are usually most concerned. Transactions between affiliated entities can be used to reduce taxes for purely domestic corporations, but their importance is much greater in the international context than in purely domestic operations. Since all the affiliated entities in the domestic case are generally subject to some kind of domestic income tax, the effects for the government concerned may not be so serious as when the profits are shifted to another tax jurisdiction. Thus, in countries where international business is relatively rare, the laws and administrative machinery have typically not been well developed to handle affiliate transactions. Even where the laws are well developed, the problem of transfer pricing has generated the need for tax authorities of host countries to constantly monitor prices for sales to affiliates. Without such monitoring of sales prices, the result has been the loss of considerable tax revenue.

Governments have followed various policies in dealing with the problem of the prices of goods sold to affiliated parties when no adequate free-market standard has existed. The posted price for petroleum, already mentioned, is only one approach of many.[19] Some countries have taken a different tack. We have described the use of the pig aluminum price for bauxite.[20] But even for ingot, few open-market transactions have occurred. The quoted ingot price itself was a basing point price.[21] In another case the Liberian Mining Company Agreement of 1945 used the average wholesale price of Bessemer pig iron at Pittsburgh, as reported by the U.S. Bureau of Labor Statistics, as the basis for royalty calculations.[22]

To avoid the imposition by the government of notional or artificial reference prices, companies have, in some cases, made efforts to establish some independent sales that would provide a basis for assigning free-market prices to sales to affiliates. The Orinoco Mining Company in Venezuela, owned by U.S. Steel, established a market for iron ore in Venezuela with nonaffiliated buyers. It has been said that this market was established largely for the purpose of demonstrating what free-market prices would be for its sales to its American owner.

Even where published free-market prices have existed, agreements have sometimes avoided using them as the basis for the calculation of gross income. The free markets were often marginal ones, with the major volume of transactions in the industry occurring between affiliates or through long-term, unquoted contracts. The prices on such a marginal market may swing widely, reflecting disproportionately the marginal needs of users who normally purchase through other arrangements, or reflecting the influence of speculators. Illustrative of this instability was the copper market in the early months of 1972. It was thought that the London Metal Exchange prices for copper were heavily influenced by small transactions by speculative buyers and sellers, rather than by regular patterns of supply and demand. Taxes from agreements based on this price varied with the speculative mood. In fact, some of the copper-exporting countries harbored suspicions that the importing countries might be manipulating the price with small sales on the open market to drive down the price at the time they were exporting major shipments whose prices would be determined by those published for the thin open market.

To avoid the pitfalls that might be associated with a particular formula or reference price, some agreements have begun to spell out the principle that is desired as the overriding rule for the determination of price. The principle has usually been based on what would be the price for transactions between independent parties. Such agreements have then gone on to specify some rules reflecting this principle at the time of negotiation. In newly producing countries, for example, a copper agreement might specify that the price will be the same as the one governing contracts in the major producing countries. Then specific—but temporary—rules may refer to refined products traded on the London Metal Exchange as a basis. The agreement might then detail deductions for costs of smelting and refining and for impurities contained in the ore. Should these rules no longer reflect the principle that is specified, new rules are to be constructed. Whether the uncertainty inherent in such an approach will result in more destructive conflict between investor and host than that which characterized the more specific arrangements remains to be seen.

To ease the administrative burden on taxing authorities, governments have attempted, on occasion, to place on the foreign firm the burden of justifying the appropriateness of prices that are recorded for transactions with affiliates. Unable to collect the documentation required to show prices ruling in an independent market, governments have insisted that the company provide copies of its contracts concerning transactions with unaffiliated parties. The increase in information seems likely to reduce somewhat the suspicions of the host government. And the company is probably more careful in its calculations when it knows it must provide a great deal of documentation.

Deductions for Calculating Net Income

Equal in importance to a careful determination of gross income are the deductions to be allowed in the calculation of net income subject to taxation. The deductions recognized for this purpose have varied considerably from country to country and in agreements within particular countries. No established list of appropriate deductions can be found, since much depends on the particular industry involved and the tax system to which the investor is accustomed.[23] Yet the areas of principal concern in most negotiations have included depreciation, amortization, depletion, and the acceptability for tax purposes of various payments to affiliates.

Depreciation. In most tax jurisdictions firms have been allowed to take as an expense of doing business each year a sum that is intended to represent a cost of capital equipment.[24] The theory is that the capital deteriorates in value, and this loss of value, or depreciation, should be charged against profits.

Depreciation for the investor is only a bookkeeping entry. He need make no cash outlay that matches the write-off. However, the result of allowing depreciation as a deductible cost for tax calculations is a reduction in taxes by the amount of the tax rate times the depreciation that is allowed. Contrary to occasional belief, there is no cash "created" through taking depreciation. The only result is that the cash outflow for taxes is reduced and the profits stated in the books are lower than they would otherwise be. Although the tax savings could lead the firm to have cash on hand, there can be no assumption that an amount of cash has been set aside in a reserve for replacement of equipment.[25]

Depreciation write-offs take on added significance when governments move to take over mineral properties that are in private hands. If the compensation offered by the government is based on book value, the compensation to the company is, of course, lower if more depreciation has been shown on the balance sheet.

The simple concept of depreciation as a bookkeeping entry to reflect the using up of capital assets would suggest that annual depreciation should be based on the yearly loss of value of the assets, if indeed there is a loss. For administrative convenience, however, tax authorities have generally estimated the life of an asset and allowed the write-off to occur in equal amounts each year, or in amounts that reflect some other simple formula, until the asset reaches its scrap value.

Since the resale value of many assets declines more rapidly in the initial years than in later years, it has not been very difficult to support a view that depreciation should be greater in earlier years and less in later years. Various formulas have been devised that are supposed to reflect the nonlinear decline in value of a firm's assets. The result of the application of such formulas is to reduce the tax burden of the firm in earlier years while increasing it in later years.

The most common practices have been for the government to specify the assumed life of the assets in a schedule, by type of asset. The firm then has taken straight-line depreciation or used the sum-of-the-years or declining-balance methods. Once the method is chosen, the firm must be consistent in its approach and must begin depreciation with the acquisition of the asset. There is usually one exception: if the declining-balance method is used, the company may shift to straight-line depreciation when it chooses.

In many cases depreciation has been used for purposes beyond those that simply reflect the using up of assets. Depreciation has been manipulated to grant incentives to investors by allowing the firm to postpone taxes. To grant tax incentives, governments have, for example, shortened the presumed economic life of assets to allow the firm to write off the assets quickly. Or they have introduced formulas that allow very high depreciation in the early years. Under most such arrangements, the host government has received the same amount of taxes as under the more traditional depreciation calculations, but in later years. Such an arrangement could, of course, be viewed as the equivalent of imposing on the firm a lower tax rate in the earlier years and a higher one later.

There are other methods that have departed from the original concept of depreciation. For example, some governments have entered agreements that allow the firm to choose its own rate of depreciation each year, subject to a few constraints. In some Indonesian concessions, for example, the company can select its depreciation rate each year, as long as the rate does not exceed 12.5 percent of the value of the assets being depreciated. Under such an arrangement the company will presumably charge depreciation in years in which there is a taxable profit or there is a loss that can be carried forward. During tax holidays or periods in which losses are incurred that cannot be carried forward, it will not charge depreciation, saving the charges until tax savings will be generated.

In another departure from general practice, some countries have permitted fixed assets to be expensed as purchased. Under the post-1969 copper arrangements in Zambia, for example, all capital expenses could be written off immediately. With unlimited loss carry-forward, the firms were assured of no taxes until the investment was recovered.

Most such arrangements to vary depreciation from the generally accepted approaches have been designed as incentives to induce the firm to do something that it would not otherwise have done by rewarding the firm with lower taxes in the earlier years, although the government generally recoups the foregone taxes in later years. Although the idea of financial incentives is appealing, empirical research has tended to show that the decisions of the investor are generally only slightly influenced by tax factors. Developing countries, placing a high value on current versus future income, would do well to adopt a cautious approach to incentives in the form of special depreciation rules.

Amortization and Depletion. In addition to allowing depreciation for fixed assets, mining agreements have also generally permitted deductions in recognition of the decline in value of intangible assets, including the costs of developing the mine. Such deductions have often been referred to as amortization deductions.

The term amortization, used in the sense of the write-off of capitalized expenditures that do not represent fixed tangible assets subject to depreciation, should not be confused with the same term applied to the repayment of the principal on debt. Repayment of debt has been allowed as a deduction for tax purposes only in very exceptional cases.[26] But development costs have generally been treated much like depreciation. Agreements may specify the number of years over which development costs can be written off. Another similar practice has been to provide for the write-off of these costs in equal annual installments over the term of the contract.[27] Still another method has been to associate the amortization with the production rate. The reserves are estimated, and the development costs are amortized in proportion to the using up of these reserves.

The handling of expenses incurred before the signing of the agreement and of expenses incurred outside the country have presented more problems. Sometimes these expenses can be amortized; sometimes not. In certain countries, national law or minerals agreements have disallowed for tax purposes the amortization of expenses incurred by the home office for the benefit of the local company. Such a policy has been justified on the ground that information as to the amount and nature of home office expenses is difficult to obtain. In other cases such deductions are acceptable if they can be shown to be associated with the local income. In other situations tax treaties have specifically called for such deductions in the pattern of the OECD Model Income-Tax Convention. Some tax treaties have also called for an exchange of information between the tax authorities. This provision has been little drawn upon, but might reduce the difficulties associated with the calculation of appropriate allocations of such expenses.

Where home office expenses are to be allowed, the government may want to spell out rules governing the expenses. Factors that might be taken into consideration in determining the amount of the deduction include the local company's gross receipts in comparison with those of the total enterprise; the number of workers employed compared with the total enterprise; or the wage costs compared with that of the total enterprise. Such factors have been considered by state tax authorities in the allocation of income among the state tax jurisdictions within the United States.

A number of countries have allowed as a deductible business expense a figure designated as depletion. A common method for computing the depletion deduction has been the so-called cost basis "by which the cost of acquiring and bringing a natural resource deposit into production is spread over the life of that deposit."[28] When depletion is based on cost of bringing the deposit into production, it is no more than amortization of expenditures. However, an alternative method available in the United States and some other countries, termed percentage depletion, is conceptually different. Percentage depletion has permitted a deduction from gross income that is calculated as a fixed percentage of gross or net income from the exploitation activities.

Where depletion is based on cost, the "cost" may include, for example, geological surveys, other exploration expenses, exploratory mining or drilling costs, costs of constructing roads, providing power, and amounts spent for obtaining the concession. The costs usually include expenditures incurred up to the point of operation. Cost depletion, of course, excludes expenditures that are currently deductible.

In some countries exploration costs have been considered part of the depletion base; in others these costs have been currently deductible. Where an agreement allows amortization and depletion, government negotiators must be careful to avoid offering double deductions for particular costs, and it is advisable to spell out the specific expenses that qualify under a particular deduction heading.

It should be noted that although the depletion allowance is often conceived of as taking into account the gradual using up of a wasting asset, the cost basis for the allowance seldom, if ever, includes the value of the asset when discovered.[29] So even in countries where the subsoil and minerals are legally the property of the state, cost depletion may be permitted.

Percentage depletion may be usefully viewed as a tax incentive to encourage mineral development rather than simply as a method for systematically calculating a deduction based on the decline in value of economic resources. Percentage depletion has generally resulted in larger deductions than cost depletion; annual deductions have tended to be larger and the total deduction over the life of the deposit has reflected not actual cost but the results of an arbitrary formula. Usually the total sum deducted under the formula far exceeds any and all nondeductible costs incurred in discovering and developing the deposit. In 1975 in the United States, for example, allowances for depletion varied between 5 and 22 percent of the value of the output at the mine or wellhead (as long as this did not exceed half the taxable profits) for hard minerals and petroleum.

Whatever the case for or against the percentage depletion allowance in the United States, where the allowance has resulted as much from political factors as from economic ones, developing countries should consider percentage depletion as a form of income tax incentive; at the same time they should ask whether such an incentive is called for at all. If the host country determines that an incentive of some sort is necessary, other techniques may prove less costly and more rational. The tax reduction that is equivalent to a given depletion allowance based on value of output is easy to calculate, *if* the average profit margin on sales is known. The difficulty in the negotiating stage is that the margin is usually very difficult for the two parties to project with any degree of confidence.

If net income is 20 percent of gross income, a 10 percent depletion allowance based on output or gross income simply reduces the taxable profits by 50 percent. Thus the effective tax rate on net income is halved. In general, the tax rate is reduced by the fraction that the depletion rate represents of the net profit margin.

The difficulties in projecting profit margins and the general confusion that surrounds the meaning of depletion allowances lead us to believe that the predictability of the results of a lower tax rate makes the rate reduction a better incentive than the granting of percentage depletion allowances, if some sort of special treatment for the extractive industry is indeed required.

The depletion allowance, cost or percentage, was not recognized as a deductible item in the early 1970s in most oil-producing countries in Africa, Asia, and Latin America, although a depletion allowance still applied to a few hard mineral arrangements in developing countries.[30] The pattern appeared to be a reduction in the allowances for depletion where they were granted, and a tendency not to apply them at all in most cases.

Purchases of Goods and Services from Affiliates. There is little controversy over the allowance of costs as deductions from gross revenue in the calculation of net taxable income. But the amount of deductions to be allowed when costs have been incurred in transactions among affiliated firms has created problems. Pricing affects not only the calculation of gross income through sales, but also the calculation of net income through purchases.

The problem faced by tax authorities in developing countries has been similar to that encountered in taxing domestic importers and exporters. The authorities of most developing countries have been well acquainted with the problems of over- and under-invoicing of imports and exports by local traders to accumulate foreign exchange in private hands and to reduce local taxes. Such over-invoicing of imports can be easily accomplished by the international firm. Mining companies typically purchase much of their equipment and inputs through affiliates abroad. The company has an option of pricing these imports so that profits are generated where the company's interest requires. That place may be outside the developing country. One study in Colombia showed the extent to which over-pricing of imports can occur in a case where the incentives are significant for the foreign firm to use this option for shifting tax burdens and to avoid exchange controls.[31]

To reduce the tax losses through price manipulation on purchases of goods, a number of mineral agreements have specified that the company report to the tax authorities prices that would govern independent purchases. Where no similar transactions take place on an open market, cost-based figures can be used. U.S. tax regulations spell out methods of calculating an acceptable resale price or an acceptable cost-plus price.[32]

The administrative problems involved in policing prices for goods purchased from affiliates has proved difficult for developing countries. In some cases host

sents a real cost to the corporate group of which the operating company is a part. To generate any tax savings, the company must incur a real cost greater than what it saves. Thus it is a reasonably safe assumption that the company will limit its outside borrowing to an amount that serves a reasonable business purpose. (The method used by a company to determine a reasonable borrowing level is complex, but is not of great concern to the government.) Affiliate loans, however, come at no extra cost to the corporate group and can generate tax savings. Strangely, at least from the government's point of view, there are a number of mining agreements that have provided specifically for the deduction of interest to affiliates.[43]

Before looking at what host governments have done about the fictitious debt problem, it is worth mentioning some of the other incentives for the company to use fictitious loans from affiliates instead of equity:

1. *Foreign exchange controls:* Some countries have given preference to payments for interest and principal on debt when authorizing foreign-exchange purchases. Thus a company could use fictitious debt as a way of obtaining foreign exchange for what would otherwise be dividend remittances.
2. *Tax in developed country:* In some of the developed countries the parent may avoid taxation on the repayment of principal. Without the debt, the payment would have been a taxable dividend. By labelling the payment as a repayment of principal, the company may postpone long into the future some tax payments in the home of the parent.
3. *Flexibility:* One of the major attractions of the use of affiliate debt instead of equity has been that the company retains flexibility; it can convert the debt to equity if it chooses; it can convert equity to debt only with much greater difficulty.

Host country governments have taken a number of steps to ensure that the foreign company does not escape tax liability through the use of debt from affiliates. At least three kinds of policies have been tried:

1. A policy that disallows for tax purposes deduction for any interest payments abroad; generally, such a policy has applied only to certain industries— for example, petroleum in Libya and Indonesia.[44]
2. A policy that disallows, for tax purposes, deduction for any interest payments to affiliates; the Carter Commission Report in Canada recommended this policy for general application in Canada.[45] Such a policy was called for in the Indonesian Corporate Tax Law,[46] although the provision of this law was overruled in practically every hard mineral investment agreement entered into by Indonesia in the late 1960s and early 1970s.
3. A policy that provides guidelines, but depends on a case-by-case analysis to determine the appropriateness of any particular deduction; this has been the

approach used in the United States. The questions asked by American courts have been:

i. Is the debt held by the shareholders in proportion to their equity?

ii. Is the debt subordinated to unaffiliated creditors?

iii. Does the debt have fixed repayment terms and does it call for interest at market rates?

iv. Does the company have a debt-to-equity ratio of greater than 4:1?

v. Does the debt serve a clear business purpose other than that of avoiding taxes?

An answer of yes to i, ii, or iv, or an answer of no to iii, has generally led to a disallowance of the interest payments for tax purposes unless there was a clear yes to v.

The Tax Reform Act of 1969 added a new section to the Internal Revenue Code giving the Commissioner authority to issue rules for distinguishing debt from stock interests. Although the Commissioner was given broad authority in formulating the various factors to be considered, the new law required that the guidelines include (1) whether a written unconditional promise to pay at a specific date or on demand a fixed sum at a fixed interest rate; (b) whether the alleged indebtedness is subordinate to other corporate indebtedness; (c) the ratio of corporate debt to equity; (d) whether the alleged debt is convertible to stock; and (e) the relationship between the alleged debt and actual stock ownership.[47]

Two other approaches sometimes used to attack the problems are: (1) limiting the overall debt-to-equity ratio a company may have; or (2) imposing a withholding tax on interest payments. Neither policy (nor that of a ban on all foreign interest payments) makes the necessary distinction between loans from affiliates and loans from independent parties. The withholding tax still leaves an incentive for the company to utilize affiliate loans, as long as the withholding rate is less than the corporate tax rate. If the two rates were equal, however, the result would be a tremendous burden on real borrowing from independent sources. Limiting the debt-to-equity ratio still gives a tax break to the firm that does not borrow from banks, relative to the firm which, for sound business reasons, does borrow from banks. Neither approach has proved completely satisfactory for developing countries.

The complex approach used by the United States requires a large input of administrative skills to be pursued effectively. Developing countries have been wise to avoid this approach.

The principle of not allowing a deduction for any interest payments to affiliates seems appropriate for many developing countries. Its application is not administratively difficult and the principle makes sufficient distinctions between kinds of loans to permit fair handling of the vast majority of cases.

There is one special case in which the limit of the debt-to-equity ratio has perhaps been the only appropriate and feasible approach. In some situations it has been virtually impossible to distinguish affiliates from independent parties. For the extractive firms from most advanced countries, the determination of affiliated parties has not been difficult. Moreover, the company itself can be required to provide a list of its affiliates. In the case of Japanese investors, however, the problem may be a difficult one.

In Japan the affiliations among the banks and major firms have been so complex that it has been almost impossible for administrators with limited time to untangle the relationships. For Japanese investors who are financed through Japanese institutions, a rule that limits the debt-to-equity ratio in a predetermined manner may be the only viable solution for the host country that wishes to control this method of syphoning off tax revenue.

We have proposed, in a situation in which a Japanese investor planned a debt-to-equity ratio of some 10:1, that the agreement specify that the debt, for tax purposes, be limited to a certain percentage of the capitalization. In this case the limit was to be that which was the average for debt from unaffiliated parties in other operations in the same industry and region. The ratio that prevailed at the particular time was calculated as 2:1 and was included in the agreement. In addition, the interest rate on the recognized debt was to be limited to the Japanese Central Bank discount rate plus a fixed amount. In the circumstances, this approach appeared to be the only workable solution acceptable to both the government and the foreign company.

Even where governments have recognized the debt problem and adopted a general policy, some confusion has often remained. The issue has concerned the company's reporting. Many governments have recognized that they do not need to attempt to influence directly the form of the investment on the companies' books. It is the deduction of interest *for tax purposes* (and, perhaps, the issuance of foreign exchange permits) that is of concern to the government. If a company can retain the tax advantages of the debt in the home country, this, in the absence of fraud, need not concern the host country. In some cases difficulties have arisen when the host country has involved itself in the approval of loans or other contracts between affiliates in ways that might imply that it is accepting the validity of the contracts for tax purposes. The restriction of any approvals to a specific purpose—for exchange controls, for example—will generally avoid such problems.

POTENTIAL FINANCIAL IMPLICATIONS OF THE AFFILIATE PROBLEM

Although most developing countries with foreign investment have faced the problems of controlling affiliate transactions, the magnitude of the financial implications is often not appreciated. A simplified description of a case on which we worked illustrates the potential scope of the problem.

An investment was made in the 1950s by a consortium of European companies, for a total of some $150 million. In the 1960s the output of the mine was 10 million tons, with a market value of $6.50/ton. The profit before interest and taxes on this level of operation was estimated to be about $20 million annually. Since the government had negotiated a tax rate of 50 percent, it was expecting an annual revenue of close to $10 million. However, the project was financed with a $25 million equity investment, a $25 million bank loan, and a $100 million loan from the parent (the European consortium). The interest rate on all the loans was 6 percent. As a result the company had generated a tax deduction for interest to itself of $6 million annually, reducing taxes by $3 million. In addition, the company was deducting sales commissions paid to one of the consortium members for sales to a company owned by another member. These fees were high, amounting in some cases to $1.40/ton, justified on the basis that the ownership of the purchasing company represented a risk to the consortium. Moreover, another of the consortium members was being paid management fees to operate the mine; the profits on these fees were discovered to be $150,000 each year. As the government began to investigate the affiliate transactions, it discovered many other transactions being used to avoid taxes, such as overcharging for shipping on vessels owned by consortium members, discounts on sales of ore to members, and legal and financial fees to affiliates. It was calculated that the government was losing close to $8 million yearly by not policing these transactions.

Throughout the range of problems created by transactions among affiliates, the basic principle involved is the government's right to reallocate income among affiliated parties to reflect where that income would have been generated in the absence of any affiliation, or, where specified, some other method of allocation. The illustrative agreement in this book (see the Appendix) includes some provisions that could enable a government to enforce this right; such provisions cannot, however, serve as a substitute for knowledge of the industry and continual auditing of such transactions. Each country must develop the required skills to avoid the loss of income through the investor's use of affiliate transactions.

EQUITY-SHARING: VARIATION ON A THEME

The term equity-sharing, as we have mentioned, can cover a variety of arrangements. Common to all, the government receives equity, drawing all or part of its receipts from dividends instead of, or in addition to, taxes.

Under such arrangements most of the issues discussed under taxation are still of importance. For example, affiliate transactions can be employed by the firm to draw off profits that would have to be shared with the government. In fact, some of the problems have been more significant under profit-sharing arrangements than under the more traditional arrangement. The provision by the foreign firm of funds under the "debt" label rather than as equity, for instance, may cost the government more under an equity-sharing agreement than would the interest deductions under an income tax arrangement. In an equity agreement a government will normally share in the repayment of the principal, in addition to sharing in the interest payment. Principal obligations would be an after-tax expense of the firm under the more traditional tax arrangements.

In the case of arrangements based on tax, the regulations covering the general tax laws can usually be assumed to apply to the concessionaire, but whether they apply to equity arrangements is often unclear. Many of the usual government safeguards found in income tax codes may be of questionable application to an equity-sharing arrangement. To protect their interests, governments have discovered that they must spell out as many or more protections in the equity arrangements than in the traditional income tax arrangements.

Not only does an equity-sharing government run the risk of sharing in the repayment of principal on loans, the government will also, in the absence of specific provisions to the contrary, share in reinvestment of earnings, since dividends are only those profits that are not reinvested. The government can, of course, include provisions for certain minimum dividends, perhaps as a percentage of profits as defined by the tax laws, or it can define the profits in which it participates in the same way that taxable income would be defined. In fact, proposals for modifications along these lines have been made for governments with old profit-sharing agreements that were not yielding the revenue originally anticipated.

Where equity-sharing is primarily in lieu of income tax, a further problem arises. Such arrangements are likely to be unattractive for investors from countries that give tax credits for foreign income taxes. Under a tax arrangement the taxes of such investors would be reduced in their home countries by approximately the amount paid to the host government. On the other hand, dividends declared to the government under a profit-sharing arrangement would not normally generate an offsetting tax credit at home. The Liberian LAMCO operation provides an example of an arrangement designed to fit the tax situation. Although Swedish partners were subject to profit-sharing, the U.S. partner paid an income tax.[48] Sweden did not have a unilateral foreign tax credit system, but the United States did.

PRODUCTION-SHARING AND WORK AND SERVICE CONTRACTS

Many of the problems connected with income tax also arise in connection with production-sharing contracts and service contracts. The host country should not be misled into believing that such arrangements are self-enforcing. In both cases the calculation of operating costs that are reimbursible in cash or kind can be affected by such factors as purchases from affiliates. The production-sharing agreement between the Indonesian government and Kyushu Oil Corporation, for example, made no provision for auditing the investors' calculation of operating expenses.[49] This could be a costly omission for the host government. The same kind of care is called for in drawing up these more modern contracts as is needed in the traditional tax arrangements.

OTHER FINANCIAL PROVISIONS

Mining agreements vary considerably in the number and kinds of other taxes to which the foreign company is subject. The revenue from these taxes has generally been low, compared to that which has resulted from royalties, income taxes, or their substitutes in equity-sharing, production-sharing, and similar contracts.

The majority of agreements have charged the concessionaire a fee for land in the concession area. In many cases the rate has been designed to change at one or more points during the course of the agreement. Typically, a low fee has governed the early contract period, when the concessionaire was involved in exploration. A higher fee is charged later to induce him to relinquish land he does not need. The Indonesian copper agreement with Kennecott, for example, called for a payment of 0.5¢ per hectare per annum in the survey period; 10¢ per hectare between the survey and operating periods; and $1 or $2 per hectare during the operating period, depending on the deposit involved.[50]

Concessionaires may be subject to general charges, such as import duties, automobile license fees, sales taxes, documentary stamp taxes, and transfer taxes, which are designed to protect local industry or to raise revenue.[51] In 1972 Indonesia imposed a dredging tax on timber concessionaires in Kalimantan, supposedly for the purpose of opening up riverways.[52]

Often the investor has insisted on a provision that guarantees that the fees will not be discriminatory. The investor insists, in other words, that he will not be singled out for payment of fees higher than those charged others, particularly local businessmen. Some agreements have excused the concessionaire from a number of charges, including import and export duties.

Occasionally special taxes have been imposed for purposes other than raising revenue or protecting local industry. In late 1971, for example, the Venezuelan government decreed that oil companies must keep their exports within a 2 percent leeway of 1970 levels. Violations were to be punishable by a surcharge that could rise to 10 percent of a company's total exports.[53]

The fact that taxes other than those based on income do not give rise to a credit in the home country of the investor has no doubt served as an inhibiting factor in the imposition of such taxes. In some cases, however, they have been used as a way of raising government revenue from a project when the agreement froze the rates for royalties and income taxes.

TAX INCENTIVES

One of the most controversial areas relating to foreign investment concerns tax incentives. We have mentioned several incentives, such as depletion and accelerated depreciation. Other forms of incentives are common.

The basic question a government should pose is whether the investor would negotiate an agreement irrespective of tax holidays, investment credits, or other fiscal incentives. Many governments have failed to pose the question and have turned to using incentives as rewards for good behavior on the part of investors who would have acted no differently in the absence of incentives.

Take, for example, the case of a Philippine company seeking a timber concession in Indonesia to support its supply of timber to the Japanese market. The investor's interest will be affected by many factors beyond tax incentives: the quality of logs in the Philippines and other nearby sources, market projections for Japan, tariffs and taxes in the Philippines and competitive sources, comparative shipping costs, comparative labor, power, water, and infrastructure data, tax credits in the investor's home country, plus the inevitable risks and uncertainties attached to each of these estimates.

The timber case is a relatively simple one. In general, additional factors, unaffected by tax considerations, will be present, such as the fear that a competitor will preempt a potentially attractive source if the firm does not succeed in completing the negotiations.

The Tax Holiday

A number of mining agreements have provided for a tax-free period for the operation of the foreign firm, ranging from one to ten or more years. The wisdom of these provisions has been questioned by many observers.[54] Indonesia's policy with regard to timber concessions in the late 1960s and early 1970s raises some of the central problems.

In 1973 a timber investor would have received a year's holiday beyond the normal tax holiday for investing outside Java, and one for increasing Indonesia's foreign exchange earnings. Yet if a timber company decided to invest in Indonesia at all, it would almost certainly have invested outside of timber-poor Java and would have exported its timber. Moreover, it is unlikely that a tax holiday would have been a primary factor in inducing a company to come to Indonesia. The company would have been influenced more strongly by factors of good sources elsewhere in Southeast Asia and by its projection of political stability.

More complex tax holiday problems arise in situations where an agreement contemplates the establishment of processing facilities at a later date. In such an arrangement it should be determined at the outset whether the incentive is being requested (and offered) to encourage extraction or processing. If processing is the goal, then the host country must determine whether a tax holiday in the early years of the arrangement will have any real bearing on whether processing facilities are established at a later date. In some cases the most reasonable approach would be to offer the incentive at the later date, when processing begins, or to hold tax savings earned in the early years in a development fund for use in the establishment of processing facilities in a later year.[55] Another approach, implemented in the Peruvian General Mining Law of 1971, would be to provide that a mining company will be granted a guarantee of tax stability if it installs or expands processing plants of a certain capacity.[56]

In addition to examining whether the structure of the industry requires some form of tax holiday, the host country should inquire whether the tax system of the investor's home country makes tax holidays entirely inappropriate. There have been a number of examples of concession contracts providing for tax holidays where neither the host country nor the investor benefited financially.

Whether a company benefits from a tax holiday (that is, whether the tax holiday reduces the company's total tax bill) depends on the home country of the firm, the tax treaties existing between the home and host countries, the use to which the investor will put his profits, and his earnings and taxes in other countries.

Take as an example a U.S. investor who carries out mineral exploitation activities through a subsidiary enterprise incorporated in the host country. In this case the local company pays no U.S. tax on its income (with rare exceptions) and its shareholders (the parent company) pay no U.S. tax until the income is repatriated or remitted in the form of dividends, interest, royalties, or other payments. If the income remains in the host country, then the U.S. tax liability is postponed until the income is eventually repatriated.[57] If it is used to pay debts, that portion is never subject to U.S. tax. In these situations the company will benefit from a host country tax holiday and postpone or escape a tax liability in the United States.

If, however, the hypothetical U.S. investor operates through a branch (that is, does not incorporate locally), or if the locally incorporated company remits all of its earnings immediately to the United States, the situation changes. As long as the host country tax rate is not more than the U.S. tax rate, the U.S. investor, because of the U.S. foreign tax credit, generally pays less tax in the United States.[58] Only the excess of the U.S. tax over the host country tax is payable in the United States. The income taxes saved in the United States will offset the income taxes paid in the host country. In this case a tax holiday or a reduced tax rate would simply mean that the U.S. Treasury collects what the host country forgives.

There are several qualifications to this simple U.S. example. Moreover the situation varies for investors from other industrialized countries. The U.S. foreign tax credit system is statutory and is applied unilaterally, not through tax treaties.[59] Most other advanced countries do not give unilateral tax credits. Instead, their laws call for an exemption of foreign income, for the deduction of foreign income taxes in the same manner as other costs, or for an investment credit or for reduced tax rates on foreign source income.

The exemption method places the foreign investor in a tax position equal to that of a local investor in the host country, since the company's tax burden is determined solely by the level of taxation in the host country. The incomes of subsidiary and branch operations are generally treated equally under the exemption system. Tax holidays or reduced tax rates fully benefit such a company.

The exemption method and the investment credit may be granted by treaty as well as statute.[60] A further treaty device is the tax-sparing credit. This method provides a credit for host country income taxes that are forgiven by the host country through a tax holiday or reduced tax rate. Thus, where a tax holiday is given, the benefit accrues to the foreign investor rather than foreign investor's home country.

There have been some attempts to arrange taxes imposed on the foreign investor in such a way that the host country imposes taxes up to the amount that does not add to the total tax burden of the company. Liberia attempted this in 1969.[61] Panama has attempted similar legislation. Egypt's 1974 foreign investment law appeared to contain another attempt along these lines. The theory is simple. Where the United States, for example, reduces the tax by the amount of the tax paid in the host country up to some limit, then the host country taxes up to that limit. But this approach has proven to be an administrative jungle. Such issues as what happens when the savings in the home country are not *exactly* equal to the taxes paid in the host country, as is the case with the U.S. foreign tax credit for less-developed countries, have been difficult to settle. In addition, there has been no adequate way to handle income that could be used as an offset to excess tax credits generated in another country. Tracing through all these complexities has proved simply impossible for the administrative machinery of developing countries.

One compromise solution has been suggested. It involves the exclusion from tax of income reinvested in the host country. An approximation of this approach is reached by setting a low income tax (or even a tax holiday on retained earnings) and a high withholding tax on dividends paid abroad. This approach is also not without administrative difficulties and problems of definition, but the problems appear to be less than those of more liberal rules.

Even where there is a net saving in taxes to the company from a tax holiday, it is not clear that the tax holiday is worthwhile from the host country point of view. The results of empirical research should be given serious consideration. These studies suggest that firms are not very often strongly influenced by tax factors in their investment decisions.[62] And if the holidays do not increase investment incentive, they are of no value to the country.

The conclusion that tax factors have little influence in the investment decision is not particularly surprising. Substantial uncertainty faces the investor considering a mineral source in a less-developed country. It is difficult to know in advance whether the source will be commercially viable or whether it will be secure from expropriation. These are primary concerns that are not answered by tax relief. Fear of disaster causes the investor to hesitate. If the worst happens, there will be no profits to be taxed anyway. The prospects of a somewhat higher cash flow in the event of success have done little to decrease the basic fears of the investor.

There are qualifications, however. Clearly, where the uncertainties are minor and there are opportunities open to the investor elsewhere, the country that generates a larger cash flow would be the more attractive. This may be the case especially if the industry is one where costs are critical because of intense price competition. The manufacturer seeking an offshore location for an assembly plant to supply the United States cheaply, for instance, may choose his location on the basis of costs. This has rarely been the case for the investor in hard minerals whose shopping list of new sources is a short one.

Nevertheless, company representatives have sometimes bargained hard for tax holidays. Why is this so? In many cases, tax holidays have become symbolic. They may suggest that the country really wants the investor, and they may serve as evidence that the negotiator can carry to the firm's top management to show that he did a good job of bargaining. If liberal tax holidays are provided for in the incentive code of the country, it is a worried negotiator who has to report to his superiors that he could not obtain them for his company. One answer to this problem would be for a country to limit the terms of its investment code concerning the availability of tax holidays and other incentives such as loss carry-forward and accelerated depreciation. Reducing the options open to negotiators may reduce the demand for special incentives. Those limited incentives that are available can retain their symbolic value with less cost to the host country. The exceptions—where tax holidays appear to be essential, such as assembly operations for export—can be clearly defined in the laws. And their costs can be limited through carefully constructed loss carry-forward regulations, depreciation scales, and other rules.

Investment Credits

In some countries, agreements have called for another incentive designed to reduce tax, a tax credit for investment.[63] When an investment is made, the company can subtract a certain portion of the cost of the investment as an expense, or more commonly, direct from its taxes. This deduction is in addition to that gained from depreciation. The Indonesian Nickel Agreement[64] provided a credit of 8 percent of investment, presumably to be subtracted directly from taxes.

The investment tax credit is supposed to have two effects: (1) as an incentive to induce the investor to come to the country; and (2) as an incentive to induce the company to use modern mining methods. Both of these assumptions bear examination.

On the first point the same arguments apply to the investment credit as apply to the tax holiday. For most mining operations such minor tax provisions are hardly likely to have a significant effect on the flow of investment to the country.

It is also doubtful that the investment credit will significantly change the technology employed by the mining company. But if it did, it is not clear that the shift toward the more capital intensive technology which would be engendered would necessarily be of benefit to the less-developed countries, many of which have a surplus of labor.

Where investment credit provisions are included in agreements, difficulties of interpretation have arisen. These agreements have sometimes not been explicit as to whether replacement of worn-out equipment is to benefit from an investment credit, or whether the benefits are to come solely from original investment (and, perhaps, investment that expands volume).

LOCAL INCORPORATION AND TAXATION

Many hours have been spent in negotiations, particularly with U.S. investors, over the issue of local incorporation of the mining enterprise. Local regulations in developing countries have, in many cases, provided that investors must be incorporated locally.[65] The foreign company has often refused. In most cases the firm was not simply being obstinate. The issue has been one of taxation.

In the case of a U.S. firm conducting mining operations abroad there may be a tax advantage in operating as a branch instead of as a locally incorporated subsidiary. A U.S. entity having an "interest" in oil, gas, or other minerals may normally deduct against its U.S. income intangible drilling costs of oil and gas wells, mine exploration expenditures up to $400,000, and mine development expenditures. It does not matter that the mine or well is outside the United States. In addition, such an entity holding an "economic interest" can normally claim U.S. percentage depletion allowances for its mining operations overseas.[66] If the entity is not a U.S. firm, the company loses these privileges. Although the depletion allowance benefits from overseas operations have been steadily reduced beginning with the 1969 Tax Reform Act,[67] there was still some benefit to be gained from the U.S. depletion allowances for many mining companies.

In the situation where the host country requires local incorporation and the investor wishes to retain the tax benefits accruing to branch operations, competing interests can sometimes be reconciled. One proposed solution has involved a so-called cost company. A group of manufacturers may, for example, join together to develop a mining property for ore necessary to their operations. They buy stock in a corporation (the cost company) established to own and operate the property in the host country and agree to provide all funds needed by the cost company. The mining operations remain under the control of the manufacturers and the cost company does not sell any ore. The manufacturers share in the ore in proportion to their contributions to capital and operation.

The underlying assumption is that the depletion allowance will be permitted on the justification that the cost company does not own the "economic interest" (as defined in U.S. tax law), since the transfer of ore to the participants by the cost company does not have a profit objective.[68]

Frequently the concession has been held by an unincorporated contractual joint venture. One of the partners may even be a government agency. The National Iranian Oil Company has, for example, participated in such joint ventures. The output of the operations passes to the members of the joint venture as it is extracted, according to a predetermined formula, satisfying the requirements of U.S. tax rules.

The complexity that can be generated is illustrated by the Liberia LAMCO arrangement already mentioned several times.[69] The interest in the ore body was held by an unincorporated partnership between a local corporation, LAMCO, owned by a Swedish group, and Bethlehem Steel Corporation, incorporated in the United States. The management was in the hands of a local entity. Bethlehem retained U.S. tax benefits by not being incorporated in Liberia; on the other hand, for the Swedish group there were no benefits in avoiding incorporation in Liberia.

THE EFFECT OF TAX CODES AND TAX TREATIES

Although the two parties to a mining agreement may be free to negotiate various tax provisions, a general income tax code governing foreign investment in natural resources or a double taxation treaty between the host country and the investor's home country may limit options.

In some cases where modern income tax codes exist, many important tax provisions have not been negotiable on an *ad hoc* basis. This has been true in a number of petroleum-exporting countries, for example. In other countries the general tax law has sometimes permitted all or part of the income tax regime governing the concession to be negotiated in a case-by-case approach. While one income tax code might require that a tax holiday be granted if certain conditions are met, another code might give the relevant ministry discretion to grant such a holiday. In spite of the appearances of rigidity, most countries have been willing to pass special legislation when it was essential to a major project.

Where an income tax treaty has existed and has covered income from natural resource development, a number of issues may be predetermined. The treaty might cover such issues as the business profits that will be subject to tax in the host country and certain of the deductions that will be allowed for the tax calculation of the mining operation. An income tax treaty may also provide for the exchange of tax information between the investor's home country and the host country, thus facilitating the policing of such matters as affiliate transactions and the deduction of home-office expenses. It appears, however, that few countries have taken advantage of the opportunities to exchange tax information. The treaty may, of course, provide for some sort of tax exemption or tax sparing, thereby affecting, perhaps, the host country's policy with regard to the granting of certain tax incentives.

THE FINANCIAL PACKAGE

The issues in the financial arrangements for a natural resource agreement are invariably complex. The result of attempts to arrive at a satisfactory division of rewards and risks almost always means that a particular agreement contains a package of various tax and other financial provisions. The package reflects bargaining powers, attitudes toward risk, and technical issues, such as home-country tax laws.

In many cases complex financial packages are an almost inevitable result of the international business environment. Complicated provisions may be the only way to satisfy the needs of both parties. For example, the renegotiated LAMCO Agreement in Liberia did not eliminate the varied financial instruments. In fact it added preferred shares to the old package of two classes of common shares and various classes of debt. But the result was forecast to be a 20 percent gain in government revenue, only about one-quarter of which would come out of the pocket of the private company. The rest comes out of taxes that would have been paid in Canada and Sweden.

The complexity and the variety of financial packages tailored to particular situations make it difficult to compare terms of different agreements. Similar nominal royalty and tax rates may result in very different effective rates. And agreements may include royalties of different rates, varying with quality of ore or the prevailing price. Income tax rates may vary with the size of the operation, the size of the profits, or the rate of return. In addition, equity participation may provide a significant portion of revenues. The complexities make it difficult to estimate the effects of seemingly minor changes in an existing arrangement. Calculations become more complex when one attempts to compare agreements under alternative assumptions about prices and costs, or under alternative assumptions about such matters as expansion and reinvestment needs and debt availability and repayment schedules. Nevertheless, tools of financial analysis are available to both the host government and the private investor that enable such calculations to be made. The clarity created for the negotiating process is a worthwhile product of attempts to do a thorough analysis of the financial flows under alternative arrangements. Comparisons become more complex when one introduces the factor of economic development provisions that are designed to provide other benefits to the host country. These important provisions are dealt with in the next chapter.

NOTES

1. David Sassoon, "World Bank and the Mining Industry," paper presented to the Interregional Workshop on Negotiation and Drafting of Mining Development Agreements, Buenos Aires, November 2-18, 1973, ESA/RT/AC.7/13, p. 12.

2. For an illustration of how an investor calculates the expected rate of return, see Raymond F. Mikesell, "Financial Considerations in Negotiating Mining Development Agreements," paper presented to the Interregional Workshop on Negotiation and Drafting of Mining Development Agreements, Buenos Aires, November 2-18, 1973, ESA/RT/AC.7/4, pp. 2-3, 18.

3. The "basic royalty" of the original *Liberian Government-Liberian Mining Company Agreement* (1945) was 5¢ per ton on all iron ore shipped. (Art. 9.)

4. In addition to the royalty based on tonnage shipped, the 1945 Liberian Mining Concession called for an "excess royalty" per ton based on a percentage of increase in price over a previous ten-year average price. Ibid.

5. H.J. Maidenberg, "Jamaica Outlines Bauxite Tax Plan," *New York Times,* May 17, 1974, p. 1.

6. Muhammad A. Mughrabi, *Permanent Sovereignty over Oil Resources: A Study of Middle East Oil Concessions and Legal Change* (Beirut: Middle East Research and Publishing Center, 1966), pp. 138 ff.

7. Ecuador, *Mining Development Law* (Supreme Decree 101 of January 24, 1974; published in *Official Register* No. 484, dated January 31, 1974); translated in *Mineral Trade Notes* 71 (April 1974): 7. See Title VI, Arts. 83-88.

8. Peter L. Harrigor, "Nigeria's Tin Mines—Progress, Prospects and Problems," *West Africa,* December 18, 1972, p. 1685. Bolivia, in mid-1972, shifted from a royalty for gold based on gross production to one based on international price quotations. The stated purpose of the shift was to encourage production. "Gov't of Bolivia's Gold Policy," *Mineral Trade Notes* 69 (October 1972): 15.

9. On the question of whether the levy is based on income or whether it is a true tax, see Boris Bittker and Lawrence F. Ebb, *United States Taxation of Foreign Income and Foreign Persons* (Branford, Connecticut: Federal Tax Press, 1968), pp. 212 ff, 223 ff. See also footnote 18, below.

10. United Nations, Department of Economic and Social Affairs, *United States Income Taxation of Private Investments in Developing Countries* (New York: United Nations, 1970). This monograph was prepared for the U.N. by the Harvard Law School International Tax Program and was written by Arie Kopelman under the direction of Elisabeth A. Owens.

11. Speaking of the Indonesian situation, one commentator has observed that "most of the existing tax law dates back to prewar years and lacks definition." Murray Clapham, "Some Difficulties of Foreign Investors in Indonesia," *Bulletin of Indonesian Economic Studies* 6 (March 1970): 73.

12. See, e.g., *Nova Scotia Pulp Ltd. Agreement Act,* (5-3-58), as amended, 1960; and the *Hamersley Iron Pty. Ltd./Kobe Steel Ltd. Contract* (September 3, 1965).

13. Some arrangements concluded in the 1970s raise a number of issues hardly covered in the literature on taxation. For example, the revised Bougain-

ville agreement calls for progressive taxation, with an attempt to relate the rate to the company's return. An effort is made to allow for adjustment in exchange rate, for limited depreciation, and for the acquisition of new assets. The adjustments were sufficiently complex that they had to be expressed in algebraic terms. And in the "Heads of Agreement" the formulas contained mistakes. See the "Heads of Agreement for Variation of the Agreement of 6th June 1967 between the Government of Papua New Guinea and Bougainville Copper Limited," Port Moresby, 1974.

14. Henry Cattan, *The Evolution of Oil Concessions in the Middle East and North Africa* (Dobbs Ferry: published for the Parker School of Foreign and Comparative Law by Oceana Publications, 1967), p. 8.

15. U.S. *Internal Revenue Code,* Sects. 861–64.

16. United Nations, *Ad Hoc* Group of Experts on Tax Treaties between Developed and Developing Countries, *Tax Treaties between Developed and Developing Countries* (N.Y.: U.N. Department of Economic and Social Affairs, 1969), p. 63.

17. Norman Girvan, "Making the Rules of the Game: Company-Country Agreements in the Bauxite Industry," *Social and Economic Studies* 20 (December 1971): 409.

18. On the question of whether a tax based on posted prices in the oil industry is a true income tax, see Morris A. Adelman, "Is the Oil Shortage Real?— Oil Companies as OPEC Tax-Collectors," *Foreign Policy* (Winter 1972–73), pp. 69, 78. Adelman states that the tax per barrel is "completely independent of actual receipts, and only very slightly affected by costs, [and] hence almost completely independent of profits. Therefore it is an almost pure excise tax." Despite this, taxes based on posted prices are creditable against U.S. income tax under the foreign tax credit. See footnote 9, above. This may not be the case in other countries.

19. For the effect of posted prices on the profit-sharing concept in petroleum agreements, see Cattan, op. cit., pp. 79, 51–52.

20. For price behavior generally for bauxite and aluminum, see Zuhayr M. Mikdashi, *A Comparative Analysis of Selected Mineral Exporting Industries* (Vienna: OPEC, March 1971), p. 18 (mimeo.).

21. "Alcan Drops its Crown," *The Economist,* January 8, 1972, p. 68.

22. The 1971 *General Mining Law of Peru* provided that the selling prices of the mineral products will be those corresponding to the "Peruvian Producers' Quotation" which will be set by the Ministry of Energy and Mines for each mineral product with reference to the representative international quotations deemed most suitable for the country and within the general conditions of international transactions. In the absence of representative international quotations, the selling price will be established following the usual international norms. *Peru General Mining Law: Decree Law No. 18880* (Lima: Ministry of Economics & Finance, Office of Public Relations, 1971), Art. 36.

23. For a general overview of the problem, see William D. Popkin, *The Deduction for Business Expenses and Losses* (Cambridge: International Tax Program, Harvard Law School, 1973).

24. See generally, Alan P. Murray, *Depreciation* (Cambridge: International Tax Program, Harvard Law School, 1971).

25. Under the Liberian LAMCO Agreement there is a provision for deductions from gross profit for "equipment replacement" at the rate of about 30¢ per ton. This is an allocation from profits in addition to that allowed for depreciation. *The Liberian Mining Concession Collateral Agreement* of March 12, 1953, provides for a deduction for depreciation and a "reasonable reserve for replacement."

26. Apparently such is the case with the *Liberian Mining Concession.* See *Collateral Agreement* (March 12, 1953). In calculating profits subject to tax, the company may deduct "interest on indebtedness and amortization of debt."

27. *The Agreement between the Ethiopian Mineral Development Share Company and Duval Corporation* (June 15, 1969) provides that development costs can be written off at a rate of 20 percent per year. Art. II(1)(2)(i).

28. See A. Murray, op. cit., p. 81. For a comprehensive examination of the depletion problem, see pp. 81–97 of Murray.

29. Ibid., p. 87.

30. For a comment on the petroleum situation in the Middle East and North Africa see Henry Cattan, op. cit., p. 58. The Trinidad and Tobago ordinances provide for a "submarine well allowance computed on the gross value of production at wellhead." V. Mulchansingh, "The Oil Industry in the Economy of Trinidad," *Caribbean Studies* 11 (1971): 73, 80. For depletion allowances for hard minerals, see, for example, The Zambian *Income Tax Law,* 1966, Fifth Schedule, Part VII; and *Liberian Iron and Steel Corporation Concession* (1967), Art. 8.

31. C. Vaitsos, "Transfer of Resources and Preservation of Monopoly Rents" paper presented at Harvard Development Advisory Service Dubrovnik Conference, June 20–26, 1970 (mimeo.).

32. U.S. Treasury Regulations, para. 1.482, are summarized in *International Allocations of Income: Problems of Administration and Compliance* (New York: U.N. Secretariat, 1973), ST/SG/AC.8/L.5.

33. Kennecott Copper Corporation, "Confiscation of El Teniente: 'Expropriation without Compensation,'" Supplement, 1971, p. 6.

34. *Production-Sharing Contract between P.N. Pertamina and Phillips Petroleum Company* (1968), Exhibit C, Art, II, sec. 2.2. See also *Agreement between Ethiopian Mineral Development Share Company and Duval Corporation of Ethiopia* (June 15, 1969), art. II(f)(v)(9), which appears to incorporate this principle.

35. The Indonesian production-sharing contracts provide several variations. Under the Mobil agreement of October 16, 1968, no commissions are to be paid on sales to affiliates; the Japex agreement of October 6, 1966, and the Australian Drilling agreement of April 1, 1967, permit commissions paid to affiliates as long as the commission does "not exceed the customary and prevailing rate." Several contracts make no mention of commissions on sales to affiliates. See, e.g., the Union contract of January 26, 1968. The Ethiopian Duval Corporation agreement disallows the deduction of any commission paid to any affiliated party in connection with the handling of funds, Art. II(f)(v) (20).

36. *The Contract of Concession between the Imperial Ethiopian Government and Ethiopian Potash Company* (November 4, 1968) provides that com-

missions paid in connection with loans from affiliated parties may be deducted only with the "prior written approval of the Government." Annex B, Sec. C (21).

37. Article 13(d)(D)(iii) of the *Contract of Work Between Republic of Indonesia and P.T. Kennecott Indonesia* (November 1, 1969) provides: "Operating Expenses shall include . . . (6) amounts for royalties and other payments including those to Affiliates for patents, designs, technical information and services."

38. Ibid. Exhibit C, Article III: "A fair rate shall be charged for technical . . . services . . . provided such charges shall not exceed those currently prevailing if performed by outside . . . companies. . . ."

39. Brazil, for example, has taken this approach generally. See *Information Guide for Those Doing Business in Brazil* (New York: Price, Waterhouse, & Company, 1970), p. 25.

40. India and Brazil have taken this approach. See ibid. and "Taxation in India," in *International Tax and Business Services* (New York: Haskins & Sells, 1969), p. 39.

41. For a general discussion of the debt/equity problem in the United States, see "Thin Capitalization and Tax Avoidance," *Columbia Law Review* 55 (November 1955): 1054; and Richard B. Stone, "Debt-Equity Distinctions in the Treatment of the Corporation and its Shareholders," *Tulane Law Review* 42 (February 1968): 251.

42. See *Agreement between Ethiopian Mineral Development Share Company and Duval Corporation of Ethiopia* (June 15, 1969), Article II(f): "Deductible Costs shall . . . include . . . (iii) interest on loans. . . ."

43. Article 13(d)(D)(vii) of the *Contract of Work between Republic of Indonesia and P.T. Kennecott Indonesia* (November 1, 1969) provides that "Interest Expenses paid . . . with respect to interest on any capital borrowed for the purposes of the Enterprise, including interest on capital borrowed from Affiliates, are deductible from income according to actual rates. . . ."

44. See *Libyan Petroleum Law, 1955,* as amended to 1965, Schedule, Clause 8, Section 4; *Production-Sharing Contract between P.N. Pertambangan Minjak Nasional and Phillips Petroleum Company* (1968), Exhibit C, Article I, sec. 8 (company may deduct certain expenses "excepting interest on monies borrowed after the date the Contract becomes effective").

45. Kenneth Carter, ed., *Report of the Royal Commission on Taxation* (Ottawa: R. Dahamel, Queen's Printer, 1967), Vol. 4, p. 549.

46. *Indonesian Corporation Tax Law of 1925,* Article 5, para. 2, item 3.

47. See articles cited in note 41 and *United States Tax Reform Act of 1969,* Part VI, Sec. 385.

48. *Concession Agreement between the Government of Liberia and the Liberian-American Mining Company* (April 28, 1960).

49. *Production-Sharing Contract between P.N. Pertambangan Minjak Nasional and Kyushu Oil Company, Ltd.* (November 22, 1966), Exhibit C.

50. *Contract of Work between Republic of Indonesia and P.T. Kennecott Indonesia* (November 1, 1969), Art. 13(b). Under Trinidad law, as of 1971, oil companies paid 96¢ per acre in the first year, through $2.16 in the fourth. Submarine leases were charged 10¢ per acre in the first year, to 80¢ in the

seventh year, to $3.60 in the tenth and subsequent years. V. Mulchansingh, "The Oil Industry in the Economy of Trinidad," *Caribbean Studies* 11 (1971): 73, 87.

51. See *P.T. Kennecott Indonesia Agreement,* op. cit. at Article 13(a)(V) and (VI).

52. The "dredging tax" was not provided for in the agreements.

53. "Venezuela Shaping Added Taxes on Oil," *New York Times,* April 17, 1973, p. 49.

54. See footnote 62, below.

55. See Albert O. Hirschman, "Industrial Development in Brazilian Northeast and the Tax Credit Scheme of Article 34/18," *Journal of Development Studies* 5 (1968): 5. See Martin Norr et al., *The Tax System in Sweden* (Stockholm: Skandinaviska Enskildabanken, 1972) for a related "investment reserve for economic stabilization."

56. Decree Law No. 18880, Art. 126. See also note 22.

57. See U.N., *United States Income Taxation of Private Investments in Developing Countries,* op. cit., pp. 27 and 55. The use of a provision allowing for the tax-free remission of income by a developing country holding company was severely limited in 1975.

58. Ibid., p. 12. See also *U.S. Internal Revenue Code,* secs. 901–905.

59. Some other capital exporting countries also give tax credits by statute. See U.N., *Tax Treaties between Developed and Developing Countries,* op. cit. p. 40.

60. On tax treaties generally, see ibid.

61. United Nations, *Foreign Investment in Developing Countries* (New York: United Nations, 1968); G. Lent, "Tax Incentives for the Promotion of Industrial Employment in Developing Countries," *IMF Staff Papers* 18 (July 1971): 399–419. See also Milton C. Taylor, *Industrial Tax Exemption in Puerto Rico* (Madison: University of Wisconsin, 1957); Murray D. Bryce, *Policies and Methods for Industrial Development* (New York: McGraw Hill, 1965).

62. Yair Aharoni, *The Foreign Investment Decision Process* (Boston: Harvard Business School Division of Research, 1966); Helen MacGill Hughes and You Poh Seng, eds., *Foreign Investment and Industrialization in Singapore* (Madison: University of Wisconsin Press, 1969); George E. Lent, "Tax Incentives for Investment in Developing Countries," *IMF Staff Papers,* 14 (July 1967): 249.

63. See *Contract of Work between the Government of Indonesia and the Indonesian Nickel Development Company, Ltd.* (April 1969).

64. Ibid.

65. See, e.g., the *Indonesian Law Relating to the Investment of Foreign Capital,* Law No. 1/1967, Ch. II, Art. 3: "An enterprise . . . which is operated wholly or for the most part in Indonesia as a separate business unit, must be a legal entity organized under Indonesian Law. . . ." In late 1972 the government of Ghana announced that, to ensure effective control over the mining industry, all operating companies would be organized as Ghanaian companies. "Ashanti, CAST Takeover," *West Africa* (December 18, 1972), p. 1705.

66. Under U.S. tax regulations the depletion allowance applies to one who "has acquired by investment any interest in mineral in place and secures, by

any form of legal relationship, income from the extraction of the mineral . . . , to which he must look for a return on his capital." Reg. Sec. 1.611-1(b)(1). The taxpayer must own a "working interest" to deduct intangible drilling costs for oil and gas. Reg. Sec. 1.612-4(a). See generally *U.S. Taxation of International Operations* (Englewood Cliffs: Prentice-Hall, 1972), pp. 9521-32 and 9541-53; and U.N., *United States Income Taxation of Private Investments in Developing Countries,* op. cit., pp. 120-25.

67. Elisabeth A. Owens, "An Analysis of the New Law's Impact on Foreign Income and Foreign Taxpayers," *The Journal of Taxation* 32 (April 1970): 250, 252.

68. See Paul Pommier, "How You Should Set Up Your Overseas Extractive Operations," in *U.S. Taxation of International Operations,* op. cit., pp. 9521, 9528. See also Walter W. Brudno, "Tax Considerations in Selecting a Form of Foreign Business Organization," in Institute on Private Investments Abroad, Southwestern Legal Foundation, *Proceedings* (Albany: Matthew Bender and Company, 1959), Vol. 1, p. 105.

69. See note 48, above.

Chapter Four

Economic Development Provisions

In the mid-1970s developing countries were becoming increasingly concerned about the role of raw-material production in their overall plans for economic development. Even though prices of commodities appeared to be on the rise—stifling the usual arguments that the terms of trade move inexorably against raw-material exporters—many producing countries believed that they were not benefiting from their resources to the extent they should. In a quest for a new economic order, developing countries sought still higher prices for their commodities and what they considered more just and equitable relationships between the prices of raw materials exported by them and the manufactured goods imported by them.[1] In addition, they sought from the industrial nations financing for industrial projects, particularly involving export-oriented production, as well as access, on better terms than in the past, to modern technology.

Many developing countries had earlier taken modest steps in some of these directions by attempting to broaden and multiply the contributions to development made by investors in natural resources. While such efforts did not promise the large-scale stimulation of the economy anticipated by those supporting the establishment of the proposed new economic order of the 1970s, these efforts did promise relatively immediate and concrete contributions.

The history of such efforts has been mixed. Economists and other commentators disagree about the results of efforts to extend the contributions of natural resource development beyond increases in foreign exchange and government revenues. Foreign investors have been accused of establishing economic and social enclaves with little spillover into the rest of the economy. "Growth without development" is one label that captures the spirit of the attack. Indeed, some observers have argued that foreign investment in natural resources actually retards economic development.[2] On the other hand, there are those who have argued that no matter how accurate the enclave concept is as a description of the early years of an extractive operation, the beneficial spillover effects during the life of the concession almost inevitably grow to be very important as the years pass.[3]

As the debate continues, governments of most developing countries have considered it desirable to take steps to maximize the possibilities that: (1) natural resource investment will generate income as soon as possible after the signing of the agreement; and (2) it will provide benefits in addition to government revenue and foreign exchange. No matter what the structure of the agreement, most concession arrangements provide, either through the agreement itself or through general laws, that the investor engage in a broad range of "development activities." Ironically, as they have become more successful in involving foreign investors in broader development activities, some countries have begun to have second thoughts about this involvement.

PROMOTING LINKAGES

Most governments have looked to extractive operations as ways of generating benefits to the economy that are external to the project itself. Four kinds of linkages have been pursued in particular. First, natural-resource investments are seen as providing an opportunity to develop industries to process these raw materials, contributing to national income and, where these objectives are separate, to stimulate employment and to earn foreign exchange. Second, the extractive operations can provide the critical market needed for the start-up of local industries. Third, the operations are looked to for training of manpower that can be used in other activities within the country. Fourth, the natural-resource project may provide both the increment of demand and the funds required for the development of infrastructure, the benefits of which may extend far beyond the extractive operations themselves.

Encouraging Processing

In a number of countries, the prospect in recent years that the investor in natural resources would establish processing facilities has become a major consideration in bringing in the investor. Not only have governments viewed the establishment of processing facilities as a significant step in the industrialization of the country, but some have also thought that local processing may mean that the country would face a more stable world market than if it were to export unprocessed materials.

Whether the establishment of processing facilities is a rational goal is a question subject to the same analysis as any other project that uses domestic resources. The various approaches to social cost-benefit analysis are as appropriate for this kind of activity as for import-substituting investments. With or without the analysis, many concession arrangements have been designed to encourage the establishment of such facilities.

Timber concessions provide an illustration of the difficulties frequently encountered in negotiations for processing facilities. Various governments have found timber-processing facilities to be desirable projects, once the officials have calculated the net benefits using social costs and social benefits. For the investor who sees the project in terms of private costs and benefits rather than social figures, however, the same project may appear unattractive. The different outcomes may result from market wage rates that differ from shadow costs, from taxes that are omitted from the social analysis, or other sources. Regardless of the source of the difference, once the fact is recognized, some effort is usually made by the parties to make the socially attractive project attractive to the private investor. The firm may seek concessions on tariffs, export duties, or other taxes to make the project profitable, in exchange for a commitment to build processing facilities sometime in the future. But the government may fear that the concessionaire will "cut and run," shipping the choicest logs for a few years, depleting a significant portion of the concession area, reaping the benefits of a tax holiday, and then abandon operations at the end of the tax holiday or logging period. Given the fact that investments in timber harvesting need not, in many instances, be very large, a concessionaire may have little hesitation about abandoning the operation at the end of the allowed logging phase. Resolving such conflicts of interest and fears presents a formidable problem in negotiations.

The risks are usually less substantial in the area of hard minerals. Governments have attempted a number of approaches in these cases. One technique that relies on the agreement itself has been straightforward: the parties agree that processing facilities are to be established by a certain date, or at the point at which raw-material production reaches a certain volume. Failure on the part of the investor to establish the requisite facilities then constitutes a breach of contract. The 1970 OMRD copper agreement in Ecuador, for example, required the investor to construct processing facilities when a sufficient volume of reserves was discovered to support a production of 150 million pounds of metal per year. Such a provision may be adequate if the investor has a reputation or a significant amount of capital at stake so that failure to comply with the commitment will be costly.

Some agreements have been less specific about the establishment of facilities, but have required feasibility studies to be undertaken at a later date. The 1967 iron ore agreement between the Republic of Liberia and the Liberian Iron and Steel Corporation illustrates this approach:

[The] Concessionaire agrees that within fifteen (15) years from the effective date . . . it shall establish iron ore processing, smelting and manufacturing facilities in Liberia if then found economically feasible. To this end, the parties agree to jointly consider this economic feasibility at the end of each three (3) year period following the effective date. If and when any of such facilities are constructed, the parties agree to thereafter discuss and consider, in good faith, the feasibility of subsequent additional facilities.[4]

Another example is the 1969 timber agreement between the government of the Republic of Indonesia and A. Soriano y Cia, which provided that the general policy the company would pursue would be directed toward the establishment of a forest-based industry that would be optimally integrated:

> In furtherance of the general policy of optimal integration, the establishment of log-processing plants such as sawmills, veneer plants and plywood plants is contemplated. Such plants would be justified economically either because the logs they use for raw material cannot be successfully marketed as such, or because such local processing of logs would improve the overall economic efficiency of the Project.[5]

Both of the above provisions were premised on the assumption that, at the time of the initial negotiation of the contract, the parties did not have sufficient information to determine whether construction of a processing facility would be justified at a future date.

A feasibility study may provide useful information to the government as to why processing is not viable from the private viewpoint. The government may discover, for example, that duties on processed products in the importing country are serving as a barrier to local processing. The host country may have to seek tariff reductions in the market nation. Assuming, however, that local finishing is feasible from the private cost side, or can be made so, the question remains whether provisions of the type quoted above do the job for which they are intended. The answer would appear to be, "Not necessarily."

In many cases the host government has been willing to negotiate a particular agreement only if the establishment of processing facilities was a likely component of the arrangement. In fact, many specific provisions may have been negotiated under the assumption that processing facilities would be established. In the Soriano agreement, for example, significant tax incentives were offered during the early timber-harvesting stage. It appears that such incentives were offered only because the government expected the substantial economic benefits of an integrated forest industry involving sawmilling and veneer and plywood operations. The agreement, however, provided neither certainty that such facilities would be established nor clear penalties for the firm if they were not built. To ensure the establishment of processing facilities, if they are economically feasible, the contract must incorporate enforceable standards.

The difficulty has been that those standards have been hard to define. The result has usually been a vague economic-feasibility provision of the LISCO and Soriano types. The former provided no meaningful standard at all. The Soriano agreement provided two standards—that raw material cannot be successfully marketed and that local processing would improve the overall efficiency of the project—but neither standard, without more detail, would necessarily accomplish what the government intended. They invoke private rather than social criteria, and do not appear to be binding. In the Indonesian example there was no assurance that processing facilities would be established if the company determined that it was more profitable for the firm to ship unprocessed logs to Japan or the Philippines than to process them in Indonesia. Indeed, a firm that had already established—in Japan or the Philippines, for example—processing facilities not utilized to capacity, might find it more profitable from its point of view to ship logs to one of those countries for processing rather than to construct new facilities in Indonesia. Likewise, if the tax rate on corporate profits is lower in the Philippines than in Indonesia, the company could find it more advantageous to pay Indonesian tax only on unprocessed logs and to pay Philippine tax on the higher income from processed timber. Such factors could, in some cases, be examined in advance to determine whether a finding of economic justification (from the investor's viewpoint) for construction of processing facilities is apt to be made. Careful specifications of standards in the agreement may help to avoid later disputes.

A provision calling for the future review of the economic justification or economic feasibility of a project connected with the concession should recognize the interests of both parties. There are several techniques that may contribute to dealing effectively with the processing problem.

First, economic justification and economic feasibility can be defined in such a way that profit maximization is not the sole governing criterion. Though the project must be economically viable (that is, provide a fair rate of return to the company), the test can also include considerations of the country's interest in fostering economic development. Standard social cost-benefit calculations can be called for to supplement the private profitability analysis.

Second, it can be required that feasibility tests provided by the company meet the standards of such tests set by an independent organization, such as the World Bank or the U.S. Agency for International Development. It is conceivable that provision might be made to have an independent third party, such as an approved consulting firm, conduct the test. From a high-quality study the government is likely to learn what barriers to local processing exist.

We have recommended to some host governments that tax or other fiscal incentives offered in the early years of a concession to promote the establishment of processing facilities be supplemented by a provision for the forfeiture to the government of such tax savings in the event that processing facilities are not established. The "conditional tax holiday" incorporated in the Brazilian plan to encourage the development of the Northeast Region illustrates a similar approach.[6] Under such an arrangement all or part of the taxes from the first year of the mining or timber operation is refundable to the enterprise at a later date for use in the construction of processing facilities, if the enterprise constructs the facilities within a certain period and provides part of the funds itself.

Another approach has been to offer tax holidays only for profits that arise from processing activities. The administrative details of such an arrangement, as we noted in Chapter 3, can become complex unless the agreement adequately provides for the allocation of income between extraction and processing. As we have observed earlier, however, there is substantial evidence that tax holidays have little effect on most investment decisions. This evidence raises doubts about the value to the government of tax holidays in connection with processing as well as with exploitation.[7]

If tax incentives can be considered to be the fiscal carrot, a fiscal stick has also been utilized occasionally. There can, for example, be provisions for a tax on the export of unprocessed materials, which would not apply to processed output. Such an export tax has been applied to timber in the Philippines. In fact, export taxes differentiated by degree of processing have a long history. In 1903 the Federated Malay States took action to support local tin processing plants against possible competition from plants located elsewhere. That action came in the form of a higher export duty on tin ore exported for smelting outside the Straits Settlements than for ore to be smelted in the region.[8]

Some countries have gone further. They have, under the aegis of general trade regulations, placed absolute quotas on exports of unprocessed raw materials. The quotas may be allocated according to the company's exports of processed material. In other countries similar provisions may apply in particular concessions. Japanese investors have in some cases agreed not to export concentrates after a certain time period, for example.[9]

Fearful that neither the carrot nor the stick will induce the investor to establish local processing, some governments have tried still another method. They have included in the agreement a guarantee that the foreign investor will offer output to any processor who establishes local facilities, at a price that is not higher than the investor's f.o.b. price to other buyers. The objective of such provisions has usually been to allow another firm to set up processing facilities in the country if it is economically attractive and if the concessionaire himself fails to act. Another company might possibly respond to the guaranteed supplies by establishing the desired facilities.

Although such provisions may be useful, some care must be exercised in their drafting. The purpose of the provision may be thwarted if they are qualified by conditions such as those found in the Indonesian Alcoa agreement, which called on Alcoa to sell to other processors only until Alcoa set up its own facilities.[10] No independent investor is likely to build a processing plant if the mineral investor can establish his own facilities and cut off ore sales to the existing plant once the feasibility of the project has been conclusively demonstrated.

In some cases provisions for local sales have made their way into the general laws. For example, the 1974 Mining Development Law of Ecuador provided that any company that exploits a mine but does not install a processing plant must sell the ores to government processing plants if they exist.[11] Other countries have included similar provisions in their mining laws or concession agreements, although the usual provision is that the company must provide only part of its production to the local company. Some of these provisions would probably not do much to support local processing. For example, under its 1968 agreement with Costa Rica, Alcoa was required to provide 50,000 tons of alumina per year to any local smelter that might be established. One observer estimated that this tonnage would permit a smelter of approximately 25,000 tons per year capacity only, and that it is doubtful whether a smelter of this size could support a hydroelectric scheme large enough to be economical.[12] The same problem was thought to exist in the 1967 Revere Copper and Brass Company agreement with Jamaica.[13]

Some concession agreements have encouraged the foreigner to cooperate with related local processing industries in more limited ways. A foreign investor in forestry might be required to supply secondary species, sub-export grades of primary species, slabs, edgings, and sawdust to local processors. In the absence of such provisions nonexportable products may be destroyed. With further processing, this apparent waste may be avoided. We encountered in one developing country a furniture manufacturer who was finding it difficult to obtain high-grade wood for furniture, despite the fact that the country was a major exporter of quality wood. The concessionaires had established transportation facilities directly to the ports and were unwilling to sell small quantities locally. Eventually the manufacturer managed to obtain access to pieces too small for export. The local firm used these pieces to make furniture parts, which were then exported for assembly abroad. The business held out promise of becoming a significant exporter of furniture in the future.

Ultimately the establishment of processing facilities depends to a great extent on the interest of the foreign firm. The provisions of the agreement can play some role in influencing what those interests are. If the penalties for not establishing processing facilities outweigh what may be the extra costs in building facilities in the country of extraction, the firm may yield. But wise selection of investor may be more important than sticks and carrots. The timber firm that is running out of processing capacity abroad is, for example, a better candidate to build local facilities than is a firm that has excess capacity abroad. Similarly, a firm that plans to market output in a country which has a tariff structure that does not discriminate heavily against the processed resource is more likely to do its processing locally than is a firm that will export to a country that imposes barriers on the import of the processed product.

The prospective establishment of processing facilities is often a difficult issue to deal with in concession negotiations. Occasionally the barriers the investor faces in the form of discriminatory tariffs in the consuming country, and shipping and marketing problems for the processed product, are not well understood by the host government. Sometimes neither party recognizes that private and social benefits may differ dramatically. And, in many cases, the uncertainties at the time of the signing of the agreement are so substantial that any concrete planning is difficult. Although concession agreements have sought to overcome these problems in numerous ways, the agreements that have been the most specific have resulted from at least some discussion of the basic issues between the parties. No doubt by encouraging discussion of the different views, such contracts go further in reconciling expectations than do contracts incorporating vague standards and ignoring the real issues.

Local Purchasing

In addition to encouraging foreign firms to establish processing facilities, most governments have sought to induce the foreign firm to purchase locally made goods and services rather than imported products. The goal has been to expand the market for domestic industry and agriculture.

Government pressures for local buying have often led to the development of local businesses to supply the needed items. Often the foreign firm has provided substantial direct assistance to local businessmen. In other cases the foreign extractive firm has brought along its suppliers from abroad; these suppliers have themselves then become investors in the host country.

Most modern agreements have required that the foreign company purchase its needs locally as long as certain conditions are met. In such provisions some limitations on the price that the firm must pay for local products have been common. One finds in agreements at least three kinds of price limitations:

1. A price not above the c.i.f. price of imported goods, excluding duty.
2. A price not above the local price of imported goods, including duty.
3. A price not above the c.i.f. price of imported goods plus a certain percentage (say, 15 to 20 percent).

In addition, the company has usually been provided with a safeguard concerning the quality of the goods and the delivery schedule. These are not to be substantially less favorable than for imported goods.

Provisions to encourage linkage between foreign investors and local firms can, of course, take other forms. There have been many cases where local firms have produced the same raw material produced by the foreign firm. Tin is produced in Malaysia by foreign and local firms; rubber is grown on foreign and domestic plantations side-by-side in Liberia. If processing facilities are largely in the hands of foreign firms or if marketing contacts are crucial for exporting, success of local firms may require that the foreign enterprise provide processing or marketing services to local producers. Tin ore may be most efficiently processed by large-scale smelters tied to the foreign mines. Firestone in Liberia has processing facilities and marketing contacts that may be critical to small holders' rubber farms.[14] In the case of other plantation crops, new seed varieties or new methods of disease control developed by the foreign firm may be important for local growers. In such cases the government may want to support local firms by requiring the foreign firm to process their materials, market their products, or provide technical help. When such linkages are to be promoted the government may want to reduce the possibility that the foreign firm will take advantage of what may be a monopoly position. A provision guaranteeing a particular formula price for the processing and other services can be included in the concession contract.

Employment and Training of Nationals

Foreign investment in the extractive industries may foster other development goals. In most developing countries employment of nationals has been of particular concern. At the same time, countries have sought to use the foreign firm as a source of training to increase the level of skills available to the nation.

For decades it has been common for agreements with foreign investors to require the firm to give preference to the hiring of nationals of the host country, to meet minimum goals of local employment, and to provide training. Most governments have depended on requirements that locals be hired for certain posts as an incentive for the company to establish training programs. To compel training, a common provision—and one that has worked well on occasion—has been a clause requiring a higher percentage of local workers for the jobs requiring less skills, and setting a timetable that requires progress toward turning over jobs to local workers. One such timetable for a range of extractive operations might be:[15]

Skill Category	By 3rd year	By 5th year	By 10th year
Unskilled	100	100	100
Skilled	50	75	100
Clerical & supervisory	50	75	90
Technical	50	75	85
Management	50	75	85

Similar provisions have occasionally been included in the country's mining or petroleum legislation. Although a study showed that oil operations in Nigeria had made only a minimal contribution to the provision of skilled manpower in the early years,[16] there was promise of change. The 1969 Nigerian Petroleum Decree provided that recipients of mining leases must guarantee that within ten years they would employ Nigerians in 75 percent of the management, professional, and supervisory positions, and in 100 percent of all other jobs. The decree also required that holders of post-1969 prospecting licenses submit a detailed program for recruitment and training of Nigerians within the first year of operation.[17] The changes were designed to ensure that the earlier pattern of little training was not continued into the future.

Clauses that leave to the company the determination about the availability of qualified personnel to fill employment quotas have generally been unsatisfactory to host governments. And provisions that have called for the employment of nationals have probably worked best when they have required the company to submit to the government its reasons for any request for exceptions, while demonstrating the adequacy of its past training programs.

Although preferences for the employment of local nationals have long been common in concession agreements, an additional employment issue came to the fore in the early 1970s. Governments became concerned about the kind of technology used by the foreign investor. Large-scale unemployment led governments to appeal for labor-intensive technology to increase employment. This concern has spilled over from manufacturing to the extractive operations, even though mining, plantation, and timbering projects may be in sparsely settled regions with little spare labor. Although the mining firms in particular have responded to government pressure by claiming that they have little alternative to capital-intensive technology, there is some evidence that there are feasible alternatives for some extractive operations. Whether host governments will be successful in their efforts to induce foreign extractive firms to employ more labor-intensive technologies than they have to date remains to be seen. But the prognosis is not very good.[18]

Infrastructure and Community Services

Extractive enterprises can often assist the economic development of the country through the infrastructure they build and the community services they provide. Host governments took an early interest in this kind of contribution as they recognized the potential of the roads, ports, and power facilities constructed by foreign firms for their own use. Governments began to insist that the facilities be made available for other purposes.

Access to mining roads or railroads has become of particular importance to the development of agriculture. Reduced transportation time and costs due to mining roads or railroads have resulted in increased employment and production in the agricultural sector. In Liberia, for example, the long access roads to the iron ore mines are dotted with small rubber farms and other cash cropping that did not extend into the interior before the roads were built. Access to roads and railways has also stimulated medium- and large-scale timber harvesting operations in areas in which lumbering would not otherwise be economically feasible. For example, the building of the first section of the Trans-Gabon Railway, which was intended to take iron ore from eastern Gabon, was expected to benefit the timber industry by opening up the okoume timber-rich Booué section.[19]

Infrastructure may also be useful for other purposes. It was thought, for example, that the proposed road linking Arlit with Niamey in Niger would open the Air country, with its mountains and neolithic rock carvings, to tourism.[20] The operations of the Ghana Timber and Plywood Company were expected to open up areas for the establishment of forest villages.[21]

Concession agreements now regularly call on the company to grant rights of access to infrastructure on terms that will avoid interference with the company's operations. In most cases the facilities are to revert to government ownership and control when they are no longer needed by the company for the extractive operations.[22]

Mineral and timber developers have not typically been called upon to create new rail links or roads for government or third-party use. They have simply been asked to make the rails and roads associated with their operations available to others. But concession-holders have been asked to provide community service beyond what is normally required for the concession's "community." It was probably inevitable that schools and hospitals would be demanded of foreign firms that operated in remote areas. Few governments have felt able to pay for the cost, in financial and administrative resources, of extending services into such areas.

Governments have recently taken a more aggressive approach toward infrastructure development. They have used the extractive project as the base for financing developments that might otherwise be difficult to initiate. The Roan Selection Trust investment in Botswana is one example. The development plans for the mining project called for a total investment of about $200 million: $121 million for development of the mines, mill, and smelter; $7 million for working capital; $67 million for the township, rail links, power supplies and dam, reservoir, and water pipelines. The Shashi Infrastructure, as it was known, was considered important to the general development of the area. With the Botswana government as a partner in the general enterprise, it was possible to isolate the Shashi Infrastructure from the sectors of the agreement to be financed from commercial fund-raising. The funds for the Shashi sector were to be loaned by the World Bank, the Canadian International Development Agency, and USAID. Botswana would service the loans out of revenue it would receive from the mining operation for power, water, and municipal services.[23]

The importance of infrastructure to regional development has meant that governments are making efforts to try to blend the company's infrastructure into the regional plans. In many cases the government insists on minor rerouting of roads and rail lines to conform to these plans.

Infrastructure developed for extractive operations sometimes has international implications as well. The government of Guinea hoped that the railroad that ran through Liberia from the LAMCO mine near Guinea could be utilized to carry iron ore from Guinea to a Liberian port.[24] It was also hoped that a manganese development in Upper Volta's northeast region would provide a rail link between the ore site and the capital at Ouagadougou, and that there would then be prospects of completing a long-desired rail connection to Niamey in Niger. Many believed that this link could be a key factor in encouraging crop and cattle enterprises in both countries.[25] Similarly, a proposed copper project in Papua New Guinea would use the Fly River, parts of which are an international waterway serving as a border with West Irian. The development of this transportation route could benefit countries on both sides of the river. Bilateral or regional cooperation in building infrastructure or processing facilities has been the exception, however, in economic planning in many parts of the world.

The access to remote areas that extractive operations provide can promote economic development; it can also have important effects on population location. It was claimed, for example, before the drought of the Sahelian region forced Taureg migrations southward, that the uranium agreement between the government of Niger and German and French interests would bring several thousand Tauregs out of the desert into towns where they would come under more direct government control. Often, however, improved communication routes that induce large population movements have undesirable effects. Infrastructure construction may bring people from the subsistence sector into the money sector, and the subsequent decline in employment that typically follows the construction stage may leave many of these workers unemployed in overcrowded urban areas. And the new roads may provide the immigration routes to more urbanization. But most governments have felt that the economic benefits from open roads and railroads outweigh the resulting urban problems.

PROTECTIVE PROVISIONS

In earlier days little attention was paid by governments to the interests of residents in the area of the concession. But as governments have become more concerned about the effects of extractive operations on economic development, they have become increasingly concerned with protection of local interests in the concession area. Concern with protection of rights of local residents has led to concern with protecting the natural resources themselves and the environment.

Local Residents
Governments have insisted on guarantees not only to give residents access to infrastructure constructed by the foreign firm, but also to the concession area so that they may carry on traditional economic activities. In timber contracts, for example, provisions may allow access to forest areas for wood traditionally needed by villagers for firewood, local crafts, local construction, and canoes.[26] Similarly, access to traditional sources of water and to sacred sites has usually been guaranteed.[27]

In addition, attention has been given to the "ownership" or comparable rights of local citizens.[28] Some agreements have spelled out the kind of compensation that would be made to local inhabitants for their loss of rights to, and interest in, land. The Lesotho Maluti Diamond Agreement of 1971 provided, for example, that any "diggers" within the concession area would be compensated for the withdrawal of their prospecting rights. The agreement also required the operating company to provide relocation and housing for those diggers who wished to operate in another location. Similarly, arrangements were made to compensate clans with claims to land or to the right to harvest wild crops or fish in areas that were affected by the development of the copper mine in Bougainville. Even when careful attention has been paid to these matters, local residents have often complained that they were not being fairly treated. Perhaps clear specification of rights and duties at the outset removes some of the onus from the company for what is almost inevitably an unpleasant task: that of relocating people from their traditional homes for what is hoped to be the national good.

Some governments have paid attention from the beginning to the use to which land may be put as the extractive operations are completed on various tracts. In regard to forest operations, for example, governments have attempted to ensure that if the land is not to be returned to forest use local farmers can begin planting agricultural crops as soon as the trees are harvested in a particular tract.

Scientific Development

There are many other areas in which protection of the nation's economic and social interests have been sought. The requirement of "scientific and modern" development techniques has become common in mining agreements.

Such techniques have been of particular importance in forestry operations where reforestation and sustained-yield principles are essential to the continuing economic life of the concession area. And the use of methodical cutting techniques may be important for the most effective utilization of the concession area. Where the general laws are silent or inadequate, timber agreements have commonly included provisions relating to minimum girth requirements, cutting of timber on a tract-by-tract basis, cutting of timber on contiguous tracts, and the intensive harvesting of each tract. Such provisions have facilitated government inspection and permitted the return of tracts to the government on a progressive basis after the area has been cut and seeded. They have also encouraged the most economic use of timber resources by compelling the company to harvest all eligible timber within a given tract before moving to another tract.

There have been similar provisions in mining agreements. Companies have been required to extract ores of a minimum grade, for example. Low-grade ore left behind can only rarely be extracted economically later. In addition, provision has frequently been made for the safe and economic disposal of overburden and tailings. The objective has been to avoid the deposit of overburden and tailings in an area or manner that causes the danger of slides, damages the tourist appeal of an area, or destroys economically useful land.[29]

Provisions concerning the ecological impact of mining can be extremely valuable, as is illustrated by the attempts in 1972 of Banada, one of the Gilbert and Ellice Islands, to invoke a clause in its agreement on phosphate mining. The mining operations were leaving the island useless for agriculture. The islanders claimed some $25 million in compensation, since the original 1913 agreement called on the company, the British Phosphate Commission, to restore the areas with new soil and plants "whenever possible."[30]

Yet, traditionally, little attention has been paid in concession arrangements to the social and ecological impact of mining or timbering operations on the exploitation area.[31] As developing countries begin to take a broader view of their development goals,[32] they may become interested in requiring prospective concessionaires to present reports, perhaps by an independent consulting group, on the social and ecological implications of their proposed projects, as well as requiring concessionaires to take steps to protect the environment. In the early stages of development, the need of the country for income typically has outweighed concern for the environment. Further development and the influence of changing concerns in other countries have begun to shift the emphasis. The 1972 Selebe-Pikwe agreement in Botswana, for example, includes a detailed provision requiring the concessionaire to prevent or mitigate "consequences adverse to the environment." The problem is determining how far such efforts can go before the costs to the economy exceed the benefits. Even the advanced countries are far from being able to deal adequately with this issue.

LIMITS ON THE ROLE OF THE FOREIGNER

In earlier periods probably the most complex issues in concession negotiations were those relating to the direct division of profits. Yet as developing countries have become increasingly concerned with the wider range of benefits a foreign investor might offer, agreement on terms to govern these wider contributions is proving no simpler than on those that cover the allocation of financial rewards. To the extent that the private interests of the firm coincide with the social interests of the country, the negotiating problems may not be formidable. Training of local workers may, for example, increase the profitability of the enterprise by cutting costs of expatriate personnel while it contributes to local development. A clause in the agreement may be required simply to overcome managerial inertia. But in many cases the social demands may decrease private profitability.

Unlike increased taxes, the benefits to the country may be difficult to quantify, although the costs to the company may be all too obvious. Faced with an implicit trade-off between measurable increments to revenue and more complex contributions to development, government negotiators have often been unable to sort out their own priorities. In fact, the decision is made more complex by the fact that the agreement must be explained in simple terms to the public. The local press has the habit of reporting the financial provisions in considerable detail (and in comparison to agreements elsewhere), while the development provisions are glossed over with a few sentences. At the same time the company may be able to calculate the costs of the alternatives with a reasonable degree of certainty. Faced with such difficulties in a negotiation, many a government official has retreated to the more measurable benefits from taxation.

The trade-off between quantifiable and unquantifiable benefits has always been a difficult problem. The problem is made more complex by a new major dilemma: on the one hand, officials may wish to maximize the investor's contribution to development; on the other hand, they may be sensitive to incursions into the host government's realm of "sovereignty." The host government would like to operate its own schools, hospitals, and railroads. Schools in the hands of foreign firms are likely to be difficult to control. Hospitals run by foreign firms, although probably free from the ideological ramifications associated with education, can upset national health plans by offering salaries that attract local medical personnel away from areas that are accorded higher priority by the government. Even projects that appear to offer little challenge to government planning can evoke fears that the foreigner is going too far in usurping government prerogatives.

In one case with which we are familiar a foreign mining firm, in an effort to improve its public image, offered an African government a plan to provide massive assistance to agricultural development along its access railroad. The government felt compelled to turn down the offer, since the government thought the proposed program represented an invasion of the government's field of responsibility. The rejection of the offer was based on concepts of sovereignty, not doubts about whether the foreign firm could or would carry out its plan adequately. In fact, fears on the part of the government that the company would embarrass government programs by being very successful probably influenced the response.

In the 1974 renegotiations of the Bougainville Copper Agreement in Papua New Guinea, the government considered and rejected provisions that would put pressure on the company to hire more local managers and to expand its training efforts. The government apparently preferred not to encourage the company to compete in the tight local market for skilled personnel. And training, negotiators decided, should be done as much as possible by the government. They decided that the company should increase its financial contribution so that the government could undertake more activities, such as training.

Some governments have already determined not to have foreign firms move beyond the kinds of involvement mentioned in this chapter. Like Papua New

Guinea, they prefer increased financial contributions, which they can employ themselves to promote development. Many agreements are now calling for contributions by the foreign investor to "development funds." Although in reality no more than another tax, such a fund may create the illusion of an additional contribution to development, which may be important to some governments. But other countries have continued to seek new ways to link the foreign firm directly to development efforts. Illustrative are the requirements that Malta has imposed on enterprises interested in petroleum in that country. To gain access to petroleum, the firm must bring along manufacturing investment. In 1975 a number of oil companies were scrambling to promote and finance investment by American and European manufacturers in Malta.

RAPID EXPLOITATION

As governments have become more concerned about the broader effects of foreign investment, they have taken steps to assure that the benefits, financial and other, begin quickly. Most governments put a high premium on obtaining income and other benefits early in the life of the concession arrangement. Until recently only a few countries have even thought of the storage of raw materials in the ground as a possibly attractive alternative to immediate income. Yet many governments have not paid sufficient attention to the two most critical factors affecting early results: (1) the choice of the firm; and (2) the imposition of strict working requirements.

There is a serious danger in certain extractive industries that the foreign firm will attempt to retain control of the resource while delaying exploitation activities. In some cases the control may be purely speculative, in hopes of a strike of, say, oil nearby. However, the danger is greatest in industries where control of raw materials is an essential part of the strategy of the major firms. The raw material need not be in short supply for such a strategy to exist; if the majority of the good sources are in the hands of a small number of companies, they can ration the output as they wish. In such an industry a major threat to stability would occur if sources of raw materials were to fall into the hands of firms that are not part of the traditional oligopoly. If an outsider were to gain control of a good source of the raw material, he might disturb the oligopoly arrangement by cutting prices to gain outlets for his product. The general price structure could be eroded as a result.

In addition, an individual firm in such an oligopoly may fear that another firm within the group might obtain a cheaper source of ore, upsetting the status quo. Even though a firm may have subscribed to the implicit pricing rules of the oligopoly in the past, once it obtains a cheaper source it may be tempted to break the rules by cutting prices to gain a larger market share. The result is the pattern we described in Chapter 1. If one member of the group enters a particular geographic area, others are likely to follow to make sure that the original firm does not obtain a source that is lower in cost than those of the other firms.

Some governments have recognized such patterns of behavior and have put pressure on the latecomers for better terms. But there still remains the task of gaining some reasonable assurances that the source will be used, or, if unused, will be surrendered. Illustrative of the difficulties encountered was the slow development of nickel deposits in Latin America under some concessions granted in the late 1960s. As we pointed out in Chapter 1, in an industry where there is substantial danger that the foreign firm is interested primarily in tying up the resource—and these industries can be identified once their structures are analyzed—the criteria for selecting firms can go beyond the simple standards of whether the company has the capital and the technology. The government might analyze whether the company already has sufficient resources to supply the markets to which it has access. A bauxite mining company with large bauxite resources but little smelting capacity, for example, may have difficulty disposing of a large volume of bauxite. In many industries the larger, traditional members of the oligopoly have an abundance of reserves of the raw material. A smaller firm or a new entrant into the industry, on the other hand, may need sources of raw materials to exploit as soon as possible. Company data on reserves and sales are available for many industries, and provide a source for screening at least some firms.[33]

The second line of defense against the nonproductive tying up of the resource lies in the agreement itself. Agreements may, for example, include provision for minimum expenditures, minimum production goals, or the performance of certain activities at various stages of the life of the concession. Such provisions have a long history. An 1877 agreement in Pangkor, a Malay state, called for a forfeit of the concession if production was not started in one year, if a specified minimum labor force was not employed, or if work stopped for more than three months.[34] Similar provisions appear in present-day agreements and in general mining legislation. The 1971 Peruvian General Mining Law, for example, provided first for minimum annual investments "in the period of execution of the project and start of exploitation," to be stipulated in a schedule to the concession contract. The first year's investment had to be, in any case, not less than 30 percent of the amount of the total planned investment divided by the number of years programmed. Other percentages were applied to the declining balance in other years. The law also provided for minimum production levels related to the estimated mineral reserves contained in the concession. If, for example, the reserves totalled 50 million metric tons, the company was to produce 1/40 of the reserve per year and not less than 1.67 million metric tons.[35]

The amount of time granted to the company for survey, exploration, and construction of production facilities has varied by industry, but four to six years has been adequate in most cases.[36] Where exploration or prospecting licenses have been issued separately, their terms have also been limited. In Zambia, for example, the maximum period of validity has been four years. In some agreements, there have been rather complete timetables that covered exploration, exploitation, and the establishment of processing facilities.

It has become common practice to limit the type of expenditures that can be taken into account in the performance requirements. Many agreements have required that qualifying costs include only expenditures directly related to the project and not "general overhead expenses" that might be incurred in the home office of the parent company. This common practice in agreements has been incorporated by some countries in their general legislation. The 1969 Mines and Minerals Act of Zambia, for example, limited the qualifying expenditures for all mining firms operating in that country.

Some governments could give more care to the drafting of working provisions. The Indonesian Soriano Timber Agreement, for instance, gave the appearance of having performance standards, but did not in fact guarantee performance or assure that the contract could be revoked if the standards were not met. The agreement stated that "it is estimated" that the investment required to meet the Scope of Work would run in the order of US $235 million, as shown in the following tabulation (all figures in US $1 million):

	Year			
	1	2	3	Total
a. Logging, road construction and maintenance equipment, and wood base camps	14.4	14.9	23.4	52.7
b. Log-processing plants with maintenance and power facilities and their base camps	0.5	6.5	6.5	13.5
c. Pulp and paper plant	0.6	33.5	135.0	169.1
	15.5	54.9	164.9	235.3

But nowhere in the agreement was there a firm requirement that the company spend these amounts or carry out production activities at a particular level. There was no provision for cancellation or other penalty should the firm fail to meet the schedule.

Particularly in negotiations conducted at the pre-exploration or survey stage, it has proved difficult to predict exactly what expenditures and production levels will be appropriate. Yet the absence of precise data need not prevent the guarantee of *minimum* expenditures and *minimum* production levels. And in cases where agreement on a set of figures at the outset appears to be impossible, arrangements have been made for negotiation of these figures on the conclusion of the exploration or survey stage.

Performance bonds may also be useful as a mechanism for enforcing working provisions in mineral and timber-exploitation contracts.[37] If specified performance levels are not reached, the bond is to be forfeited. Bonds may govern all phases of the agreement: production and processing in mining agreements; logging, log-processing, and pulp and paper production in timber agreements.

The LISCO Agreement in Liberia provides an alternative mechanism. If production is unduly delayed, the company is to make annual payments to the government, and these payments are supposed to approximate the tax revenue that would accrue to the government if the mine were in operation.

Careful determination of the date on which the agreement takes effect may help in accelerating the benefits to the government. Agreements have differed on this point. In some cases the effective date is the date of signing the agreement. In other cases the effective date is the date of first production, which could be a considerable number of years after the signing.[38] Since such production is itself a major concern of government, most contracts have started at the time of signing or ratification. Thus, if the firm delays in the start of production it faces a shorter period during which production can be undertaken under the agreement.[39]

Not only the beginning of production but also the rate of production must be considered. Tax provisions have occasionally been designed for the purpose of affecting this rate. In the Middle East, for example, there have been experiments in lower tax rates on the profits from oil output that exceeds a certain level. And, as noted earlier, Venezuela enacted a tax in 1972 that would rise to a high rate—up to 10 percent of the company's total exports—if the exports of an oil company were to fall more than 2 percent below those made during a particular base period.[40]

Governments have, on occasion, carried out their threats of contract termination when production activities have been unduly delayed or certain levels of production have not been maintained. In 1893 the Malay state of Pahang cancelled 21 tin concessions for violation of working provisions.[41] In 1970 Peru cancelled concessions for a mine at Michiquillay when Asarco did not start production within the specified time.[42] In 1974 the Nigerian government asked Texaco to cease oil production, reportedly because the government considered oil production too low. And Dahomey nullified an agreement made in 1964 with Union Oil Company, charging that the company had unduly delayed bringing an oil deposit to production. The Cameroun government put five oil companies on notice in 1974 that any attempts to keep oil deposits in reserve would result in the revocation of exploration licenses,[43] and in the early 1970s Ethiopia took action to cancel several agreements because of slow progress. At least one company responded with a defense of *force majeure.*[44]

Of course, the host government's interest is not always in the direction of maximizing production levels. Where a commodity appears to be in oversupply or where prices are depressed, governments have occasionally directed, or put pressure on, companies to cut back output. The year 1974 provided several examples. Venezuela announced that it would cut oil output in 1975 to dry up "excess" supply.[45] Threats by Kuwait to cut production were reportedly behind the decisions of two foreign oil companies to raise the price they would pay for state-owned oil.[46] The Indonesian government, in an effort to check declining prices for timber, ordered timber companies to reduce production 15 percent.[47] As in the question of foreign involvement in local activities versus sovereignty, the question of establishing production rates is often not as simple as it appears.

Host governments can be expected to take an increasing interest in the development-related issues raised here. And these issues are likely to become as much a subject of dispute and misunderstanding as questions of sharing of financial benefits have been in the past. Methods of conflict avoidance and resolution as they relate to these and other issues are the subjects of the next chapter.

NOTES

1. See "Declaration on the Establishment of a New Economic Order," Resolution adopted by the Sixth Special Session of the U.N. General Assembly (A/RES/3201 (S–VI), May 9, 1974).

2. H.W. Singer, "The Distribution of Gains between Investing and Borrowing Countries," in *Papers and Proceedings of the American Economic Association,* supplement to the *American Economic Review* 40 (May 1950: 473–85. See Chandler Morse, "Potentials and Hazards of Direct International Investment in Raw Materials," in Marion Clawson, ed., *Natural Resources and International Development* (Baltimore: published for Resources for the Future by Johns Hopkins Press, 1964), pp. 380 ff. With regard to petroleum it has been written: "To date there is no clear correlation between oil revenue per capita and the level of development at the regional level." Kamil Salib Sayegh, *Oil and Arab Regional Development* (New York: Praeger, 1968), p. 81. Note also Robert W. Clower et al., *Growth without Development:An Economic Survey of Liberia* (Evanston: Northwestern University Press, 1966).

3. Raymond Vernon, *Sovereignty at Bay; The Multinational Spread of U.S. Enterprise* (New York: Basic Books, 1971), p. 49. See also K. Georg Gabriel, *The Gains to the Local Economy from the Foreign Owned Primary Export Industry: The Case of Oil in Venezuela,* unpublished D.B.A. thesis, Harvard Business School, May 1967.

4. *Concession Agreement between the Republic of Liberia and Liberian Iron and Steel Corporation* (May 5, 1967), Art. 10A.

5. *Agreement between the Republic of Indonesia and A. Soriano y Cia* (December 4, 1969), Art. 1, para. 3.

6. See Albert O. Hirschman, "Industrial Development in Brazilian Northeast and the Tax Credit System of Article 34/18," *Journal of Development Studies* 5 (1968): 5.

7. See Chapter 3, note 62.

8. Wong Lin Ken, *The Malayan Tin Industry to 1914* (Tucson: University of Arizona Press, 1965), p. 229.

9. Zuhayr Mikdashi, *A Comparative Analysis of Selected Mineral Exporting Industries* (Vienna: OPEC, March 1971) (mimeo).

10. *Agreement between the Ministry of Mines of the Government of Indonesia and Aluminum Company of America* (1969), Art. 7.

11. Ecuador, *Mining Development Law* (Supreme Decree 101 of January 24, 1974; *Official Register* No. 484, dated January 31, 1974), translated in *Mineral Trade Notes* 71 (April 1974): 7. Sales were to be at prices determined by the Directorate General of Geology and Mining on the basis of "the international prices for such ores and processing costs." Although smelting and refining plants "will be installed by the Government," companies may also install them.

12. Norman Girvan, "Making the Rules of the Game: Company-Country Agreements in the Bauxite Industry," *Social and Economic Studies* 20 (December 1971): 402.

13. Ibid.

14. Wayne C. Taylor, *The Firestone Operations in Liberia* (Washington: National Planning Association, 1956), pp. 93–95. Many of these small holders have, however, been members of the Americo-Liberian upper class rather than indigenous planters.

15. The Mamut copper agreement in Sabah, Malaysia, had a provision similar to this.

16. Scott Pearson, *Petroleum and the Nigerian Economy* (Stanford: Stanford University Press, 1970).

17. *Africa Report*, March 24, 1972, p. 343.

18. For an analysis of factors influencing choice in manufacturing, see Louis T. Wells, Jr., "Economic Man and Engineering Man" in *Public Policy* 21 (Summer 1973): 319–42.

19. "Letter from Port Gentil," *West Africa*, April 14, 1972, p. 443.

20. R.W. Apple, Jr., "Niger's Meager Economy Aided by Discovery of Uranium Vein," *New York Times*, April 14, 1969, p. 71.

21. *Daily Graphic* (Ghana), April 12, 1969, pp. 8–9.

22. See *Concession Agreement between the Government of Liberia and Liberia Iron and Steel Corporation* (May 5, 1967), Art. 12.

23. *Mining Journal* 277 (July 23, 1971).

24. Richard G. Powell, "LAMCO: A Case Study of a Concession Contract," *Proceedings of the American Society of International Law* 61 (1967), p. 93.

25. *Topic* No. 32 (no date), cover page. See also comments on the importance of the lack of international communications in Chad: Phillipe Decraene, "Chad at World's End," *Africa Report*, January 1968, pp. 54–58.

26. The United Nations report, *A Design for Development in West Irian*, states that the "rescue of Asmat carving and its development as a village industry is important not only for the sake of preserving a distinctive art form but could be the means of introducing a cash economy to villages that have virtually nothing to offer [and] it could generate a significant income...." United Nations Fund for the Development of West Irian, *A Design for Development in West Irian* (New York: United Nations, 1968), p. 112.

27. See the "savings of rights" provisions, secs. 7 and 17, of the *Government*

of Alberta (Canada)–Northwestern Pulp and Power Ltd. Agreement (1954) as amended to 1961 (June 29, 1961).

28. In the United Nations report, *A Design for Development in West Irian,* op. cit., it is noted that in West Irian "there are virtually no forest reserves and it is argued by the forest administration that timber-cutting rights can be assured in return for the provision of employment opportunities. Such an attitude is naive and fails utterly to recognize the complete dependence of the local people on the forest habitat and the complexities of local attributes of ownership. In all occupied areas of West Irian, successful forest development will depend on the provision of equitable and acceptable compensation for alienation of usufruct."

29. The (Lesotho) *Maluti Diamond Agreement of 1971* includes detailed provisions relating to the disposal of any waste from the mining works and the prevention of water pollution and erosion. For a description of several land restoration projects, see Donald McLoughlin, *Social Considerations and Environmental Protection* (paper prepared for U.N. Interregional Workshop on Negotiation and Drafting of Mining Development Agreements, Buenos Aires, November 2–18, 1973, ESA/RT/AC.7/7).

30. See Robert Trumbull, "Micronesians in Fight Over Strip Mining," *New York Times,* October 10, 1972, p. 61.

31. See Luther J. Carter, "Development in Poor Nations: How to Avoid Fouling the Nest," *Science* 163 (1969), p. 1046; and George Appell, "Partial Social Models and their Failure to Account for the Pernicious Effect of Development" (paper presented at Symposium on Education and Economic Development, Society for Applied Anthropology, April 1, 1970, Boulder, Colorado). There have been proposals, for example, to limit cuttings along waterways in Kalimantan to protect the usual paths for wandering wildlife.

It has been stated that should pollution controls in the developed countries become stricter there is a strong possibility that mining companies will "listen more favorably to demands for the establishment of smelters and refineries at the mine site where pollution controls are more likely to be less severe or even nonexistent." "The Cost of Pollution Control," *Mining Journal* 277 (November 26, 1971): 473–74. See *The United Nations and the Human Environment* (New York: Commission to Study the Organization of Peace, 1972), p. 21. See, e.g., Robert Trumbull, "Timber Venture Alters Samoan Life," *New York Times,* June 16, 1973, p. 33.

33. Annual reports of the companies, financial analysts' reports, and industry studies often provide such information.

34. Wong Lin Ken, *The Malayan Tin Industry to 1914* (Tucson: published for the Association for Asian Studies by the University of Arizona Press, 1965), p. 54.

35. Peru, *General Mining Law; Decree Law No. 18880* (Lima: Ministry of Economics and Finance, Office of Public Relations, 1971), Articles 84 and 86.

36. The total of 12 years granted in the *Contract of Work between the Government of Indonesia and the Indonesian Nickel Development Company, Ltd.* (April 1969) is clearly too long.

37. The *Agreement between the Government of the Province of Alberta
(Canada) and North Western Pulp and Power Ltd.* (June 29, 1961) provides,
for example, that:

> The Company shall, on the signing of this agreement, deposit with the
> Minister the sum of Ten Thousand ($10,000) Dollars . . . and shall, be-
> fore any timber is cut or purchased for the mill, deposit with the Minister
> an additional sum of Fifteen Thousand ($15,000) Dollars, and at any
> time thereafter may substitute for the two deposits Bearer Bonds . . .
> having face value of Twenty-five Thousand ($25,000) Dollars which
> shall be held by the Minister for the period of the agreement, or any
> renewal or renewals thereof, as security for the due performance by
> the Company of its obligations hereunder.
>
> * * *
> * * *
>
> In the event of the Company making default by failing (to perform its
> obligations under the agreement) . . . the Minister may declare the rights
> of the Company under this agreement forfeited, and thereupon the cash
> deposit or Bearer Bonds . . . shall be forfeited. . . .
>
> * * *
> * * *
>
> In the case of such forfeiture of deposit . . . the Company shall make good
> the default . . . and re-establish the guarantee deposit. (Section 2)

38. The first practice has been usual in the case of Liberian agreements.
See *Liberian Mining Concession* (January 22, 1946), Article 6. The second
practice has been common in Indonesia. See *Production-Sharing Contract
between Pertamina and Phillips Petroleum Company* (1968), secs. XV and I.

39. The 30-year *Contract of Work between the Ministry of Mines of the
Republic of Indonesia and Overseas Mineral Resources Development Company,
Ltd.* (1968) runs from the date of commencement of production, although
the Agreement "takes effect" on ratification by the Government (Art. 23).

40. "Venezuela Shaping Added Taxes on Oil," *New York Times,* April 17,
1972, p. 49. In some cases, of course, the government's goal may be to restrict
production to maintain high prices or conserve the resource. See William D.
Smith, "Libya Intensifies Oil Restrictions," *New York Times,* August 14, 1973,
p. 43 and note 45 below.

41. Wong Lin Ken, op. cit., p. 144.

42. "Peru Cancels Concessions Hold by Asarco on Copper Deposits," *New
York Times,* October 2, 1970, p. 49.

43. *Africa Report,* May–June, 1974, pp. 18 and 28.

44. For a useful discussion of what constitutes *force majeure* in concession
agreements, see G.R. Delaume, "Excuse for Non-Performance and Force Majeure
in Economic Development Agreements," *Columbia Journal of Transnational
Law* 19 (Fall 1971): 242.

45. "Venezuela to Cut Oil Output in '75," *New York Times,* August 28, 1974, p. 37.

46. Clyde H. Farnsworth, "Kuwait Threat Cited in Gulf and BP Deal," *New York Times,* July 20, 1974, p. 41.

47. "Indonesia Ordering Cuts in Production of Timber," *New York Times,* August 27, 1974, p. 45.

Chapter Five

Dispute Settlement and Contract Revision

Concessions disputes appear to be inevitable. Given the high financial stakes, the complexity of financial and development issues, the continually changing concessions environment, and the host country's constantly nagging doubts about yielding too much sovereignty, it would be remarkable if conflicts did not arise. Disputes are of two basic types: (1) those concerned with interpretation of the contract; and (2) those involving the appropriateness of the terms themselves. Either type of dispute may result in action by one party which the other interprets as a breach or a threatened breach, but the distinction in types of disputes is critical if one is to develop an approach to dealing with the problem of potential conflict. Concession agreements have traditionally provided some mechanisms and guidelines for settling disputes involving interpretation and enforcement of existing provisions. Less well developed and utilized are mechanisms for handling situations where certain terms no longer reflect the current bargaining positions and perceived interests of the parties to the agreement. It is this latter type of dispute, which goes to the heart of the concessions relationship, that is our chief concern in this chapter.

Much of the concessions literature of the last two decades has focused on dispute settlement issues as they are framed in a context of adjudication. In contrast, major emphasis in this chapter is on conflict avoidance, and conflict resolution in a context other than formal adjudication. We are not concerned primarily with those areas of the law that have traditionally attracted the attention of lawyers concerned with concessions-related litigation. These include exhaustion of local remedies, sovereign immunity, the act of state doctrine, compensation for nationalized property, valuation of nationalized property, *pacta sunt servanda, rebus sic stantibus,* the law to be applied in arbitrations, and arbitration in general. To the extent that we do deal with these issues, it is essentially for the purpose of giving some perspective and for providing a brief introduction to issues with which some readers may not be familiar. For those who are familiar with these issues our very limited reference to them will no doubt cause some discomfort. For those unfamiliar with these issues, but anxious to learn more, there exists a vast literature, some of which is mentioned in our footnotes.

ARBITRATION

The Usual Approach

Historically, concession agreements have relied on arbitration provisions as the principal mechanism for settling disputes between the host government and the foreign investor. The interest of lawyers in arbitration clauses has meant that these clauses are frequently the longest and most detailed provisions in agreements. In fact, the legal literature about concessions deals far more extensively with arbitration than with many technical issues—royalties, taxation, land use, employment, processing, and the like—which have been at the heart of most concession negotiations.[1]

The emphasis on arbitration as the primary technique for dispute settlement has directed the attention of some negotiators away from other, perhaps more satisfactory, approaches to conflict resolution. In addition, the emphasis on arbitration clauses in the literature and in contracts may give both parties to concession arrangements a sense of security that is largely unjustified.

Illustrative of a typical arbitration provision in a concession contract is the dispute-settling provision in the 1964 agreement between the government of Liberia and the Kitoma Mining and Trading Company, for the exploration and development of iron ore:

> Any dispute arising between the government and the Concessionaire with respect to the interpretation, exercise of rights or compliance with the obligations under the terms and conditions of this Agreement, shall be submitted to arbitration for decision. . . .[2]

The settlement mechanism in this agreement was clear as long as the dispute arose from "interpretation, exercise of rights or compliance." As has commonly been the case, however, the agreement did not deal with the problems of settling conflicts that might arise because certain terms—relating to such matters as pricing, taxation, royalties, control of concession land, and utilization of the concessionaire's transportation facilities—either were not considered when the agreement was concluded or were no longer acceptable to one of the parties.

Although the traditional arbitration clause has been useful on occasion in dealing with questions of interpretation of contract provisions,[3] such a clause, at least as traditionally conceived, has not proved to be a dispute-settling device capable of dealing effectively with the most serious concession disputes. As a result it is perhaps not surprising that actual arbitration proceedings have not been especially frequent in the history of relations between host governments and foreign mining companies.

There have been efforts to provide arbitration mechanisms to deal with the more fundamental conflicts, but such attempts have been rare. The Sierra Leone Tonkolili Iron Ore Agreement of 1937 offers one example:

> If either the Government or the Company shall request a revision under paragraphs (a) or (b) of this clause and the two parties shall be unable to agree as to the extent of the revision, the question shall be submitted to arbitration.[4]

The inclusion of a set of standards to guide arbitrators in reaching their decision could turn such a clause into a powerful instrument. The criteria to be used by the arbitrators might include contracts recently negotiated in the host country or contracts that govern similar operations in other countries for the same industry. Such a provision, with adequate standards, holds some promise of turning arbitration, still an acceptable settlement mechanism for some developing countries, into an effective tool for dealing with the most difficult concession disputes.

Simple Procedures for Simple Disputes

Not only has arbitration not been utilized to a significant extent in dealing with questions of contract reform, but it is unclear that arbitration has been very effective in dealing with less fundamental problems of interpretation and enforcement. The expense and time involved in arbitration proceedings have generally discouraged governments or investors from resorting to this mechanism to settle questions of interpretation and enforcement. To an extent, arbitration has proved inadequate for both the big job of revision and for the small jobs of interpretation. On the other hand, the mere presence of an arbitration mechanism may have assisted in the nonlitigious settlement of minor contract disputes. In many cases the awareness that one aggrieved party might carry an unsettled issue to cumbersome arbitration proceedings has probably meant that both parties would attempt to avoid arbitration by settling their difficulties in a mutually agreeable way.

Although traditional or modified arbitration provisions may be of some value in leading to settlements, other mechanisms have been tried in some contracts to provide alternative methods of resolving conflicts. While retaining an arbitration clause, a few concession contracts have made attempts to categorize types of disputes and to differentiate the settlement mechanism according to the nature of the particular dispute. In such contracts the negotiators have sought means to handle the "simple" types of disputes in a rapid and economic way.

The Pan American-Iranian Oil Concession Agreement of 1963, for example, distinguished between disputes of a "technical and accounting nature" and disputes relating to "legal questions" that deal with the execution and interpretation of the agreement.[5] The first type of dispute would be handled expeditiously by one or three experts in a proceeding that was to be more streamlined than a full-scale arbitration. The second type of dispute would go to a regular arbitration.

A rather similar mechanism was included in Lesotho's 1971 Maluti Diamond Agreement. The agreement provided that disputes involving "any expenditure sought to be deducted" were to be referred to a single expert acceptable to the parties to the agreement. The decision of the expert, who was to determine his own rules of procedure, was to be final and binding.[6]

The attractiveness of such distinctions as those drawn in the Pan American and Maluti agreements is the relative speed and efficiency with which "technical and accounting" disputes can be settled outside the costly and time-consuming arbitration procedures. On the other hand, provisions simplifying settlement of minor technical matters may have their disadvantages, at least for the host government. An investor will probably be more willing to accept the decision of the government's ministry of finance or other agency concerning an accounting or "technical" matter if the alternative to acceptance is a complicated, expensive arbitration proceeding. A government may feel, in any case, that on matters of taxation and accounting it should not be subjected to third-party supervision on what would normally be an internal administrative matter.

Some agreements have used another form of third-party dispute settlement. They have designated the use of an independent firm of accountants as final arbiter in accounting disputes. Such a provision is particularly attractive to the investor when the foreign firm doubts the capability or fairness of local tax administrators. The Collateral Agreement of 1953 between the government of the Republic of Liberia and the Liberian Mining Company, Ltd. provided that:

> The Government's participation in "net profits" of the Company . . . shall be determined from the books of account of the Company. . . . The Company shall cause its books to be audited within three (3) months after the close of each fiscal year by such independent certified public accountants as may be chosen by the Company and approved by the Government, and such audit shall be conclusive in determining the Company's "net profits."[7]

Despite the condition that the government approve the accounting firm selected, such a provision could be detrimental to the government's interests. The standards of an independent accounting firm are not generally those of a government taxing authority. A North American accounting firm would, unless there are clear instructions to the contrary, generally audit under standards of a conservative reporter to the shareholder. Where alternative solutions to accounting problems are acceptable, the independent accounting firm would probably choose those that understate profits. For example, "conservative" accounting principles would allow many outlays of the firm to be expensed currently. The government's interests and common tax policy in most countries, however, require that some of these expenditures be capitalized and depreciated over the expected life of the asset. Given the possibility of reasonable differences on such matters, governments have generally wanted to retain the authority to decide accounting questions from the point of view of a governmental taxing authority.

Yet the use of an independent accountant provides the company with some degree of predictability regarding norms covering tax issues. Whether this benefit to a foreign investor and the relief from some administrative burden for the government is worth the price in terms of a possible reduction or retiming of tax receipts and the yielding of some sovereign power must be judged by the host government.

SETTLEMENT IN THE HOST COUNTRY'S COURTS

Many modern concession agreements have abandoned completely the principle of calling on nonnational third parties to resolve disputes.

Especially in Latin America, many concession contracts require that disputes be settled in local courts, according to local law.[8] The Peruvian Constitution, for example, requires that in "every state contract with foreigners, or in the concessions which grant them in the latter's favor, it must be expressly stated that they will submit to the laws and tribunals of the Republic. . . ."[9] In other countries, as we have mentioned, certain specific disputes—such as those relating to taxation—must go to local courts. Where a contract makes a distinction between "technical" and "legal" disputes, the contract may call for submitting both types of dispute to local courts. As a consequence, adjudication as a potential source of conflict resolution has become increasingly less attractive to foreign investors, and lack of trust in the fairness of local courts in dealing with disputes between the government and a foreign enterprise has been the primary reason for reluctance in accepting the local judiciary for dispute settlement.

Where the forum for dispute settlement is not stated in an agreement, the parties usually must exhaust the remedies offered by the courts of the host country before resorting to an international forum. Where there is provision for arbitration, this is usually considered a waiver of the need to exhaust local remedies.[10]

Regardless of the forum for settlement, parties to a concession agreement are generally free to select the law that will govern their contractual relationship.[11] Increasingly, whether the concession agreement calls for resort to arbitration or to host country courts, the law of the host country is explicitly invoked.[12] Where the law of the contract is not stated, the arbitrators or judges determine what the parties' intention may have been. In such a case, the law of the contract is usually presumed to be the law of the host country and/or "general principles" of law.[13] Often the contracts leave little choice, even when there is no specific choice-of-law provision invoking the law of the host country. Major legislation (such as mining laws, company laws, and tax laws) may be incorporated by reference, or such legislation may be drafted to cover all concession contracts. The choice of law left to the arbitrator or judge may only relate to rules of interpretation. The probable invocation of local law and local courts may be sufficient to encourage more serious efforts by investors to reach accommodations outside of court.[14]

INSTITUTIONALIZING MECHANISMS
FOR CHANGE

The problem of dealing with terms that are no longer acceptable to one of the parties is a more difficult one than that of handling technical and interpretive issues. Such disputes over basic terms have been frequent; and they will continue to arise in a world of change and imperfect information. The negotiation of a concession contract is not an isolated, discrete event.

Occasionally concession agreements have been referred to as "living contracts" and the phrase does capture much of the essence of the arrangement. The meaning of the phrase was perhaps best described by a lawyer who represented the Bethlehem Steel Corporation in negotiations with the Liberian government for the LAMCO Agreement.[15] He wrote that:

> the signing of a concession agreement is only the invitation to the ball. . . .
> [T]he foreign investor may feel at times that he has entered into a contract to make concessions rather than a concession contract.[16]

The LAMCO Agreement has been the object of almost constant negotiation and discussion since 1960. Continued discussions between firm and government have ranged from such matters as the use of railroad and harbor facilities by the government and the firm's education and employment of concession personnel, to possible restructuring of the entire arrangement.

> The negotiations have all taken place under the umbrella of the basic Concession Agreement and are governed in the last analysis by the spirit in which that Agreement was negotiated. Actual textual reference to the Concession Agreement is, however, relatively rare.[17]

The ongoing process of negotiation is not unique to the concession contract. It is becoming increasingly recognized in the law of contracts in the United States, for example, that:

> In the actual carrying out of a complex agreement between friendly parties, the written contract often furnishes a kind of framework for an

ongoing relationship, rather than a precise definition of that relationship. For that definition we may have to look to a kind of two-party customary law implicit in the parties' actions, rather than to the verbal formulations of the contract; if this is true of contracts that are eventually brought to court, it must be much more commonly so in situations where the parties make out without resort to litigation.[18]

In some instances domestic contracts are actually revised.[19] In other cases of contracts between "friendly parties" the two-party customary law that grows out of and alters the contract may remain only implicit and unwritten. It is, however, no less a "revision" of the contract than if the changes were incorporated into writing. In some concession contracts the developing relationship of the parties, carrying with it a two-party customary law of the contract, has been made explicit, and the subject of codicils to, or changes in, the agreement. In other cases the terms have been developed implicitly through the parties' "interactional expectancies,"[20] rather than through explicit contract revisions.

The contract relating to the Senegalese Taiba phosphate mining operation is one example of implicit revision. In 1973 and 1974, after some fifteen years of low phosphate prices, prices increased rapidly. Benefits from higher prices were not passed on to the government because of the special terms of the agreement. In 1974, however, the company agreed to make a lump-sum payment of 3.5 billion CFA francs to the government as part of a settlement that recognized the government's low tax receipts over the years. Although the contract was not changed immediately to call for such a payment, implicit revision was a prelude to later explicit revisions, calling for 50 percent equity ownership by the government.[21]

Some of the changes in the LAMCO Agreement in Liberia have been of this nature:

> A great deal . . . depends on the working relationships between the foreign investors and representatives at all levels; on the ability of the foreign investors to remain in communication with those representatives, to understand and appreciate their needs and concerns. . . . These goals cannot be achieved simply by pointing to the small print in the Concession Agreement. . . .[22]

Few contracts have been as "interactional" as concession agreements. Not only is the concession arrangement often an extremely complex document, but it may extend over a long time period, usually several decades. In this respect the concession contract is quite different from most agreements for the sale of goods, for example, where the transaction may be precisely defined and may be quickly concluded. Major uncertainties prevailing at the time a concession contract is negotiated generally make it necessary to reexamine the terms at a later time. In addition, the bargaining powers of the parties to the agreement are likely to change over time, creating tensions that generally lead to revisions. In fact, the need for change is so frequent and compelling that revision or updating are probably more apt terms to describe the process of evolution than is the frequently used term renegotiation.

The process aspect of concession agreements has meant that historically contract revision has been the rule rather than the exception. Much has been written by international lawyers about the character and renegotiability (or nonrenegotiability) of international investment contracts. Arguments have been presented on both sides about the legal justification of renegotiation of a concession contract when the conditions under which the concession was first negotiated have changed.[23] Whatever interest such arguments may attract, the fact is that the history of concession contracts in many countries has been one of constant revision and updating.

While the alteration of concession contracts has received the most publicity in the oil industry, the practice has had substantial impact in other industries. Iron ore, copper, bauxite, and other mineral contracts have been the subject of revisions in much the same way as oil agreements.[24]

Revision of contract terms has most often focused on fiscal provisions, but other provisions have been subject to change: allocation (and future reduction) of land area; the use of transport facilities by the government and third parties; equity ownership; management; employment of local workers; and local processing.

The need for regular change in concession agreements suggests the possibility that contracts can and should include institutional arrangements to regulate the timing, scope, and nature of changes. Provisions facilitating and regulating contract changes have appeared only infrequently, and usually in connection with specific items in concession agreements.

Provisions for change fall into two classes: (1) clauses that call for the automatic, nonnegotiable adjustment of certain terms of the contract; and (2) clauses that provide for the future negotiation of selected terms of the contract. We have already discussed, in Chapter 4, another vehicle for changing contract terms. Provisions relating to tests for determining the economic feasibility of establishing processing facilities have sometimes resulted in the reopening of negotiations to reexamine concession terms.

Provisions for change can be useful in institutionalizing changes that are predictable and in smoothing the way for negotiation of other provisions. They can be deceptive, however, if one of the parties fails to recognize that negotiations are likely to be reopened from time to time even when such negotiations are not triggered by an express contract provision. The danger is that such provisions may give a misleading sense of permanence to both the terms to which the change provisions refer and the terms to which no allusion is made.

Moreover, provisions that purport to change only limited terms in a predetermined fashion at a later date often have been misleading. Some of these provisions have operated almost completely automatically. Others, such as the most-favored-company and most-favored-country clauses—which usually purport to be concerned with levels of taxation—in practice have led to a reopening of a broad range of issues covered in the original contract.

Two examples of the virtually automatic change provision include periodic reductions of landholdings of the concessionaire and periodic increases in government equity holdings.

Progressive Reduction of Concession Area

Widely accepted in international oil contracts and only somewhat less widely utilized in hard mineral and timber contracts have been provisions requiring the periodic reduction of concession land. One writer stated in 1967 that "all new [oil] concessions have included a relinquishment obligation as a matter of course."[25] Such provisions have helped in avoiding disputes over how much land the foreign firm should continue to hold. In some cases the subject has been covered in the general laws, as in Libya, where the 1955 Petroleum Law provided:

Within a period of five years from the date of the granting of a concession, the concession holder shall reduce the concession area to 75% of its original size, within eight years from the said date, the concession holder shall further reduce the concession area to 50% of its original size and within ten years from said date the concession holder shall further reduce the concession area to 33 1/3% of its original size....[26]

With regard to hard mineral and timber contracts, reduction provisions have been included primarily in the agreements negotiated in the 1960s and early 1970s. The 1969 agreement between the Ethiopian Mineral Development Share Company and Duval Corporation of Ethiopia (for the development of a number of hard minerals, including gold, copper, lead, and nickel) provided that the investor:

shall, on or before one (1) year from the effective date hereof and annually thereafter, reduce each of the Subject Areas in the amount of not less than ten percent (10%) ... the location of such reduction to be determined by Operator in its sole discretion....[27]

From the point of view of the host country, land-relinquishment clauses have two advantages: (1) they may prevent the tying up of land that could be used for exploitation by the government or a third party; and (2) they may encourage the speedy exploration and development of the concession area. Although the foreign firm may need access to large areas during the exploration period, it will not usually find equally attractive reserves in the whole area. Or it may not be able to exploit all the reserves immediately. It may be quite willing to give up land voluntarily in the first case. In the second a conflict between the investor's and the government's interests may develop if the investor wishes to treat the excess concession area as a reserve to be used at some future date when its other sources of supply are depleted, or if the investor wishes to keep the concession area out of the control of a competitor. By helping to settle these differences early, automatic relinquishment may assist in avoiding a potential source of friction between the host country and the investor.

The relinquishment clauses typified by the 1955 Libyan Petroleum Law and the Ethiopian Duval Agreement have normally contemplated the release of land that has not been exploited. Most relinquishment provisions for minerals are of this type. A somewhat different type of relinquishment clause has been typical of timber contracts. Such provisions, mentioned in the previous chapter, call for the relinquishment of timber tracts after the tracts have been harvested. If the government does not intend to have a particular tract reforested, relinquishment will release the land for other purposes such as agriculture. If reforestation is contemplated, the government may wish to leave the area in the hands of the investor so that he may oversee the reforestation process, with the land area reverting to the government at the end of the reforestation period.

Although the relinquishment clauses for timber and mining have differed in content, their purposes have been similar. In either case a relinquishment clause, precisely timed, may help to avoid disputes concerning the control of land area. Of course, they do not do anything to deal with disputes about division of financial rewards and the basic political problem of foreign ownership.

Phase-In of Host Country Equity Ownership

Host country dissatisfaction with concession arrangements has frequently stemmed from political concern that the country is not controlling its own resources and hence its own economic destiny. Service contract arrangements have offered one response to the problem of sovereignty, since they put the foreign investor in the posture of a contractor to the government. Another response to the issue of ownership has been arrangements whereby equity is shared between national investors and the foreign investor.

Although local private ownership is encouraged in some countries, only occasionally has the local partner in mineral contracts in developing countries been an indigenous private company. There are examples, however. The work contract between the Indonesian government and P.T. Asia Mining Company (1971) was the first joint-venture mineral agreement negotiated in Indonesia. The equity in P.T. Asia Mining was owned by P.T. Togor Corporation Martapura Ltd., an indigenous Indonesian company, and Asia Mining Enterprises, a private Brunei company. Joint ventures between local companies and foreign enterprises have, of course, been common in the manufacturing sector, where the local company's contributions may take the form of goodwill, access to local markets, or small amounts of capital. The large requirements for capital, however, have generally made significant private participation in mining ventures very difficult, if the private partner must provide his total share of funds at the outset.

Joint-venture arrangements in mining between a government (or a state enterprise) and a foreign company have been more common than arrangements involving local companies. Many of the arrangements in the 1960s for oil exploration and development were joint ventures in which some development costs and profits were shared. In some instances the form of arrangement has been production-sharing. In others it has been the purely conventional joint venture, with equity held by both parties. Yet in many instances it may be neither economically feasible nor wise for the host government to invest in substantial equity at the beginning of a mineral development arrangement.[28] The government would usually prefer to take its ownership position at a later date.

One answer to the problem of local ownership is for the concession agreement to provide for a gradual phasing in of local participation. Sometimes such an arrangement allows the accretion of ownership in local private hands. In other cases the government is the partner. Although programmed changes in ownership became particularly fashionable in the early 1970s, the concept appeared in much earlier agreements. The iron ore concession granted by Peru to the Marcona Mining Company in 1952, for example, provided for the right of the Peruvian state-owned steel company, Corporacion Peruana del Santa, to exercise an option to acquire 50 percent ownership in 1982.[29]

By the mid-1970s schemes for programmed changes in ownership were evident in a large number of agreements. In late 1971, OPEC established guidelines suggesting that its member countries receive an initial 25 percent participation in the equity of local petroleum operating companies and that this participation increase by stages to an eventual 51 percent control.[30] The equity was to be paid for by the producing country. Many other arrangements, such as the Papua New Guinea copper agreement for Bougainville and the Indonesian Kennecott copper agreement, have called for the sale of some shares to local parties in the future. These agreements allowed for private participation in the mining enterprises.

One goal of some of the phase-in arrangements has been to place the initial risk of the project on the foreign investor. Since local capital is introduced at the option of the local party, it will be forthcoming only if the venture appears to be profitable. In most cases the host government can successfully manage political sensitivity to foreign ownership until the uncertainties inherent in the early stage of a project have been resolved.

Proposals have been made for more sophisticated provisions to transfer ownership in foreign investments. One scheme would allow the local partner, at his option, to increase his ownership up to a specified portion of the shares. If local ownership reaches the key percentage figure, the foreign firm has a "put" option whereby it can require that the local partner take all of the outstanding shares of the enterprise. One rationale behind such arrangements is that they allow the foreign firm to retain its position as long as it is making an essential contribution to the country. Presumably, if the foreign firm's participation is considered essential, the local partner would not acquire shares up to the level that would encourage the foreign firm to leave. On the other hand, the foreign firm is protected from having to remain in a situation where local ownership is sufficiently great that the foreign firm has lost effective control. We are not aware of any actual agreements that have been formulated on this basis, but such provisions do hold some promise of reducing one area of dispute.

Although provisions for ownership change provide a mechanism for altering apparent control in concession arrangements and, in many cases, for shifting the allocation of financial benefits, they do pose problems. When a local party is to buy shares, valuation of the shares or assets to be taken over has almost invariably created difficulties.

In ordinary joint ventures between private firms, provisions for a change in the allocation of shares are not uncommon. Pricing formulas here have typically referred to: (1) the original cost of the assets; (2) book value of the shares; (3) fair market value of the shares; or (4) a multiple of the average earnings for a certain time period. Occasionally a combination of these factors has been used.[31] Other formulas, including replacement cost or a valuation based on an estimate of what the corporation would actually realize if it were to sell the physical assets, are, of course, possible.

The 1969 Indonesian Asa oil production-sharing contract suggests one approach for an extractive operation. The agreement provided that the foreign contractor must offer to Indonesian citizens 5 percent of the rights granted to the contractor, as soon as commercial sales were started. The price of the offer was to be based on the higher of two figures: the average cost to the original shareholders, or the value determined by a security analyst who was a member of the New York Stock Exchange. The agreement left open the question of what standard the analyst should apply.[32]

The problem of valuation arises not only in programmed changes in equity ownership, but also in unscheduled partial or full nationalizations. The valuation of assets in such takeovers may offer some lessons for programmed changes.

Total nationalization has often raised the larger question of whether compensation is to be paid at all. Two major theoretical standards, and a significant body of practice, have developed in this connection.[33] The United States and certain other Western countries have long advocated a standard of "prompt, adequate and effective" compensation. By this is normally meant full compensation. The 1962 U.N. General Assembly Resolution on Permanent Sovereignty Over Natural Resources rather ambiguously called for the payment of "appropriate compensation."[34] The theoretical standards have done little to restrain the disputes relating to compensation.

In actual practice some compensation has been paid in the majority of nationalizations. It has been suggested that the only rule arising from recent international practice is that "the parties to a taking are under an obligation to negotiate the level of compensation for the seizure."[35] In the majority of cases the standard has been book value. Where book value is agreed upon as the basis of settlement, payment is for the owners' equity, defined as the book value of total assets minus total liabilities.[36] A settlement based on book value is illustrated by Zambia's takeover of 51 percent interest in two mining companies in 1969. The Zambian government determined that the price for the assets would be based on the "book value as at December 31, 1969."[37]

The term book value, however, has not always been used consistently and may have a number of meanings, depending on the context. Book value is generally considered to be the actual historical cost of the assets less amounts historically deducted for depreciation. Whether depreciation is that taken for tax purposes or some different amount that might be shown on the company's books is not clearly indicated by the term book value. Occasionally, reference is made to updated book value, which recognizes the appreciated value of assets. In some instances companies have revalued their assets before an impending nationalization in order that the books show a larger value for the enterprise.

While governments have usually favored book value as a standard, the companies have generally sought a basis that would provide for more compensation. A favored approach has been to discount the stream of earnings that would accrue to the company if it were to retain ownership.[38] Company lawyers have usually argued that the company is entitled to payment for the value of what they are losing. Government lawyers have usually responded that the stream of earnings is an unreasonably high standard, reflecting monopoly rents, and the resource, in any case, belongs to the state. The argument is sometimes supplemented by the claim that the host government would have been free to increase taxes in later years, thus decreasing the stream of earnings.[39] The 1972 takeover of 20 percent control of oil operating companies by five Persian Gulf countries illustrates claim and counterclaim. Originally the companies had asked for a price based on the market value of the assets plus payment for the profits lost up to the date of the expiration of the concession. The governments were willing to pay "normal book value." The governments finally announced they would pay something in excess of book value as recorded by the firms.[40]

There have, of course, been cases where governments have refused to pay any compensation. In 1968 Peru expropriated the LaBrea y Parinas oil complex, property of the U.S.-owned International Petroleum Company and for years refused to pay compensation for these assets.

The 1971 Chilean takeover of several large copper mining concerns provides a complex case, where compensation was withheld (until a change of policy, by a new government, in 1974)[41] because of previous "excess" profits. For the properties owned by the Kennecott Copper Company and Anaconda Copper Company, the Chilean nationalization prescribed a detailed formula for valuation based on the 1964 book value of the assets. Provision was made for deductions for amortization, depreciation, writeoffs, and excess profits earned by the companies between 1955 and 1971. Excess profits were defined as those profits exceeding: (1) the average return on the company's worldwide copper investments outside Chile; (2) the return allowed foreign investors under international agreements to which Chile was a party; or (3) the level established as the base for preferential dividends payable to the Chilean government corporation, Codelco, under a 1967 agreement with the companies. The government determined that the excess profits of both Kennecott and Anaconda exceeded any compensation otherwise due. Owners of other, smaller mines nationalized at the same time did receive compensation.[42] It has been suggested that the measure of reparation guiding the Chilean government in dealing with the two major mines was what was fair and appropriate under the circumstances and that there was a concept of unjust enrichment underlying the standard.[43]

The companies, of course, disagreed with the valuation. The Kennecott Copper Company argued that deductions for what the Chilean government called excess profits and some other charges were unfair, and that the valuation standard adopted by the government was inappropriate because it failed to take into consideration the replacement cost or the operation's value as a going concern with potential to earn future income. "Costs of assets acquired in past years will not reflect replacement costs, appreciation by reason of inflation, scarcity, or other factors. Balance sheets do not reflect ore reserves or the intangible value of marketing practices, contracts, technical expertise, experience and the like."[44] The company distinguished (a) businesses that have relatively short-lived assets or assets whose depreciated costs approach current values and mining operations that are relatively new from (b) mining companies that have been in operation for an extended period of time. Only in the case of the former, the company argued, would the difference between original cost less depreciation and going-concern value be modest. In addition, the company added that the Chilean expropriation legislation denied compensation for the value of any interest in advisory and management contracts. And Kennecott protested the failure of the government to take into consideration the value of mining rights lost by the operating company. The government, of course, considered the minerals, the source of this wealth, to be the property of the state.

Whatever the standard of valuation in a programmed or unprogrammed change in ownership, the method and rate of payment are important. Where ownership has been transferred to government hands, a common provision for the purchase has been for the government to pay for its shares out of future dividends. This was the method of payment proposed by the government of Ghana in 1972 in connection with its projected takeover of 55 percent of the equity interest in the Consolidated African Selection Trust and Lonrho's Ashanti Goldfields.[45] Bonds have sometimes been issued. For example, the government of Sierra Leone's compensation of £2,555,000 to the Sierra Leone Selection Trust for 51 percent interest in that company's operations was to be paid in bonds bearing 5.5 percent interest. The bonds were to be retired by the government in sixteen equal half-yearly installments beginning in 1971. The funds were to come out of future dividends accruing to the government from ownership in the company.[46]

In other cases, the payment explicitly combined features of bonds and deductions from dividends. The government of Zambia's 51 percent share in the operations of the Zambian Anglo-American group, taken over in 1969, were to be paid for with 6 percent "loan stock" to be paid off in installments every six months over twelve years. The interest in Roan Selection Trust, taken over at the same time, was paid with 6 percent bonds to be retired in installments every six months over eight years. Accelerated payments were to be made if two-thirds of the government's dividends totalled more than the annual compensation payment.[47]

In fact, payment from future dividends may only be a form of delayed expropriation. Where the government does not pay a market interest rate and has no commitment to pay unless dividends are earned, the same economic results could be obtained by expropriating the shares at some later date. But the political benefits of this form of payment appear to overwhelm the economic realities. Indeed, the businessman has only rarely protested this form of payment, perhaps because he considers the implied delayed expropriation as being better than the likely alternative, an immediate expropriation.

Although equity changes could be programmed without compensation, negotiators usually are not able to foresee the kind of shifts in bargaining power in the future that would lead them to agree to such changes at the outset. In most concession arrangements where programmed ownership changes are to be a basic aspect of the agreement, the parties must specify in the agreement the basis for valuation of the shares, the currency in which the shares are to be paid, and the mechanism for resolving disputes relating to valuation and payment.

Where equity change is programmed, the shifts in ownership, if significant, may be effective in reducing the political tensions associated with a continued foreign presence. And the programmed changes generally mean a shift in financial benefits from the investor to the host government when operations are successful.

Opinions differ among investors on the desirability of planning for possible, but unprogrammed nationalizations. Some investors have believed that the possibility of nationalization should not be mentioned in order not to plant a seed for later unfavorable action. Others have considered it best to guard against all eventualities and to include provisions that maximize the protection of the investor's interests, should nationalization be undertaken in the future.

Most-Favored-Company and Most-Favored-Country Provisions

Most-Favored-Company Provisions. Another type of automatic revision clause that has come into fairly general use is the provision for most-favored-company treatment. An example of such a clause, in its simplest form, is contained in the 1966 agreement between the government of Jamaica and the Aluminum Partners of Jamaica, Ltd.:

> In the event of the Government of Jamaica making any arrangement or agreement with any other person in respect of . . . royalties, income tax, other taxes, mining leases, land use and/or any other terms and conditions relating to mining of commercial bauxite . . . different from herein contained, the Companies shall be entitled at their option to substitute such terms and conditions . . . for the terms and conditions herein contained.[48]

Similarly, an agreement between the Imperial Ethiopian government and the Ethiopian Potash Company provided:

> During the term of this Agreement the Government grants [the concessionaire] Most Favored Concession rights and privileges. . . . Upon written request of the [concessionaire], the Government shall enter into an appropriate amendment [to] this Agreement in the event, in the [concessionaire's] opinion, the specific terms and provisions of any such other agreements are more favorable than the terms and provisions of this Agreement. The purpose of such amendments shall be to permit uniformity between the specific terms and provisions of such other agreements.[49]

From the host country's viewpoint, provisions such as those in the Jamaican and Ethiopian agreements have represented the least appealing type of revision clause. This kind of provision tends to inhibit a government from negotiating with other companies specific terms that are more favorable than those of past agreements.

Unfortunately, the fact is that in some circumstances a second agreement has been negotiated in ignorance of the existence of the earlier agreement's most-favored-company provision. This may simply be a result of the turnover of staff in government offices and the generally poor state of concessions administration. It may mean that the earlier agreement is in effect automatically revised without the government realizing that it is initiating such a revision.

Equally important, the language of many most-favored-company provisions is likely to lead only to the appearance of similar treatment of foreign investors. Under the Jamaican agreement, for example, a lower rate of income taxation for a second company would be substituted automatically for the rate set forth in the Aluminum Partners of Jamaica agreement. But nothing was said about the possibility that the second company may be paying a higher rate of royalties, may have given up rights to claim certain deductions, or may be making certain infrastructure contributions not made by the first company. Under the Jamaican and the Ethiopian agreements, the companies were entitled to the more favored treatment received by the second company, but need not have taken on any additional burdens assumed by that second company.

It is, of course, nearly impossible to consider any single provision in isolation from the rest of the contract. During the negotiation process, the government's negotiator may offer a particular investor more favorable tax treatment than was offered an earlier company because the mineral resource of the second agreement is not thought to be as valuable or as large as that covered in the first agreement. In the negotiation process a decision about taxes may be made in a particular way because a certain decision was taken about the company's contributions to community development. To undo automatically one provision in this complex and intricate structure without considering the rest of the structure simply defeats much of what was gained in the negotiation.

The problem is compounded if, as in the Ethiopian agreement, the contracts with which the first agreement is compared need not even deal with the same industry. The Jamaican agreement at least limits the comparison to other "commercial bauxite" agreements.

Some of the oil contracts of the 1960s dealt directly with these problems by providing that, in making adjustments, "the parties shall have due regard to the basic differences between the provisions of the respective agreements, arrangements, and circumstances."[50] Such comparisons can probably do little more than reopen concession negotiations. The outcome of the reopened negotiations is difficult to predict.

Most-Favored-Country Provisions. Provisions calling for most-favored-country treatment have been less common than those calling for most-favored-company terms. Such clauses call for the substitution of provisions accepted by the foreign company in another country, if those provisions are more favorable to the host government than those that were agreed upon in the original negotiations in the country in question. Most-favored-country provisions provide a counterbalance to most-favored-company clauses.

In 1967 Nigeria invoked a most-favored-African-nation clause, a variant of the most-favored-country clause, to bring the Nigerian oil-mining leases in line with the terms of the Libyan Petroleum Law, under which certain companies operating in Nigeria were also operating in Libya. The federal government of Nigeria passed a decree amending its 1959 Petroleum Profits Tax Act to provide for the application of posted prices and the expensing of royalties for tax purposes as provided in the Libyan law, justifying its actions under the most-favored-African-nation clause of its petroleum concessions.[51]

Some agreements have taken a somewhat broader approach based on the company's agreements elsewhere. For example, the Bahrain Petroleum Company Ltd. agreement provided that "if States other than Bahrain bordering the Arabian Gulf in which oil was then produced should receive substantially better terms than the Ruler of Bahrain, the company would be willing to review the situation."[52]

Neither most-favored-company nor most-favored-country provisions are easy to administer. Yet one cannot deny the relevance to a concessions relationship of the fact that the host government has substantially altered its policies in a later agreement with another party or that the company has accepted substantially different conditions in a later agreement with another country. These may well be factors that should be taken into consideration in a general periodic review of the agreement. The policy changes in the later agreements may reflect significant changes in the industry that should then be reflected in the earlier agreements through contract revision. Provisions that ease the reopening of negotiations in such circumstances may be useful.

Periodic Revision

Although changing circumstances have often led to contract revisions even without express provision for such changes in the agreement, specific terms that trigger the review process at fixed intervals have been useful in minimizing friction and facilitating the orderly and systematic updating of the agreement. Clauses of varying types that call for periodic reconsideration of terms have appeared in hard mineral, oil, and timber contracts. In general they have tended to limit the terms to be reviewed regularly. The calculation of export prices and of royalty rates appear to be the most common subjects of scheduled review provisions.

In some agreements the revision clauses have called for review at specific time periods. For example, the Sierra Leone Development Company Iron Ore Agreement provided:

> If at the end of the sixth, eleventh or sixteenth years following . . . the first commercial shipment . . . or at the end of any further five-year period thereafter the average cost to the Company of placing the ore from the demised areas . . . is materially less or materially in excess of the average cost during the period preceding that under review, either the Government or the Company may request a revision in the basic royalty . . . whether or not such basic royalty has previously been revised. . . .
>
> It is declared that the general object of any revision contemplated [above] . . . is to redress any hardship which may arise either to Government or Company either from a general change in world price levels or from an alteration in cost of working due to a change of labour or social conditions in Sierra Leone. . . .[53]

A 1964 amendment to the 1958 concession agreement between the government of the Republic of Liberia and the Gewerkschaft Exploration Company was also concerned with pricing. During the first ten years of operation under the agreement, the iron ore concentrate from the Bong Mountain Range was to be sold at a price calculated on the basis of the average f.o.b. price obtained from the Ruhr steel works by the Liberian Mining Company for Bomi Hills concentrate for the five years preceding commencement of production under the

Gewerkschaft agreement. It was further provided that the pricing arrangements for Bong concentrates:

> shall be subject to review after the first 10 years of operation and if, after consultation between the Government and the Concessionaire, it is considered that the 5-year average f.o.b. price of Bomi Hills concentrates is no longer a satisfactory basis for price determination of Bong concentrates then a new basis for calculation shall be established.[54]

The provisions for change in these agreements were narrow in scope. Provisions calling for a general review of the agreement's fiscal or other terms have been less common. The 1974 amendments to the Bougainville Copper arrangement provided:

> the parties will co-operate with each other in carrying out the purposes of this Agreement and will meet together during the seventh year after the year in which the Agreement which introduced this Clause into this Agreement came into force, and at intervals of seven years thereafter, with a view to considering in good faith whether this Agreement is continuing to operate fairly to each of them and with a view further to discussing in good faith any problems arising from the practical operation of this Agreement. If at any such meeting it is agreed that this Agreement is not so continuing to operate fairly to each of the parties, or the parties agree that there exist problems arising from the practical operation of this Agreement, then they shall confer together in good faith in an endeavour to ensure that this Agreement will operate fairly to both of the parties or to resolve such problems (as the case may be) and, in particular, and without prejudice to the generality of the foregoing, they shall use their best endeavours to agree upon such changes to this Agreement as may be requisite in that regard.[55]

The advantage of a general review clause is that it puts both parties on notice that a review and revision will take place and thus minimizes the possibility of surprise and misunderstanding. But determining the appropriate mechanism is not easy. The method for institutionalizing mechanisms for adaptation to change in concession agreements will necessarily vary in light of the precise circumstances of each individual agreement. The types of provisions that appear to be stabilized over the life of the agreement, the types of provisions that will be subject to review and revision, and the events or time limits that will trigger the review requirements may well depend on whether the agreement is for timber, oil, or a hard mineral, and on such matters as the size and expected economic impact of the concession. In some cases both parties realize that change will be essential. In other cases one or both parties may overestimate the life of particular terms and may be unwilling to provide, at the outset, for later revision.

One observer, in commenting on the need for good-faith bargaining provisions in oil concession contracts, has suggested three standards for triggering review and revision: (1) a fixed number of years; (2) a length of time commensurate with the company's recovery of capital investment in addition to a reasonable return on the balance of the investment; or (3) an indefinite length of time until a material change of condition occurs that makes the original arrangement inapplicable.[56]

The following provision may be suggestive of a general type of review clause with some indications of standards that could be incorporated in a concession agreement:

> The Parties shall, at five-year intervals from the effective date of this contract, review the terms of Article (   ) of this Agreement to determine whether Article (   ) shall be amended to provide for an allocation of Net Profits differing from the allocation provided for in said Article.
>
> In undertaking such review, the Parties shall bargain in good faith with a view toward providing a fair and equitable division of profits in light of the economic factors prevailing at the time of the review.
>
> In undertaking such review the Parties shall be guided by, but not limited to, consideration of the following factors:
>
> 1. The economic value of the concession.
> 2. Terms of other (nickel) agreements negotiated by the government within the five-year period preceding the date of review.
> 3. Terms of other (nickel) agreements negotiated by the Concessionaire within the five-year period preceding the date of review.
> 4. Terms of other (nickel) agreements negotiated by third parties to the extent that such agreements can be reasonably compared to this Agreement.

Although frequent reconsideration of terms has become the normal pattern in concession arrangements, with or without revision clauses, their inclusion may remind both parties of the changing nature of such agreements and may ease the reopening of negotiations at an appropriate time.

FACILITATING CHANGE

In the past, some concession arrangements have contained provisions that no sovereign government could realistically be expected to tolerate for a substantial period. Control of land area has been one example of a continuing source of friction. The land provisions from one typical concession of the first half of the century[57] were characterized by an arbitration tribunal as "so extensive as to partake of quasi-governmental powers akin to those accorded the great trading companies of an earlier concessions era."[58] Until 1962 when control of mineral rights was removed from tribal chieftains and transferred to the central government, Ghanaian mineral and timber agreements were characterized by large concession areas and—by standards of agreements in other countries—unbalanced profit arrangements favoring the investor.[59] As recently as 1969, the Ecuadorian government, in demanding the return of "vast land holdings" by two American oil companies, charged that the terms of the concession agreements were "laughable" and "must be changed."[60]

The parties to concession arrangements have come slowly to the realization that their past demands and practices have not always been reasonable in the light of later conditions. In part this realization has been prompted by action taken by foreign governments in the form of expropriation, partial nationalization, or forced revision, or by oil-exporting countries through collective bargaining.[61] But in part also foreign investors have come to appreciate the changes that have occurred in developing countries and have come to see their roles in the larger context of the country's economic development.[62] The chairman of the board of the United Fruit Company has written, for example, that:

> we have been rightly criticized for having excessively large land holdings. . . . It involved the acquisition of extensive holdings of undeveloped lands and then using a small part for producing crops. . . .
> Fifty years ago United Fruit owned or leased approximately 5,000 square miles of tropic lands. . . . Yet, at that time United Fruit was using only about a tenth of this productively.[63]

As improved understanding of the provisions and practices that are most apt to be the source of conflict is reached, steps can be taken to draft concession agreements with a view to minimizing the problem areas. In general this involves an understanding of the motivations, interests, and bargaining positions of the other party; appreciation of the technical issues that are most apt to cause difficulty; and appreciation of the administrative handicaps under which the host government may operate. Furthermore—and most importantly—it involves a recognition of the fact that the conditions that made a particular arrangement appropriate at one point are likely to change. If either party looks to the agreement for protection in the face of substantially changed circumstances, disruptive dispute is inevitable.

In spite of the attention paid to the means of dispute settlement in concession contracts, most disputes have been settled outside the framework of the dispute-settling clauses. Most revisions and updating have been undertaken as part of the parties' on-going relationship and without the intervention of third parties.

Institutionalizing change in the contract may reduce the bitterness that often accompanies unexpected demands for revision. And it may limit the negotiations to certain well-defined time periods rather than permitting negotiations to be strung out over the entire course of the concessions relationship. Brief periods of harmony between points of negotiation may be well worth striving for.

COMPANY RESPONSES TO CHANGE

Some extractive companies have recognized the inevitability of change in concession terms and have taken steps to reduce the frequency of change or to prepare themselves for change.

Some companies have thought that the most effective approach to delaying change is the negotiation of an agreement that would appear to be reasonable to future host country governments and to a host government's political opposition. Both substance and form are important. A reasonable agreement, such companies feel, is less likely to be the subject of renegotiation or expropriation than one in which the foreign investor appears to have taken advantage of the host government's poor bargaining position or poor negotiating skills. An agreement that shares benefits equitably over the projected life of the agreement may be less costly than one which yields large short-term profits but soon results in bitter renegotiation.

This approach may be a correct one. But in situations in which there is a high degree of uncertainty about prices, quality of ore, and costs, and a strong sense of investor risk, it may simply not be possible to draft an initial agreement that will be attractive to the firm at the outset and still appear equitable when uncertainties disappear, profits grow, and risks are forgotten.

Even in the face of uncertainties some public relations provisions may help. Provisions providing for increasing equity interest for local or government shareholders, guarantees of increased employment of local nationals, and clauses that guarantee assistance to local industry may possibly contribute something to the longevity of a contract. And clauses that call for periodic renegotiation in a few years may at least hold off change until the specified date.

It is doubtful that any contract provisions can do much to forestall change when bargaining powers have shifted dramatically. But companies are not helpless to take steps that protect their interests. Kennecott's strategy in Chile in the late 1960s suggests an approach to the problem of change: the minimization of risk and the involvement of third parties in the face of a declining position of power. After 1964 Kennecott took a number of steps in a "strategy of protection."[64] It offered to sell a 51 percent interest in El Teniente to the Chilean government and turned to the Export-Import Bank and the proceeds of the sale of equity to finance expansion. The loan was guaranteed by the Chilean government and made subject to New York law. It insured as much as possible of its assets under a U.S. guarantee against expropriation. The output was to be sold under long-term contracts with Asian and European customers, and the collection rights on these contracts were sold to a consortium of European banks and a consortium of Japanese institutions. The result was that customers, governments, and creditors shared Kennecott's concern about future changes in Chile. Each had a stake in the investment. When Chile acted to expropriate the operation, Kennecott was able to call all these parties in on its side. Although the properties were expropriated, the political costs to Chile came high. The evidence suggests that variations on the theme orchestrated by Kennecott are being used by other companies in other parts of the world.[65] In particular, many extractive firms are requiring the host government to underwrite obligations to third parties. [66]

Arbitration and insurance may provide some solace to the foreign investor once major changes take place. Despite the weakness of typical arbitration clauses, arbitration proceedings may result in compensation for partial or total nationalization or other redress for other host country actions. The International Centre for Settlement of Investment Disputes (ICSID) offers one vehicle for conciliation and arbitration.[67] Its rules, among other things, provide for the enforceability of awards in the territories of the contracting states.[68] Over 60 states have ratified the relevant convention, including a substantial number of Asian and African nations, although not Latin American states.[69] But the protection may be illusory. In 1974 three American aluminum manufacturers—Alcoa, Kaiser, and Reynolds—requested ICSID arbitration of their dispute with the Jamaican government over Jamaica's unilateral steps to increase government revenue from bauxite production.[70] Jamaica was refusing to submit the matter to arbitration, since it had just withdrawn from the convention.

The Overseas Private Investment Corporation (OPIC), an agency of the United States government, is authorized by the U.S. Congress to write up to $7.5 billion in "political risk" insurance, designed to protect U.S. private investors against risks of war, revolution, insurrection, expropriation, and inconvertibility of currency. At the end of fiscal 1973, OPIC had written $919 million in inconvertibility converage, $2 billion in war risk insurance, and $2.4 billion in insurance covering nationalization, confiscation and "politically motivated defaults." Of the $2.4 billion, $410 million had been reinsured with Lloyd's of London.[71] Among the extractive projects covered by OPIC insurance at the end of 1973 were the HALCO (Mining) Inc. bauxite project in Guinea, the Union Oil Company of California project in Korea, the Freeport Minerals Corporation copper project in Indonesia, and the Kaiser Cement and Gypsum Corporation fluorspar project in Thailand.

Between January 1, 1971 and the end of 1973, OPIC settled insurance claims amounting to $119 million. During 1973 OPIC denied two major claims: the Anaconda Company's claim for $154 million for the expropriation of its former Chuquicamata and El Salvador mines in Chile and International Telephone and Telegraph Corporation's claim for $92.5 million for expropriation of its investment in Chile Telephone Company. The first claim was denied on the grounds that Anaconda did not have current insurance coverage; the second was denied on the grounds that ITT failed to disclose material information and failed to preserve administrative remedies. Both cases were submitted to arbitration.[72]

OPIC has not been alone in providing overseas investment insurance. At least fifteen other countries provide similar coverage for investors. Investment insurance programs have been proposed by the Commission of the European Economic Community. And there have been proposals for an expanded program in the United States to include private insurers with OPIC.

In spite of their attraction to investors, insurance programs have been the subject of criticism. Such insurance tends, according to critics, to reinforce the investor's desire to maintain ownership interest in foreign mining operations in situations where a divestiture of equity and adoption of a new form of relationship, such as a service contract or management contract, would be in the best interests of the investor and the host country.[73] And the insurance tends to involve the home country in disputes between investor and host country.

Faced with expropriation, some investors have turned to courts in countries in which the expropriating country has commercial dealings. They have attempted to obtain compensation from assets of the expropriating government that may be found in the investor's or a third country or from the seizure of minerals being sold to a third party.[74]

The success of such an approach has been modest as courts have tended to draw on two doctrines to which we can give only brief, and oversimplified, mention here: "sovereign immunity"[75] and "act of state."[76] The sovereign-immunity doctrine raises the question of whether a court can take jurisdiction over a government or one of its agencies. The act-of-state doctrine raises the question of whether a court can examine and decide the legality of taking by a government or one of its agencies. While sovereign immunity applies only when a foreign state or its agency is to be made a party to a litigation, the act-of-state doctrine may protect private parties who assert that the act of a government is not subject to examination by a court.

In situations where the U.S. Department of State has determined that immunity is justified, United States courts have applied the doctrine of sovereign immunity in suits against governments engaging in commercial or industrial activity, even though such activities are reserved for private enterprise in many countries. The theory of acceding to such determinations has been the judiciary's unwillingness to jeopardize the proper handling of foreign relations. In situations where the U.S. Department of State does not interfere, U.S. courts decide, on a case-by-case basis, whether the doctrine of sovereign immunity is applicable.[77]

The act-of-state doctrine may arise in connection with the pursuit of "hot" (i.e., allegedly unlawfully expropriated) minerals or other hot commodities in international trade. In hot mineral cases, the company whose property was expropriated alleges that the expropriating country has not acquired good title to the mineral. If a third party attempts to purchase the hot mineral, the expropriated company sues to regain possession of the mineral or the proceeds from its sale.

A central question in most such suits is whether a local court can inquire into the merits of a claim alleging that a foreign sovereign state has acted unlawfully. In a 1964 suit involving hot sugar, the U.S. Supreme Court, in *Banco Nacional de Cuba* v. *Sabbatino*,[78] held that U.S. courts could not, in private litigation, inquire into and challenge the legality of Cuba's seizure of foreign-owned sugar properties even though the U.S. Department of State had denounced the acts as contrary to international law. Almost immediately after the *Sabbatino* decision the U.S. Congress enacted, as Section 620(e)(2) of the Foreign Assistance Act of 1961, the "Sabbatino" Amendment, which (with qualifications specified in the legislation) permits a court to presume that it may proceed with an adjudication on the merits unless the President of the United States says officially that such adjudication would embarrass the conduct of U.S. foreign policy.[79]

Suits in which an expropriated company has pursued a hot mineral or other commodity have had mixed results in other countries. In 1972 a French court, presented with the defense of sovereign immunity put forth by the Chilean Copper Corporation in a suit by a subsidiary of Kennecott against a third party and the Chilean Copper Corporation, held that the defense did not apply. The court stated that the Chilean Copper Corporation had its own legal personality, formally distinct from the central power of the Chilean government, that it pursued its activities in the manner of a private commercial business, and that its contracts of sale exclude recourse to methods usually associated with government operations.[80] The U.S. courts may respond in a similar way, since the distinction between public and commercial acts is one that is usually invoked in determining the immunity issue in circumstances where the State Department does not request the application of the sovereign-immunity doctrine.

In 1951 the Anglo-Iranian Oil Company successfully pursued, in a court of Aden (then a British protectorate), oil expropriated by the Iranian government. Similar suits by the company in Italy and Japan, however, were unsuccessful,[81] as was a 1973 suit brought by British Petroleum in an Italian court in respect of Libyan oil, and a 1973 suit brought in a German court by a subsidiary of Kennecott in respect of Chilean copper.[82]

Such efforts may receive support from a company's home government. In 1973 the Nelson Bunker Hunt Company published in a number of U.S. and foreign newspapers a notice that it would "assert its rights" against anyone dealing with oil from its expropriated Libyan properties. The company subsequently brought suit in a number of jurisdictions, including the United States, Brazil, Italy, and Greece.[83] The U.S. Department of State agreed to support the company's position through diplomatic representations where the third party was a government or a government agency and through support of the company's position that the taking was unlawful under international law.[84]

Another defense against expropriation has long been that of collusion. In oligopolistic industries, firms may agree among themselves not to purchase the output of expropriated properties. The Libyan Producers' Agreement of 1971 provides an example. Under that compact, fourteen oil companies agreed that if a party's Libyan production should fall below a designated level as a result of any action by the Libyan government, the other parties would share in such cutbacks through contributions of Libyan and Persian Gulf oil. The agreement was the subject of a suit brought by Nelson Bunker Hunt in 1974 against the Mobil Oil Corporation in a U.S. federal district court.[85] The suit alleged that Mobil Oil refused to supply the plaintiff with the crude oil to which he claimed entitlement under the 1971 agreement.

Companies have not only appealed to the courts in the developed countries, but they have attempted to invoke direct government action from their home government. Although the days of gunboat diplomacy appear to be over, private firms appeal to their home governments for other than military actions. Faced with nationalization, firms have appealed to their home government to cut off aid to the host country and to use their influence to persuade international financial agencies not to provide more funds to the country. Proposals have gone further, suggesting that the home country discourage tourism to the errant country, for example.[86] But the threat of action by the foreign investor's home country appears to have had only marginal effect in the major concessions disputes of recent years.

Although companies have proved that they are not completely defenseless in the face of demands for change in concession terms, the legal remedies mentioned here, the insurance schemes, and the appeals to the government are clearly last resorts and are useful only in the extreme case of expropriation. When demands are for changes that favor the host government but fall short of expropriation, the company must rely on other defenses and approaches. The most significant constraint on the host government usually is its need for the continual presence of the foreign firm, if that firm's technological or marketing skills are still critical. If the firm's presence is no longer essential, the only shield left is usually the government's desire to work out an arrangement that will not repel other potential investors. Since investors who feel they are in a strong bargaining position show little reluctance to enter a country that has mistreated a recent weak investor, this is indeed a thin shield with which to do battle.

NOTES

1. See, e.g., Maurice Bourguin, "Arbitration and Economic Development Agreements," *Business Lawyer* 15 (1960): 860.

2. *Concession Agreement between Government of Liberia and Kitoma Mining and Trading Company* (September 16, 1964), Article 15.

3. J. Gillis Wetter and Stephen M. Schwebel, "Some Little Known Cases on Concessions," *The British Yearbook of International Law* 40 (1964): 183.

4. *Sierra Leone Tonkolili Iron Ore Agreement of 1937,* Second Schedule, Sec. 9, CAP. 202 in *The Laws of Sierra Leone* (London: Waterlow, Government Printers, 1960), Vol. 4, pp. 2123-24.

5. *Pan American-Iranian Oil Concession Agreement* (1963), Article 40.

6. *(Lesotho) Maluti Diamond Agreement* (May 6, 1971), Section 13.

7. *Collateral Agreement between the Government of the Republic of Liberia and Liberian Mining Company, Ltd.* (1953), Clause 4. See also the *Sierra Leone Tonkolili Iron Ore Agreement,* op. cit., sec. 11(iii).

8. For the effect of such a provision in preventing resort to diplomatic intervention or in depriving an international tribunal of jurisdiction, see J.G. Starke, *An Introduction to International Law* (7th ed., London: Butterworths, 1972), pp. 299-300.

9. *Constitution of the Republic of Peru* (Washington: Pan American Union, 1962), Art. 17. The Concession 'Contract of January 13, 1972 between Getty Oil (Peru) Inc., Pan Ocean Oil Corporation of Peru, Transworld Peru Petroleum Corporation and PETROPERU, Article XIV, provides that:

14.1 Any disputes which may arise between Contractor and PETRO-PERU on the interpretation or execution of this Contract or any clauses thereof which cannot be mutually agreed upon shall be submitted exclusively to the jurisdiction of the courts of Lima, Peru. The Parties renounce the use of any foreign diplomatic claims and shall be subject expressly to the laws of Peru.

14.2 It is understood and agreed that in carrying out the operations referred to hereunder, Contractor shall comply with all the provisions which the Peruvian authorities and laws establish and may establish in connection with all aspects related to the national defense, security, and sovereignty of Peru.

10. Charles Spofford, "Third Party Judgment and International Economic Transactions," *Recueil des Cours de l'Academie de Droit International* 113 (1964): 121, 168.

11. See Georges R. Delaume, *Transnational Contracts-Applicable Law and Settlement of Disputes* (Dobbs Ferry: Oceana Publications, Inc., 1975) sec. 1.01 ff. Also see discussion of law of and about concession contracts in Henry J. Steiner and Detlev F. Vagts, *Transnational Legal Problems* (Mineola, New York: Foundation Press, 1968), p. 398 ff.

12. See, e.g. *Production Sharing Contract between Pertamina and Indonesian Offshore Operators, Inc.* (March 3, 1972), Sec. 14.2; and *Contract between the Imperial Ethiopian Government and Ethiopian Potash Company* (November 4, 1968), Art. XXV.

13. For a full analysis of the problems of choice of law where the law of the contract is not stated, see Delaume, op. cit., sec. 3.01 ff. Article 42 of the Convention of the International Centre for the Settlement of Investment Disputes states that "the (arbitral) Tribunal shall apply the law of the Contracting State party to the dispute . . . and such rules of international law as may be applica-

ble." See George W. Ray, Jr., "Law Governing Contracts Between States and Foreign Nationals," in *Selected Readings on Protection by Law of Private Foreign Investments* (New York: Matthew Bender and Company, 1964), pp. 453, 488.

14. P.J. O'Keefe, "The United Nations and Permanent Sovereignty Over Natural Resources," *Journal of World Trade Law* 8 (May-June 1974): 251-75. Nationalization, of course, raises special problems. Even where local law is declared to govern the contract, international law may be invoked by foreign or international tribunals on questions relating to the lawfulness of the taking, including questions relating to compensation.

15. Richard G. Powell, "LAMCO: A Case Study of a Concession Contract," *Proceedings of the American Society of International Law* 61 (1967): 89.

16. Ibid., pp. 89, 92.

17. Ibid., p. 95.

18. Lon L. Fuller, "Human Interaction and the Law," *The American Journal of Jurisprudence* 14 (1969): 15. See also, generally, Stewart Macaulay, "Non-Contractual Relations in Business: A Preliminary Study," in Richard D. Schwartz and Jerome H. Skolnick, eds., *Society and the Legal Order: Cases and Materials in the Sociology of Law* (New York: Basic Books, 1970), p. 161.

19. See, for example, "Broken Promises: Many Contracts Now Aren't Worth the Paper They're Printed On," *Wall Street Journal*, March 26, 1974, p. 1.

20. Lon L. Fuller, op. cit., p. 27.

21. *West Africa*, June 17, 1974, p. 741.

22. Richard G. Powell, op. cit., p. 95.

23. Jean-Flavien Lalive, "Recent Trends: Abrogation or Alteration of an Economic Development Agreement between a State and a Private Foreign Party," *Business Lawyer* 17 (1962): 434. See also Simon G. Siksek, *The Legal Framework for Oil Concessions in the Arab World* (Beirut: Middle East Research and Publishing Center, 1960), pp. 62 ff.

24. See discussion of the 1945 Liberian Mining Concession Agreement in Chapter 2 and the history of that agreement in Robert F. Steadman, *Report on the Fiscal System of Liberia* (Monrovia, July 11, 1952); and Russell McLaughlin, *Foreign Investment and Development in Liberia* (New York: Frederick A. Praeger, 1966), p. 85. See also "Who Will Control the Mines?" *West Africa*, December 18, 1972, p. 1677.

25. Henry Cattan, *The Evolution of Oil Concessions in the Middle East and North Africa* (Dobbs Ferry: published for the Parker School of Foreign and Comparative Law by Oceana Publications, 1967), p. 12.

26. *Libyan Petroleum Law*, as amended to 1965 (November 20, 1965).

27. *Agreement between the Ethiopian Mineral Development Share Company and Duval Corporation of Ethiopia* (June 15, 1969), Article IV (b).

28. See Chapter 3, above.

29. C. Robinson, "Competiton in the Sale of Iron Ore in World Markets," *Convencion de Ingeneiros de Minas del Peru* 11 (December 1969):2.

30. *1971 African Research Bulletin*, p. 2158. See Clyde H. Farnsworth, "Oil Producing Lands Weigh Nationalization," *New York Times*, June 6, 1972, p. 55. Increasing equity shareholding is not, of course, always gradual. In late 1972

Ghana laid plans for taking over 55 percent of the equity capital of two major mining enterprises—presumably Lonrho's Ashanti Goldfields and the Consolidated African Selection Trust. The policy was understood to apply also to other major foreign mining and timber operations. Earlier, Sierra Leone announced plans for taking over 51 percent control of four mines. "Who Will Control the Mines?" *West Africa*, December 18, 1972, pp. 1678 ff. It is of course common for a total transfer of equity to take place at the end of a concession arrangement. See "Hanna Mining, Unit of California Standard Sign Pact With Colombia to Exploit Nickel," *Wall Street Journal*, July 24, 1970, p. 8.

31. See *Manual on the Establishment of Industrial Joint-Venture Agreements in Developing Countries* (New York: UNIDO, 1971), pp. 60–61.

32. The Asa contract and other Indonesian oil contracts are reproduced in Robert Fabrikant, *Oil Discovery and Technical Change in Southeast Asia—The Indonesian Petroleum Industry: Miscellaneous Source Materials* (Singapore: Institute of Southeast Asian Studies, Field Report Series No. 4, March 1973).

33. For a concise statement of the problem and reference to other literature, see J. Rohwer, "Note on Nationalization of Mining Property in Chile," *Harvard International Law Journal* 14 (1973): 378. On the problem of compensation for rights in service contracts, see D.T. Ackerly, *The Status of Oil Service Contracts in the Event of Nationalization*, unpublished thesis, Harvard Law School, 1969.

34. U.N. Resolution No. 1803 XVII of December 14, 1962.

35. J. Rohwer, op. cit., p. 386.

36. Joseph McCosker, "Book Values in Nationalization Settlements," in Richard B. Lillich, ed., *The Valuation of Nationalized Property in International Law* (Charlottesville: University of Virginia Press, 1973), Vol. II, p. 36. See, e.g., "Mining Industry in Peru Alarmed," *New York Times*, May 13, 1973, sec. 1, p. 15.

37. Mark Bostock and Charles Harvey, eds., *Economic Independence and Zambian Copper: A Case Study of Foreign Investment* (New York: Praeger, 1972), p. 221.

38. See "In the Matter of the Claim of Nicaro Nickel Company," Doc. No. CU-6247, U.S. Foreign Claims Settlement Commission, *Annual Report to the Congress* (Washington, U.S. Government Printing Office, for the period January 1–December 31, 1971).

39. Norman Girvan, "The Question of Compensation: A Third World Perspective," *Vanderbilt Journal of Transnational Law* 5 (Spring 1972): 351.

40. Fuad Itayim, "Overhaul for Mideast Oil," *New York Times*, October 15, 1972, sec. 3, p. 1.

41. A settlement between Anaconda and the Government of Chile was reached in 1974. See Decree Law No. 601 of the Junta de Gobierno, Approving Settlement with the Copper Companies, published in *Diario Oficial de la República*, July 24, 1974, and reproduced in *International Legal Materials* 13 (September 1974): 1189 ff.

42. With regard to the takeover of Cerro Corporation's copper holdings in Chile, a special tribunal declared that Cerro was entitled to $13,254,000 for its 70 percent interest in Compañiá Minera Andia. The Company announced that

the figure was relatively close to the property's book value. Gene Smith, "Cerro is Owed $37,554,000 for Chile Copper Holding," *New York Times*, December 2, 1972, p. 49.

43. J. Rohwer, op cit., pp. 386, 388 ff. See Gene Smith, "Size of U.S. Copper Profits in Chile Disputed Here," *New York Times*, May 5, 1973, p. 45.

44. Kennecott Copper Corporation, "Expropriation of El Teniente, the World's Largest Underground Copper Mine," (1971), p. 86.

45. "Who Will Control the Mines?" *West Africa*, December 18, 1971, pp. 1678 ff.

46. "Opting Out of Iron Ore," *West Africa*, March 5, 1973, p. 303.

47. Mark Bostock and Charles Harvey, eds., op. cit., p. 146. In mid-1972 President Kaunda announced that some of these terms were to be renegotiated. "Zambia Seeks More Control of Copper," *New York Times*, September 1, 1973, p. 29.

48. *Bauxite Mining Agreement between the Government of Jamaica and Aluminum Partners of Jamaica Ltd.* (1966), Sec. 3.

49. *Agreement between Imperial Ethiopian Government and Ethiopian Potash Company* (November 4, 1968), Article XXIX. See also *Agreement between the Government of the Republic of Liberia and Gewerkschaft Exploration Company* (September 16, 1958), Article 13 (h).

50. Henry Cattan, op. cit., p. 97.

51. See *Collective Influence in the Recent Trends toward Stabilization of International Crude and Product Prices* (Vienna: OPEC Information Department, 1967), p. 11.

52. Henry Cattan, op. cit., pp. 99–100.

53. *Sierra Leone Tonkolili Iron Ore Agreement* of 1937, Second Schedule, Sec. 9, CAP. 202 in *The Laws of Sierra Leone* (London: Waterlow, Government Printers, 1960), Vol. 4, pp. 2123–24.

54. Sec. 1 of the 1964 Amendment to the *Concession Agreement between the Government of the Republic of Liberia and Gewerkschaft Exploration Company*, September 16, 1958.

55. Item IVD of "Heads of Agreement for Variation of the Agreement of 6th June 1967 between the Government of Papua New Guinea and Bougainville Copper Limited," Port Moresby, 1974.

56. Michael C. Johnson, "A Legal Alternative to Instability in International Oil," *Natural Resources Journal* 6 (1966): 376.

57. The agreement was between the Compagnie du Katanga and the Independent State of the Congo, June 19, 1900.

58. Quoted in Wetter and Schwebel, op. cit., p. 193.

59. *Report of the Commission of Enquiry into Concessions* (Accra-Tema: Ghana, Ministry of Information, 1961).

60. "Ecuador Rebuffed by Texaco and Gulf," *New York Times*, March 7, 1969, p. 3. See also Paul L. Montgomery, "Ecuador's Economy Awaits Outcome of Oil Dispute," *New York Times*, April 28, 1969, p. 55.

61. Recent nationalizations have occurred in Chile, Peru, and Zambia and Venezuela. See William D. Smith, "Shotgun Wedding for the [Oil] Companies," *New York Times*, October 8, 1972, sec. 4, p. 3.

62. See Chandler Morse, "Potentials and Hazards of Direct International Investment in Raw Materials," in Marion Clawson, ed., *Natural Resources and International Development* (Baltimore: published for Resources for the Future by the Johns Hopkins Press, 1964), p. 386.

63. John M. Fox, "United Fruit and Latin America," *The Harvard Review,* 4 (Fall 1968): 32–33.

64. Theodore H. Moran, "Transnational Strategies of Protection and Defense by Multinational Corporations: Spreading the Risk and Raising the Cost for Nationalization in Natural Resources," *International Organization* 27 (Spring 1973): 277.

65. Ibid., pp. 284–87.

66. In 1973 Pacific Nickel Company sought to have the Indonesian government guarantee an IBRD "enclave loan."

67. See Aron Broches, "The Convention on the Settlement of Investment Disputes between States and Nationals of Other States," *Academie de Droit International,* Recueil des Cours, 1972, No. II (1973), p. 331.

68. Ibid., p. 349.

69. Ibid., p. 347.

70. "Arbitration Asked in Bauxite Dispute," *New York Times,* June 25, 1975, p. 59.

71. Overseas Private Investment Corporation, *Annual Report,* Fiscal 1973, p. 8. Also Committee on Foreign Affairs, U.S. House of Representatives, *The Overseas Private Investment Corporation: A Critical Analysis* (Washington: U.S. Government Printing Office, 1973).

72. Ibid., pp. 12–13. The ITT dispute was settled in 1974. See "In the Matter of the Arbitration between International Telephone and Telegraph Corporation Sud America and Overseas Private Investment Corporation," arbitration decision reproduced in *International Legal Materials* 13 (November 1974): 1307 ff. The Anaconda dispute was settled in favor of the company in July 1975, see American Arbitration Association, "In the matter of the Arbitration between the Anaconda Company and Chile Copper Company and Overseas Private Investment Corporation," Washington, July 17, 1975 (mimeo).

73. Theodore H. Moran, "The Evolution of Concession Agreements in Underdeveloped Countries and the United States National Interest," *Vanderbilt Journal of Transnational Law* 7 (Spring 1974): 315.

74. See Gene Smith, "Cerro Is to Be Paid for Chile Copper," *New York Times,* December 2, 1972, p. 53. (Kennecott action in Paris civil court); "Iraq Offers Nationalized Oil at Cut Rate; Consortium Warns Buyers of Legal Battle," *Wall Street Journal,* June 5, 1972, p. 6; "French Seek Embargo on Algerian Oil," *New York Times,* April 27, 1971, p. 3.

75. See Henry J. Steiner and Detlev F. Vagts, *Transnational Legal Problems* (Mineola, New York: The Foundation Press, 1968), pp. 517 ff.

76. Ibid., pp. 584 ff.

77. For a statement of the role of the sovereign immunity doctrine in judicial proceedings in the United States as of 1974, see Monroe Leigh, "Sovereign Immunity-The Case of the 'Imias,'" *American Journal of International Law* 68 (April 1974): 280. In 1975 there was before the United States Congress a bill

152 Negotiating Third-World Mineral Agreements

that would establish rules relating to the sovereign immunity issue and some aspects of the act-of-state doctrine. Under the proposed legislation the restrictive theory of sovereign immunity (precluding the defense where "commercial activity" is involved) would be codified and the task of determining whether a foreign party is entitled to immunity would be left entirely to the courts, with the State Department no longer expressing itself on requests for immunity. Immunity would also be denied in cases where rights in property taken in violation of international law are in issue and where that property is used in connection with commercial activity. This exception would cover "hot" mineral cases. For discussions of the proposed legislation see R. Jacobsen, Jr., and F.E. Snyder, "The Impact of S. 566 on the Law of Sovereign Immunity," *Law and Policy in International Business* 6 (Winter 1974): 179; and H.M. Sklaver, "Sovereign Immunity in the United States: An Analysis of S.566," *The International Lawyer* 8 (April 1974): 408.

78. 193 F. Supp. 375 (S.D.N.Y. 1961), *aff'd* 307 F.2d 845 (2d Cir. 1962), *reversed and remanded*, 376 U.S. 398 (1964).

79. In 1972 the United States Supreme Court held that the act-of-state doctrine did not preclude First National City Bank from asserting a counterclaim against Banco Nacional de Cuba. *First National City Bank* v. *Banco Nacional de Cuba*, 406 U.S. 759, 92 S. Ct. 1808 (1972).

80. *Braden Copper Company* v. *Le Groupement d'Importation des Metaux* (Court of Extended Jurisdiction of Paris, September 30, 1972) reported in *International Legal Materials* 12 (January 1973): 182.

81. Department of State Statement on "Hot" Libyan Oil (May 7, 1974) reported in *International Legal Materials* 13 (May 1974): 769.

82. *B.P. Exploration Company (Libya) Ltd.* v. *Astro Protector Compania Naviera S.A. et al.* (Court of Syracusa, Italy, February 15, 1973), reported in *International Legal Materials* 13 (January 1974): 106 ff. *Sociedad Minera El Teniente S.A.* v. *Aktiengesellschaft Norddeutsche Affinierie et al.* (Superior Court of Hamburg, January 22, 1973), reported in *International Legal Materials* 12 (March 1973): 251.

83. Department of State Statement, op. cit. pp. 771–72.

84. Ibid., pp. 772–73.

85. Reported in *International Legal Materials* 13 (May 1974): 661 ff.

86. See The International Economic Policy Association, *Interim Report of the Study on "U.S. Natural Resource Requirements and Foreign Economic Policy,"* (July 18, 1974).

Chapter Six

Organizing for Negotiation

Although the structure of the industry, the requirements of the particular firm, and economic and political forces in the host country set boundaries on the kind of agreement that can be concluded, the information available to each side and the negotiating skills and strategies of the parties are nevertheless significant determinants of the kind of bargain that is struck within those boundaries.

Many developing countries have lacked the skilled manpower to do an effective job of negotiating and administering agreements with foreign investors, or they have been unwilling to allocate the requisite financial and human resources to these tasks. And in many cases officials have not formulated adequate negotiating strategies and have not brought together teams capable of effective bargaining.

Recognizing these weaknesses, some countries have recruited foreign advisors to assist in negotiations and in the administration of agreements. In Liberia, for example, resident foreign advisors were provided, under U.N. Development Program auspices, to assist the Concessions Secretariat, itself the result of recommendations made by foreign advisors in past years. But foreign assistance has not, over the long term, been a satisfactory substitute for well-trained and organized local government officials.

The weaknesses of foreign firms in approaching negotiations have been found less in organizational skills than in a failure to understand thoroughly the criteria used by government officials in evaluating investment proposals. Companies have often relied largely on engineers and lawyers as their negotiators. As a result, many company teams have lacked the critical economic, business, and political data on which the governments of developing countries rely, either implicitly or explicitly, in negotiations. For similar reasons companies have on occasion been slow to recognize and plan for inevitable change.

There is no substitute for experience in building a good negotiating team, but there are some basic principles of negotiating strategy and technique that can be usefully taught to the inexperienced. This chapter is designed to reveal some of the problems that occur repeatedly in the way governments or companies have conducted negotiations in mineral concessions, and to suggest some approaches to these problems.

THE GOVERNMENT SIDE

As foreign investors soon discover, approaches to negotiation vary widely from one country to another. The organizational structures of government negotiating teams may reflect various local colonial heritages and consequently attitudes toward hierarchy. Negotiating postures and ripostes tend to mirror, to some extent, the cultural patterns that characterize the legal process, or govern dispute settlement, in the local environment. In cultures where direct argument is avoided, for example, the approach to negotiation with foreign firms tends to avoid confrontation. In other countries the adversary process may be open and direct, and much more familiar to many Western negotiators.

Although the negotiating approach must, no doubt, continue to vary from country to country, there are still some techniques and approaches that can be adopted successfully by many countries. Care in the way provisions are drafted, for example, can help in assuring that the investor understands and fulfills his obligations.

Precision and Completeness

Concession agreements differ dramatically with regard to what subject matter they cover and the precision with which particular issues are handled. In some countries, concession contracts state only the general intent of the contracting parties and deal with but a few issues beyond those concerned with government revenue. In other countries contracts spell out in considerable detail the rights and obligations of the investor and host government in a wide range of areas of concern to the firm and the country.

Often the absence of coverage of particular issues or the failure to deal with an issue in a precise manner seems to reflect the host government's inexperience in the particular industry and a corresponding failure to perceive the terms that are crucial for the government's protection. The impact of experience is obvious when one compares those agreements negotiated in Liberia in the 1940s, 1950s, and 1960s[1] with the government's much more clearly defined proposals put forth in the early 1970s for dealing with future concession agreements.[2] Or one may compare the agreements negotiated in the early 1970s in Indonesia for oil exploration and development with those for timber. In petroleum, Indonesia had considerable experience and had developed a technical staff of high caliber.[3] For timber, experience was limited and the responsible ministry had no personnel with training in the intricacies of the industry.[4]

In some cases, vague and—at least by Western standards—inadequate provisions stem in part from the legal traditions and legal framework of the host country. In a number of jurisdictions codes of law, such as tax and company laws, have been of the most general nature, and this style has often been carried into the negotiation of concessions.[5] In fact it is often the inadequacy of the local laws in dealing with the foreign investor that leads to the negotiation of an *ad hoc* agreement. But much of the anticipated gain from an *ad hoc* arrangement is lost by carrying over the tradition of imprecision into the agreement.

In countries where local laws tend toward general principles, the legal tradition of a particular country may be used constructively to generate effective concession arrangements. Consider Indonesia again. Although the major legal codes of the country have tended to be statements of general policy and intent, these laws have usually been amplified by detailed administrative regulations. Conceivably this practice could have been carried over into concessions negotiations. The agreements could have been elaborated with additional regulations or the agreements themselves could have been viewed as regulations within the framework of the general laws. Neither approach was followed in timber and hard mineral agreements in Indonesia. Rather, concession arrangements reflected Indonesia's traditional reliance on the concept of good faith in commercial transactions. The central position of this philosophy in Indonesian law has meant that Indonesian negotiators have shown less concern with protective clauses drafted to deal with specific contingencies than have the Western firms with whom they have bargained.[6]

In addition, the legal traditions of many developing countries do not call for lawyers to play the same role they play in many Western countries. American lawyers, for example, see their role, in part, as one of seeking an agreement that leads to stability and predictability. Consequently they have sought detailed provisions in concession agreements. Moreover, the adversary system that characterizes much of U.S. law practice has placed considerable emphasis on the role of the lawyer in maximizing the protection of *his* client. He typically makes little positive effort to protect the rights of the other party; he expects the other party's lawyer to perform this task. In the domestic setting of the United States, where both parties are playing by the same implicit rules, this system often works tolerably well. Commercial contracts are often characterized by well-balanced provisions guaranteeing the rights of each party and specifying the obligations of each party. In a number of other countries, where the adversary system does not prevail, the lawyer may see his role as one in which he tries to work out a satisfactory arrangement for the two parties, rather than as one in which he works primarily for either one. In some ways this is an appealing system. But whatever the merits of such traditional roles of lawyers and the role of good faith in commercial disputes in some developing countries, it may be dangerous to carry these traditions into the field of foreign investment where the other party subscribes to a different set of rules.

The case of Indonesia illustrates what can happen when traditions shape a government's negotiations with foreign firms. A number of the mining agreements of the late 1960s in that country allowed specifically for deductions for many payments to affiliates (for interest, technical fees, commissions, and the like).[7] But most of the same agreements were vague on the definition of gross income. In those agreements where the issue was covered, there were provisions that a company "may" use arm's-length prices for sales to affiliates.[8] In many agreements the company expressed its "intention" of doing something, or it promised that it would "consider" some action such as processing before export.[9] In Indonesia, as in some other countries, the meeting of two different legal traditions resulted in very specific protection for one party, but vague protection for the other's interests. The vague provisions often become the subject of later dispute.

In those relatively rare cases in which disputes reach arbitration, vague provisions provide an insufficient basis for settlement. Since the general laws in the host country are typically inadequate to provide guidelines for decisions, the arbitral body may turn to legal principles of more developed countries for guidance. These principles might not be those that the host country views as being satisfactory.

Attempts to negotiate precise, balanced provisions have had the advantage of testing the parties' good faith at the outset of the arrangement. If there are differences in expectations, efforts to be precise in the agreement will help to flush them out early. Moreover, there has probably been a certain amount of self-enforcement built into provisions that are specific. Companies are almost certainly less likely—even when government administration is poor—to violate clear provisions than they are to violate the spirit of provisions that are ambiguous. The same pressure has probably operated on the government side.

Although there is a strong case for arguing that the government should insist on precise and complete coverage in concession agreements, the case for detailing the foreign investor's rights and privileges is less clear from the company's point of view. A precise statement of the firm's entitlements and of the host country's obligations to the firm may in the long run be more harmful to the company than beneficial, especially if the rights and obligations remain unbalanced. Detailed lists of the firm's rights may make the agreement a tempting object of attack by the political opposition in the host country. And the company may find the rights unenforceable in any case. The protection may be illusory; the irritant may prove to be severe.

Improving the Starting Offer

In the bargaining process the terms of the starting offer have usually proved important in determining the outcome of negotiations. Governments have found two techniques effective in improving the terms around which the negotiations begin: (1) they have made efforts to provide the first draft agreement themselves; and (2) they have opened the concession for general bidding and have selected the best offer as the basis for negotiation.

One of the most important jobs of the government negotiating team should be the drafting of provisions to serve as the basis of discussion with the foreign firm. Yet the scarcity of persons with the requisite skills and time to prepare an effective draft has led some governments to permit the foreign investor to submit the draft provisions that serve as the basis for negotiation.

The preparation of the first draft of a concession agreement is unquestionably a long and tedious process. Turning over to the prospective investor the task of preparing the negotiating document appears to be a useful way of saving the time of scarce technicians in the host country. But the real cost may be high. First, the preparation of the initial draft document can serve as a vehicle for developing a reasoned policy for the particular negotiations. In speaking of negotiations between governments, one observer noted that "too often our demand— the decision we desire—is vague simply because our own thinking is vague."[10] He added that "we will almost always have a better chance of getting something we want if we know some specific things we would like to have."[11] No doubt these conclusions apply equally to concession negotiations.

Inevitably a draft agreement, whether the government's or the potential investor's, incorporates a point of view. A draft reflects the position of the party who prepared it. Where the government has allowed the investor to present the initial draft document, the government has usually found it difficult to negotiate away from the general framework and from a large number of specific provisions that reflect the company's point of view. Starting from a favorable first draft is particularly important because the fear of appearing obstructive often makes a party reluctant to oppose a series of provisions presented by the other side.

Our experience in observing actual negotiations suggests strongly that the party presenting the first draft begins with a significant edge. Classroom experiments have confirmed the pattern. Each class was divided into teams representing government and company sides. For one set of opponents, the government side was allowed to write the first draft. For another, the company was given this opportunity. The outcome was consistently more favorable to the party that wrote the first draft for the negotiations.

The difficult task of writing the first draft is complicated by the fact that the preparation involves a good deal more than simply writing the sort of agreement the government ultimately desires. There are matters of strategy involved. The very nature of the negotiating process suggests that each party will have to yield on certain issues. Thus, at the very least the initial drafter must prepare back-up provisions to be used in the likely event that agreement cannot be reached on one or more of the initial proposals. In the initial draft the government must ask for more than it really wants in the final agreement, in hopes that through negotiation it will end up with what it in fact desires and considers reasonable.

In some countries and industries the government combines its first-draft agreement with bidding procedures. For the tender, the government prepares a draft agreement. It then asks potential investors to bid on certain terms, such as the tax rate, a royalty rate, and a bonus. Some governments have found this type of approach to be a useful method of beginning negotiations from a set of favorable terms. Where successful, the procedure has eliminated a number of negotiating problems.

Some countries have turned the tender into a general policy. For example, in 1973 the Dominican Republic adopted the policy of exploring for all mineral deposits at government expense and awarding concessions "through a bidding process to those individuals or organizations who offer the most favorable terms to the state."[12]

In some situations competitive bidding has not been feasible. The government of Indonesia may have been fortunate in 1966 in attracting *one* potential investor to develop a copper mine in the remote area of West Irian. After years of Sukarno's policies against foreign investors, many firms would have been reluctant to enter into a mining agreement in 1966 in Indonesia.

Some attempts at using the tender technique may also fail because of the structure of the industry. When, after substantial improvement in the investment climate, Indonesia attempted to attract interest in the Asahan aluminum smelter a number of firms showed some interest. But when the government opened the project for tender in 1972, all of the interested aluminum companies joined together to submit a single bid as a consortium. There was no competitive bidding.

On the other hand, in instances where an investment appears attractive to a number of firms, and where the industry is not characterized by tight oligopolistic cooperation, a number of firms may be attracted to bid on a potential concession. Pertamina, the Indonesian state oil company, has used bidding procedures successfully. In 1969, for example, Pertamina invited 28 companies to bid for off-shore exploitation rights, stipulating that each offer be accompanied by a check for $10,000 and a complete record of the company's financial standing and operating history.[13] The response was satisfactory.

Where a bidding process is used, what a government does with the bids can be important. In some cases the field has been narrowed to one firm on the basis of the tender. But once a firm is selected, it realizes that the government will find it difficult to go back to other potential investors should the firm refuse to yield on a point. In some cases the selected firm, in a splendid negotiating position, has bargained hard on aspects of the agreement not covered by the tender and has threatened to withdraw if its demands are not met. In other cases governments have continued to negotiate with more than one firm after tenders have been made.

A case from Portuguese Angola illustrates the effectiveness of negotiating with several companies at once. In 1971 the Angola Diamond Company (Diamang) was due to release about one million square miles of concession area it had held for some time. Two U.S. companies held marginal concessions in Angola and were waiting to extend their exploration rights upon the expiration of the Diamang contract. The Portuguese government, however, opened negotiations with several potential investors. The concession was ultimately awarded to a consortium formed by DeBeers Consolidated Mines Ltd. and Diamang. The government negotiated what were generally regarded as terms favorable to itself (including a 50 percent share in profits, a 12.5 percent royalty on the value of the production at the mine pit, a premium of $245,000 on the signing of the contract, and an annual development contribution of $70,000) in large part because of the interest displayed by the American companies.[14]

Apart from oil,[15] the use of bidding procedures in the allocation of mining and timbering rights was not very widespread in the early 1970s. Yet it is clear that where a concession area can be opened up to bids from a number of prospective investors, the bargaining position of the host country can be substantially strengthened.

In some countries "middlemen," often resident foreigners, have taken over part of the tender function. Using their government contacts, the middlemen negotiate concession arrangements with the host government and then peddle their concession rights to the highest bidder. Sometimes these middlemen have benefited from the type of bidding that the government should have undertaken. But middlemen may perform a useful role. Although the costs can appear to be high, in some instances they search for and attract investors the country would not have discovered on its own. In fact, in some countries the arrangements worked out between middlemen and investors have demonstrated to the host government the kinds of agreements the country could negotiate itself if it had a more effective strategy. Some governments, however, have reacted to the costs and the affront to sovereignty represented by middlemen and have taken steps to reduce their role.[16]

Another approach to obtaining a good starting offer is for the governments to wait until the initial uncertainty is reduced before serious negotiations are undertaken. A number of countries have refrained from negotiations relating to exploitation until after the mining firm has made substantial progress in its exploration work, conducted under an exploration or survey license. These governments have assumed that they would be able to negotiate more favorable terms if negotiations could be delayed until more information was forthcoming.

In 1973 an exploration contract was concluded between Cobre Panama S.A. (made up of a consortium of Japanese firms) and the government of Panama. The agreement provided that on completion of exploration and a demonstration that the project was commercially viable, the government would give first option for 90 days to the consortium to negotiate an exploitation contract. The government agreed to reimburse the consortium for exploration costs if no agreement could be reached.[17] In 1970 the Malaysian government waited until a Japanese group had constructed substantial infrastructure and carried out major exploration work for the Mamut copper project before it even began negotiating major aspects of the exploitation agreement. Not only was more information available, but the company already had a considerable amount of investment at stake.

Such a policy has its risks. Some firms have been hesitant to invest the large quantities of money involved in exploration in remote areas until they have had some assurance of attractive terms for the exploitation stage, should it prove favorable. In certain cases the grant of the right of first refusal to the exploring company has been sufficient to induce the company to undertake the exploration, but where such assurances are given, the flexibility sought by the government is at least partially eroded. And, in other cases, only a guarantee of recovery of exploration expenses, as in the Panamanian case, is sufficiently attractive to the firm. Even then the firm may be hesitant to provide its technical skills to uncover a source that may be developed by a competitor. Some countries have attempted to reduce these problems by having an independent agency, such as the United Nations, undertake the initial exploration.

Priorities and the Agenda

Top priority should be given to collecting information about the industry and the company with which negotiations are to be undertaken. Too often this step is not done well enough to allow the kind of analysis illustrated in Chapter 1. Once industry and company background data have been collected and analyzed, and once the government's own position on major issues has been determined, the government's negotiating team is in a position to establish its negotiating priorities. Our experience has indicated that government negotiators have too often failed to establish clear priorities. The result has been that they risk expending their bargaining strength on issues of relatively minor importance in the overall picture. By allowing negotiations to start with minor issues and by taking a hard line on these issues, the negotiators have often had to take a softer line later on, yielding on important points so as not to appear obstructive.

Frequently discussion has commenced with the first clauses of the draft agreement and then proceeded through the various provisions in the order in which they appear in the draft agreement. Yet given the way many concession agreements have normally been drafted, key provisions may come toward the middle or end of the agreement. Consideration of provisions in the order they appear in the draft may mean that the requisite time and energy needed for adequate discussion of a number of important provisions is not available.

Moreover, the clause-by-clause, beginning-to-end approach as a way of opening up negotiations has tended to distract negotiators from major policy considerations in favor of wording and technical drafting points. Again, our experience has convinced us that government negotiators (frequently legislative draftsmen) gain many of their victories on points of language and punctuation at the expense of major issues of policy. This behavior is encouraged by the clause-by-clause approach.

To elevate the negotiations above discussions of minor technicalities, the government may want to use the first sessions for establishing an agenda to govern later sessions. Efforts to construct a detailed agenda may force both parties to determine which policies, principles, problems, and issues are worth the most attention. Potential areas of serious conflict can be flushed out and the opponent's priorities can be explored. The process of establishing an agenda may reveal that one's opponent is more, or less, interested in an issue than one assumed.

Some negotiators like to establish the agenda in such a way that provisions they consider "easy" are placed at the beginning of negotiations. That party can make a series of realistic offers with regard to those "easy" provisions and appear to be conceding many points early in the negotiation. When the more difficult issues are approached, that party can say, in effect: "We have been honest with you on the issues we have discussed so far. Now it is your turn to indicate your honest offer on the next issues." The opponent's success on the early issues may put pressure on him to make concessions of his own.

Strategies at the Negotiation Table

Once the government negotiating team has established priorities and an agenda, and has assembled the critical data on the industry and firm, it must determine how it will go about achieving its goals. We have already alluded to some basic strategic problems: the submission of the draft agreement on which negotiations will be based, and the agenda for the negotiations. The way in which these preliminary questions of strategy are answered may have serious repercussions for the outcome of the negotiations.

The next stage in the process should be the formulation of an approach to bargaining. There is a substantial body of literature dealing with negotiating techniques and strategy.[18] Much of the literature is theoretical, drawing on concepts from game theory and probability analysis. And much of the literature deals with negotiations between governments or with bargaining in purely domestic situations. Yet many of the basic approaches in that literature can be useful in the concession negotiation process. It is a rare negotiation in which a party does not adopt some of the techniques described in both the practical and theoretical literature. Often, however, the technique is invoked in an arbitrary and casual manner without regard to the technique's impact on the total negotiation process. It is also frequently invoked as a spontaneous reaction, without sufficient consideration to the general range of techniques that can be drawn upon.

The negotiating team should be aware of the general armory of techniques and approaches not only for the purpose of stocking its own bargaining arsenal, but also because it should understand the techniques that the other party may use. It is as important to penetrate the other party's negotiating strategies as it is to formulate one's own.

The general goal of negotiation is, of course, to attain the most favorable arrangement that can be obtained for one's side. But unless a party is prepared to take the risk of presenting a take-it-or-leave-it proposal to the other party, or unless the second party has absolutely no bargaining strength, both parties will not usually adopt one party's idea of an ideal agreement. There will be give and take on each side. While a party may begin negotiations with a vision of an ideal agreement, it will be expected to yield on certain points at the bargaining table. There is, of course, a point beyond which neither party is prepared to yield. An idea of this limit is important to have in mind at the outset with regard to one's own position and the opponent's position.

The two basic tactics of concessions bargaining are simple: to persuade the opposing party to accept a provision or principle he finds initially not to be in his interests, or to demonstrate that there is a common interest in adopting a particular provision or principle. To persuade the other party to accept a term he opposes, one must provide the other party with the motivation to accept the term. This can be done either by showing the other party that it is in fact in his interest to accept the provision (i.e., by showing him a benefit of which he was not initially aware) or by offering him an incentive to accept the provision. The incentive may involve a trade-off: in exchange for a company agreement to set up processing facilities, the government may lower the tax rate for five years. The negotiating process may be partly educational: the other party may not be aware that there is a hidden benefit to him in a particular provision or may not see how the burdens of one provision are related to the benefits of another.

Some skilled negotiators set out to alter the other party's view of his own "settling point." Party two, like party one, may at the outset establish in his own mind some concept of a point beyond which he is not prepared to yield on particular points and in general. The task of party one may be to alter the second party's concept of what this minimal level is.

It is possible to distinguish many bargaining maneuvers and techniques.[19] The opposing negotiator may be forthright in his approach, or he may bluff or lie; he may exercise patience or convey the impression that he faces a deadline; he may give the impression he has total negotiating authority or he may seem to have limited instructions; he may be flexible or he may be unyielding. Some of these stances may be unplanned and simply natural reactions based on the personality of the negotiator; others may result from a deliberate decision to use one of these approaches as a strategic weapon in dealing with one's opponent.

A number of techniques tend to recur with some frequency in concessions bargaining. They include: (1) seeking the first realistic offer from the other side; (2) the bluff to disguise one's own position; (3) the third-party ploy; and (4) the final authority ploy. A number of these techniques intersect with other maneuvers. And they can all be broken down into a number of more refined tactics.

The problem of the first offer is not simply one of determining who presents the working draft. With regard to any particular provision the task may be to get the other party to make the first *realistic* offer, within an established framework. One approach is to show the other party an agreement negotiated with another party on a similar matter and ask him how close he is willing to come to the position stated in that agreement. The bidding process is, of course, another approach.

Negotiators, almost by instinct, tend toward various degrees of subterfuge in bargaining relationships. Some subterfuge is generally accepted and widely used. The bluff ("If we do not receive this tax concession we will be forced to withdraw;" "If you are not willing to accept the concession on these terms, there are other firms who are waiting in the wings") is generally regarded as an acceptable tactic. The so-called false demand ("We must have a five-year tax holiday to make a profit") and disguising one's true position ("This concession is marginal for us; we do not really need it") are common in bargaining situations. While some statements of bluff may fall within the grey area of the ethical-unethical spectrum, it is generally accepted that both parties are aware that some degree of bluff will be employed.

The danger of bluff in any negotiation is that the bluff may be called. If the bluffing party backs down from his earlier position, his bargaining strength on other issues may be quickly eroded. This applies with even greater force to bald deception (such as the use of false statistics, for example). Lying at any stage of negotiation may endanger the total negotiation.

Recognizing the possibility that a bluff may be called, skillful negotiators attempt to make the bluff itself ambiguous. Thus, if the negotiator is forced to back down from a bluff, he may save face by pointing out the subtle qualifications in his original statement. In the same way the opponent may seek to avoid embarrassing the bluffing party by reading some ambiguity into the bluff.

There are several ways that negotiators draw on third parties, sometimes as a bluff. The government may claim that if this particular company does not accept its terms, another company will. The company may claim that it does not need this particular source of raw materials; it has other countries to which it can turn. When bids are received, the unsuccessful offers may be turned against those selected for continuing negotiations. The government says, in effect: "Company Two is prepared to go this far on this provision. If you are not prepared to approach that offer, we may be forced to turn to someone else." Occasionally a party can determine whether this claim is fact or bluff; in other cases this may be difficult. A government may also claim that its bargaining flexibility is restricted because if it yields on a particular point to this company, it will have to make similar concessions to older investors (through revision) or future concessionaires. The government says in effect, "We would like to do this, but the cost is too great for us in terms of repercussions for other agreements."

In some instances the government may actually be conducting negotiations with a third party that intersect with the negotiations in question. Sometimes the third party is the home government of the investor. At the time that the government of Liberia was examining the possibility of renegotiating the LAMCO agreement in the late 1960s, it was also preparing to negotiate a double taxation treaty with the Swedish government. Liberia was prepared to give certain concessions to the Swedish government only in exchange for a tightening of certain aspects of the LAMCO agreement. The Liberians hoped for pressure on LAMCO not only from Liberia but also from the Swedish government.

A common negotiating technique, used by both company and government representatives, is the claim that the negotiator has little or no flexibility in bargaining. The negotiator's bargaining authority, the claim runs, is limited by his instructions or his need to consult with others. The limits within which a government negotiator can operate may actually be circumscribed by directions from his superiors; or he may simply claim such circumscription for bargaining purposes. Similarly, a company's representative may have specific orders from the company's board of directors; or he may claim to have such orders. Often in negotiating sessions a party's representative will stress the amount of time it will take to consult with a superior, who may be in another country, or the head of another department. A company's representative may argue that a response to a letter to his home office would take days or weeks or that it would be difficult to assemble the board of directors. Japanese firms have been known to argue that the steps required to reach a new decision in a Japanese company may take months. A government representative may invoke the alleged "inefficiency" of his government and stress the time involved in getting a decision out of the bureaucracy. He says in effect: "My hands are tied. Either you yield on this issue or we will waste a good deal of time." The opposing party must make a calculation as to whether this claim is true or false and whether it is willing to allow more time to lapse in the negotiations if it believes the claim.[20] This strategem is often employed at the end of long negotiations when both parties are exhausted and when there is pressure to bring the negotiations to a quick conclusion.

Parties may take actions to restrict their apparent bargaining flexibility in other ways. A government, for example, may announce publicly that it is about to enter negotiations on a mineral agreement and that it expects favorable results, some of which might be spelled out in detail in press statements. It may then argue that because the public expects the government to negotiate certain terms, it can accept nothing less. An example of this occurred in 1973, when the government of Papua New Guinea apparently released to the local press the recommendations made by one of us for the terms to be reached in a renegotiation of the Bougainville Copper Agreement.

A government negotiator might also claim that while he is perfectly willing to accept a particular provision, representatives of certain government departments with which he is not associated would not accept it. He may say in effect: "This would be fine with me, but I know the boys over at the Ministry of Finance would be unwilling to accept it. They are adamant on such tax relief. I've tried it before." Such positions may also be made public, as happened in connection with the Bougainville renegotiation. The positions of the Minister of Justice and one Member of the House of Assembly from Bougainville were tougher than that which one of us recommended. They issued a press release with their demands, generating new possible constraints to which the negotiators might appeal.

A sense of timing is important in negotiations. In many cases of long debates in negotiations, the problem is not simply that one of the parties cannot accept a particular provision. It may be that the party is unwilling to accept it too soon. As one observer has noted, "Coming forward with draft language too soon may upset [the other party] which would like to feel that they had more participation in the formulation of the decision."[21] Or the yielding party may have to demonstrate to his superiors that he did not yield too quickly on a particular point.

A negotiator can benefit by analyzing the organizational pressures on the individual against whom he is bargaining. As we have mentioned, a negotiator often feels under pressure to prove to his superiors that he is an effective negotiator. To augment the evidence he carries home he may be inclined to collect a few negotiating "trophies," even though these trophies may not be of real economic or political importance to the party he represents.[22] We have, for example, encountered situations where company representatives have bargained long and hard for tax holidays, even though the tax credit system in the investor's home country would cancel most of the benefits the company would obtain. In many such cases the negotiator appears to be motivated largely by a need to prove his skills and to show that he can strike terms as good as those a previous firm in the same country managed to strike or as attractive as those the company received elsewhere. In this situation government negotiators may find it useful to resist the tax holiday, for example, but to offer other less costly concessions that the company's negotiator can present to his organization as evidence of his bargaining skills.

The Negotiating Team

A good deal of the government's success in bargaining seems to depend on the structure and makeup of the negotiating team. Yet most countries have paid little attention to developing an effective team.

Sometimes a state enterprise or a single ministry has had virtually complete authority to negotiate agreements with the foreign investor for a particular mineral. There are advantages in this. The higher salaries that state enterprises have generally been able to pay have enabled some state corporations to attract more highly qualified people than would be available to the civil service. For example, Pertamina, the Indonesian state oil company, with a large number of qualified specialists, has acted quite independently of other government agencies in reaching agreements with foreign investors for the extraction of petroleum.[23] On the other hand, such independence is considered by some to be a potential disadvantage of the state enterprise device.[24]

In other situations negotiating teams have been made up of representatives from several government ministries. While some such teams have often operated successfully, others often face difficult problems. Their record appears to be a function of factors other than whether they are cross-ministerial.

In fact, probably any of a number of variations in organizational makeup can be made to work if certain principles are followed. Our observations of a number of negotiating teams in action indicate that the ones most successful in negotiating agreements rapidly and in negotiating terms favorable to the host country have certain characteristics: (1) their membership, no matter how it is made up, does not vary from negotiating session to negotiating session; (2) they have a clearly designated chairman with clearly defined powers; and (3) they have unambiguous authority from the government to conclude agreements, subject only to executive or legislative approval.

Lest these simple guidelines sound as if they are self-evident, we would guess that the number of countries that have not followed these guidelines exceeds the number that have. On many occasions we have attended a series of negotiating meetings in which the composition of the host country's negotiation team has varied from session to session. Needless to say, the investor, under such circumstances, attempts to gain acceptance of those terms that the negotiating team of the moment is willing to accept. He attempts to gain acceptance of other terms at other negotiating sessions when different government representatives, with different priorities and unaware of the implicit trade-offs made in the previous meeting, can be dealt with.

Where individual ministries can erode the authority of the negotiating team, the team often finds the investor negotiating directly with the individual ministries concerned with particular aspects of the agreements. Such a negotiating process tends to result in a jerry-built arrangement. If, for example, each ministry determines that investment by a particular company is desirable, each ministry may offer all of the inducements it can. The resulting package may offer more favorable terms than are needed to attract the investor. On the other hand, if one ministry does not want the investor, that ministry can block the agreement merely by refusing to yield on an important provision over which it exercises control. When the investor can negotiate directly with individual ministries, an opportunity for the team to make sophisticated trade-offs that cross ministerial lines of authority may disappear.

The chairman of the most effective government negotiating team will usually designate the members of his team who are to address particular issues on the agenda. If members of the team disagree with the presentation of another team member's response, the team adjourns for a conference out of the hearing of the other party's negotiators. Again, these simple rules have often not been followed. Open disagreement has occurred among government negotiators in the presence of the foreign investor. When this happens the foreign investor tends to select, as his allies, those government representatives who support him on a particular issue. The strength of the government team can be rapidly eroded.

Governments frequently encounter two other problems in building effective negotiating teams: (1) difficulty in finding negotiators with an understanding of the technical language and approaches used by the companies; and (2) difficulty in preserving the lessons from one negotiation in a way that they can be used in future negotiations.

When government officials confront the representatives of a large foreign firm, they often are faced with technical concepts with which they are not well acquainted. The differences between cash flow and profits, the significance of depreciation in relation to profits and cash flow, and the techniques of financing are far removed from the usual experience of the government negotiators. Yet to analyze adequately the proposals of the investor and to formulate creative responses, the government negotiator must have a thorough grasp of such concepts.

In addition, governments have found it difficult to assure continuity in the membership of negotiating units from one contract to another, as well as from one session of a particular set of negotiations to another. Much is learned through experience. But too often government teams have been put together on an *ad hoc* basis without reference to experience in past negotiations. And even where experience is sought, the experienced negotiators may no longer be with the government. Sometimes they have left to work in the private sector because of low government salaries. Whatever the cause, the lack of continuity of personnel means that negotiations begin from stage one, as earlier negotiations did.

Easing Administration

Even skilled, experienced negotiators have sometimes failed to take adequate account of the need to draft provisions that can be administered by the government's staff. In fact, the first steps toward effective administration come at the negotiating stage. Some negotiators have helped ensure effective enforcement by incorporating in the agreement a number of devices and approaches to simplify administration. Recognizing the fact that the manpower and skills of the administering agencies may be limited, they have attempted to gear provisions to the administrative capabilities of the available personnel. Efforts of negotiators to ease the administrative load have led to agreements that have incorporated "guideposts" to alert administrative officers to problems that might arise at particular points; some have utilized standardized provisions, to the extent possible, for uniformity; some have incorporated provisions allocating to the company the burden of carrying out particular acts that other countries have required of the government; and many have developed clear penalties and sanctions for the company that fails to meet its obligations.

Avoidance of Nonenforceable Provisions. The limits on the manpower and skills available to enforce agreements have led some countries to avoid highly sophisticated and intricate provisions which, while in theory beneficial to the government, would in practice be too complex to be administered well.

One example of simplification for administrative purposes is the handling of interest paid on loans. A number of agreements have taken the option of simply not permitting deduction of interest paid on loans from affiliates.[25] A principal reason for such a hard rule has been that the negotiators have recognized that the policing of such loans to determine whether they are in fact "disguised equity" is a complex and time-consuming process, which the government is unable to carry out effectively. The task of administration has held governments back from conceptually more attractive approaches, such as the case-by-case approach we described for the United States.

Negotiators have been attracted by many provisions that are attractive or reasonable on paper, but would be difficult in practice to administer. Some income tax arrangements for personnel employed by the foreign investor provide examples. Since the nominal tax rates for personal income have been rather high in some countries, foreign investors have occasionally requested and received a provision that a foreign employee would not have to pay taxes in the host country that would exceed those he would pay in his home country. Stipulations of this sort have appeared in a number of Indonesian agreements, for example.[26] To administer this provision properly, the authorities would have to receive completed tax forms of the sort that would be filed in each employee's home country. They would have to understand the regulations in each country and make the judgments required in each jurisdiction. This task would simply be impossible for the administrative resources available in most developing countries.

Accommodations that adequately meet the investor's needs and simplify administration can be made on most such points. In the case of personal income tax, agreements with investors could simply include a provision that the local tax system applies, but with a guarantee that the total tax would not exceed a certain percentage of the employee's gross income earned in the host country. Such approximations, although not optimal, can provide a sensible escape from an impossibly heavy administrative burden.

Provisions on auditing of returns have also caused many administrative problems. Mining agreements in some countries have provided a time limit on the right of the government to audit the company's accounts. Some Indonesian arrangements illustrate the problem. In one example, the government agreed to make its audit within three years of the submission by the company of its financial statements. And the government committed itself not to take more than two years for the audit once it began. If the government failed to file a claim within 90 days following completion of the audit, it apparently could never file a claim.[27] Another Indonesian agreement required that the government conduct an audit each year, that the audit be completed within three years of the annual submission of financial statements, and that any tax claims be made within five years of the end of the relevant fiscal year.[28]

These limits would impose serious constraints on the ability of some developing countries to audit the tax returns of foreign companies. Even in the United States some states are more than three years behind in their tax audits. It would be surprising if the officials in many developing countries could make an adequate evaluation of the audit and decide on the steps to be taken on back taxes within 90 days following an audit. More realistic in most developing countries would be for the government to bind itself to file any claims no later than, say, five years after the end of the fiscal year. There should perhaps be no constraint on the time it takes to perform or to evaluate an audit.

The fiscal provisions of a concession agreement may be affected not only by the availability of competent tax administrators but also by the availability of trained personnel in other agencies. The problem is illustrated in the report of a commission of inquiry into the timber industry in the Gold Coast (now Ghana) in 1951.[29] In recommending the amount of royalties to be assessed in timber-harvesting operations, the commission noted that it would be reasonable to base royalties on the content of the tree in cubic feet or in Hoppus feet. Although the approach would give a fair return to both parties, the committee observed that there would be several difficulties in applying such a system:

> Perhaps the greatest difficulty of all is the fact that all trees would require to be measured and that Native Authorities would require a trained staff of considerable integrity to carry out the measurement. . . . [T]ree measurement would be impracticable at present.[30]

The committee thus recommended the retention of the stumpage system whereby the same fee would be paid irrespective of the size of the tree. Although trees of different sizes would clearly have different values, it was felt that a rough equity would be achieved if the royalty imposed was "fair and reasonable for the average tree." Most important, the simpler provision could be administered with the skills available.

Guideposts. Some negotiators have been able to ease the administrative burden resulting from concession agreements by drafting certain provisions in such a way as to draw the attention of the government administrators to particular problems. In the section relating to calculation of taxable income, some agreements have provided, for example, that "on sales to Affiliates the price shall be taken to be that which would be received in a sale between non-Affiliated parties," or that "on purchases from Affiliates the price shall be taken to be that which would have been paid in a purchase from a non-Affiliated party." At the same time the contract has provided a clear, workable definition of "Affiliate." Such provisions have at least alerted tax administrators to the possibility that a problem in pricing or deductions could exist whenever affiliates are involved. And they have served notice on the company that the government is aware of the potential leakage of tax revenue through transfer pricing.

Guideposts can also be used to aid in some of the issues that cannot be settled at the time of negotiation because their resolution depends on factors which will emerge only after exploitation or production activities have begun. Rather than ignoring these issues entirely, the agreement can make reference to them to alert government administrators at a later date. For instance, even if negotiators cannot agree at the outset on criteria for determining the economic feasibility of establishing processing facilities at a later date, mention of the problem and clear dates for reconsideration may prove helpful in the future.

Standardization of Provisions. Administrative problems have been increased when agreements within particular developing countries contain very different provisions to cover the same technical issues. Lack of standardization has been particularly important in provisions that define taxable income. In Liberia, for example, where over 100 concession agreements were in existence in the late 1960s, there were tremendous variations, from one agreement to the next, in deductions that might be permitted and in the definitions of particular deductible items acceptable for tax purposes.[31]

Tax provisions often require a body of regulations or a set of case precedents for their interpretation. When contracts vary substantially in their structure within a country, regulations and precedents develop far too slowly. No income tax department with limited manpower could be expected to cope effectively with the administration of contracts with little or no standardization of provisions.

In some countries the great variety of provisions on the same matter has resulted, of course, from the fact that the first draft of the proposed agreement has been drawn up by the prospective investor. Each investor has shaped the contract provisions to his own idiosyncracies. Sometimes they have reflected the structure of an agreement in some other country in which the company was operating. Whatever the origin, the result has been an administrative jungle for some governments. A good negotiating team will aim for as much standardization as possible. Of course, this does not mean that the tax rates, for example, must be the same.

Self-Regulating Provisions. Some negotiators have taken steps to ease the administrative burden by attempting to shift, to the company, responsibilities sometimes held by the government. In contrast to usual provisions, which stipulate that the government may require the company "to submit such reports as the government deems necessary with regard to exploration and exploitation," some agreements have spelled out the contents of reports required by certain dates in sufficient detail that the government would simply receive the information it needs without having to make any specific request to the company. The usual provisions mean that the government must take the initiative in requiring the reports and must draft reporting forms. With changes in government personnel and a myriad of agreements to enforce, many governments have simply failed to request the needed reports.

Similarly, governments can insist that the investor provide lists of firms that qualify as affiliates, according to an agreed definition. Or the company may have to submit its method of allocating home office overhead, or its calculations of deductions to change a c.i.f. price to an f.o.b. basis. Under the assumption that most companies will avoid outright fraud when they have to provide such details, the task of administration may be eased considerably.

Penalties and Sanctions. Many concession agreements have failed to provide for sanctions in the event that a party to an agreement does not carry out one or more of its obligations. As a result the investor may have little incentive to conform to the concession terms until he is pursued by administrative authorities. The problem is especially important when the provisions themselves are vague.

Sanctions have accompanied many kinds of provisions. Agreements have specified penalties for late payment of taxes, for failure to invest stipulated minimum amounts at stated periods, or for failure to establish processing facilities when economically feasible. In some cases the provisions for penalties have apparently induced the company to make a timely compliance with the terms of the contract and have helped to avoid putting the burden on the government to request compliance. Sometimes they have helped in leading the company to seek clarification of ambiguous provisions, out of fear that it might face penalties for noncompliance.

The absence of penalty provisions in concession agreements has been common. Under tax arrangements in many agreements, for example, there has been no incentive for the company to draw up its tax statements in a way that reflects what the company thinks might be the final settlement if the returns were to be audited. The company could choose the methods of calculation that would lead to the lowest tax payment and pay up if audits revealed taxes due. Although penalties for late tax payment do not remove the necessity for careful auditing, they may reduce the incentive for the company to understate its taxes. There may be less need for frequent audits or less cost in failing to conduct them regularly.

Regulations and General Laws

The development of terms covering foreign investment activities is rarely confined to the bargaining table. The applicable general laws and the provisions of the agreement must usually be amplified and clarified by administrative regulations. The expected use of regulations should be taken into account in the concessions negotiations.

When agreements are silent on a particular issue, some countries issue regulations to cover the obligations of the company. For example, if the concession says nothing about safety requirements, the issue can be covered by the issuance of regulations covering safety in mines.

Where definitions or meanings have not been made clear, or seem inappropriate to a particular case, administrative regulations have often settled the problem. Where an agreement calls for depreciation, for example, but does not spell out rates or state whether it must be taken from the date of acquisition of the equipment (under a tax holiday, the company might prefer to postpone depreciation), administrative regulations have specified rates and procedures.

Two of the most important regulations, if they are not included in the tax law applicable to concessions, have covered the right of the government to reallocate income among affiliated enterprises to reflect arm's-length transactions and to specify the criteria for determining whether debt held by affiliates is to be treated as disguised equity for tax (and, if appropriate, for exchange control) purposes.

Generally, governments have assumed that they have the right, as sovereign powers, to issue regulations on matters such as mining safety and tax administration where agreements are silent and vague. Such regulations have provided a powerful tool in the continuing development of concession terms.

In fact, government negotiators will often avoid including coverage of a particular issue in the concession so that the matter can be dealt with outside the negotiations. The tactic may ease change, since regulations and applicable laws may be altered outside the context of the agreement.

Whether an issue is intentionally or accidentally omitted from an agreement, the government may decide later to act on the issue. For example, the original Bougainville Copper Agreement did not mention withholding taxes on dividends. The agreement neither imposed them nor excluded them. After the firm had committed many millions of dollars to the project, the government imposed a general withholding tax of 15 percent on dividends. The major impact of the tax fell, of course, on this particular project. In this case it is doubtful that the government negotiators would have been successful in imposing such a tax provision in the original agreement.

The Use of Foreign Advisers

Recognizing the shortage of skilled government personnel and the importance of properly conducted concession negotiations, a number of governments have turned to foreign advisers for assistance. Their roles have varied from country to country.

Foreign assistance can be helpful at the negotiating stage. In some instances foreign advisers have actually represented governments in the negotiations, but by the late 1960s the political processes of most countries would not permit such authority to be granted to foreign advisers. In fact, such broad delegation is probably not a good alternative, since it does little to build the needed skills in local personnel.

When negotiations are conducted by local officials, foreign consultants are, in many cases, called in to assist in formulating general policy, to assist local staff for a limited period of time for particular negotiations, or to suggest specific solutions to individual problems that have already been identified by the local staff. Such advisers have provided useful assistance in helping the local negotiators to clarify objectives, to develop a strategy for negotiation, and to prepare backup papers and fallback positions. In some cases, they have aided in restarting negotiations that have stalled.

Some governments have continued contact with the same set of advisers so that the advisers can assist, from time to time, with problems that arise during the administration of the agreement and with problems relating to the revision of terms that may be required in the future. The advantage of a continuing arrangement has been the advisers' familiarity with the agreement and local conditions. Long contact can generate personal trust, easy communication, and a recognized willingness on the part of the consultants to retain a low profile. On the other hand, new advisers may bring fresh viewpoints to the process.

Rarely, however, is a foreigner in the country long enough to be thoroughly sensitive to the local values that will determine the complex trade-offs that are important in the final negotiation of a concession. And rarely will he be thoroughly familiar with the special economic, political, and social concerns of the host country. History suggests that foreign advisers often do not possess the requisite sensitivity to the country's administrative limitations. These limitations may call for a somewhat less sophisticated agreement than the adviser might recommend in another context. There is also a danger that a country will call in consultants in the hope it can avoid some tough decisions. Sometimes the government calls in one consultant after another until it realizes that the initiative for decisions and actions must rest on local officials. In 1973 and 1974, for instance, Papua New Guinea hired a string of consultants to advise on a possible renegotiation of the Bougainville Copper Agreement. The result was a catalog of options from which the government officials eventually had to choose.

Some countries have used foreign advisers on occasion for internal political purposes as well as for advice. Sometimes the consultant is called in to bolster one ministry against another. At other times the consultant is used to quiet the opposition. After we had advised one government on a mining concession, the Department of Mines of that country called a press conference explaining (it was reported) that a "Harvard brain trust" had assisted in the negotiations and that the Harvard team had characterized the final terms as the best of any agreement for that particular mineral, from the government's point of view. Although we had made no such statement, the political opposition had to take on not only the current government party, but also the reputation of Harvard University if it wanted to criticize the terms of the agreement!

THE COMPANY SIDE

Foreign investors seldom have difficulty in putting together negotiating teams skilled and experienced in certain technical aspects of natural resource development. But despite the technical competence, many prospective investors have been perplexed and confused by negotiations with developing countries.

Culture and Standards

Part of the difficulty is often cultural. We have already alluded to different cultural approaches to contracts. Negotiators from certain developing countries may be more concerned with establishing general principles than in drafting air-tight clauses. These same negotiators may expect to rely on the good faith of the other party more than a Western negotiator would. But the cultural problem goes beyond this. The representative of a new investor in a particular country may be in the country only a matter of hours before he begins his first negotiating session. Under these circumstances he cannot be expected to be familiar with the subtle social, political, economic, and bureaucratic factors that may affect the negotiations. Similarly, host country negotiators may be unfamiliar with the industry and business "culture" within which the company's representative operates.

At the same time, company negotiators may be unfamiliar with the standards that governments of developing countries adopt in establishing concessions policy. A question frequently posed by investors is this: "What does Government X consider to be fair terms for a concession agreement?" The question suggests that fairness is the predominant criterion invoked by developing countries in formulating concessions policy. But often it is not. Nor, indeed, is it a standard often invoked by private firms. Rather, most developing countries are concerned with: (1) giving the foreign investor no more than the minimum required to attract or to retain him; and (2) negotiating terms that are no less favorable, at least superficially, than those prevailing for comparable contracts in neighboring countries. Government negotiators are under severe pressure from their constituency to attain these standards.

Of course, whether a particular government negotiating team is able to bargain for an agreement reflecting these standards will depend on the skills, experience and discipline of that team. In instances where skill or discipline is absent, the foreign investor may encounter negotiators who represent the interests of their own particular ministries. Officials of a ministry of finance, for example, are likely to evaluate project proposals according to the project's contribution to government revenue, while the central bank is likely to weigh heavily the earning of foreign exchange. The ministry of manpower may be concerned with projected labor utilization more than with projections of tax revenue or foreign exchange effects.

Some investors, faced with an undisciplined government bargaining team, have been surprised and confused by the diversity of criteria invoked by different government officials. Others have turned the diversity to their advantage by seeking alliances with certain members of the government team.

Company negotiators may be unfamiliar not only with the general social, political, economic, and bureaucratic factors that enter into host country policy development, but also with the techniques used by government technocrats in evaluating project proposals. While familiar with private financial analysis, company negotiators may be unfamiliar with social cost-benefit analysis and such concepts as explicit exchange rates and effective rates of protection often invoked by government analysts. Puzzled by the purpose of questions posed by government officials, business negotiators are reluctant to ask why the data are needed. As a result of not understanding the purpose, they may fail to provide the relevant data or may modify their data to fit their erroneous ideas of what the information is being used for. As a result of their not understanding the analytic techniques, they are frequently unable to respond adequately to questions about the effect of their proposed investment on the host country.

The techniques of project analysis are not precise, and the criteria for evaluating a project from a social benefit perspective, rather than a private perspective, vary. But within a wide range of types of investment there is a growing standardization of approach. While an investor need not be familiar with the esoteric literature on matters such as the calculation of shadow rates for labor costs and foreign exchange, he should be familiar with the general principles involved in turning a private income statement into a social statement involving shadow prices and costs and benefits external to the project itself. And he should understand the basis of calculation of the effect of a project on national income and the balance of payments. Otherwise he risks a major misunderstanding in the negotiations.

Negotiating Techniques

Although the discussion of techniques available to government negotiators is applicable to company negotiators, a few special warnings should be sounded.

Company negotiators occasionally underrate the skills and experience that government representatives bring to the bargaining table. Sometimes they adopt an attitude that appears neocolonial or patronizing to the government, as they talk down to their potential hosts. Familiar with only the superficial aspects of the country and culture, company negotiators run the risk of offending host country negotiators. Even seemingly minor mistakes can cause serious irritation. We have seen, for example, a negotiation that almost broke down in a Southeast Asian country because the potential investor tactlessly inquired about the average wage for "coolie labor."

In addition, it is tempting for the foreign investor to carry to the negotiating table the techniques that get him bargains in the local bazaar, pasar, or mercado, where ridiculously low offers and threats of breaking off negotiations are acceptable techniques. Yet in a number of countries the rules of the street markets do not apply in government circles. In some cases the differences simply reflect the norms of the elite as compared with those of the common people. As the humor and style of the elite Britisher differs from that of the London Cockney, so the negotiating customs of the elite Indonesian differ radically from those of the traders on the street.

Moreover, the government negotiator may be influenced by his colonial heritage. In the past, "final offers" from the colonial authority may have indeed been final. A government negotiator may accept a "final offer" at face value, putting an end to negotiations before a successful conclusion is reached.

Cultural misunderstandings can begin on either side. In some cases the government negotiator may attempt to mimic the culture of the foreign investor. Having heard that Westerners do not generally bargain intensely, and unfamiliar with the used car or antique markets of most Western countries, he may adopt a technique with which he thinks the Westerner is at home, while the Westerner adopts a technique with which he thinks his opponent is familiar. The result may be similar to the two camel trains that pass in the night, as the two parties adjust right past each other.

Investors have frequently misunderstood delays, when the reasons were not immediately apparent. Often the conclusion reached by the potential foreign investor has been that someone was seeking a bribe. The reasons for the delay may, however, lie elsewhere. We have seen cases in which delays result from the need for government officials to settle their differences and to test the possible political consequences for a set of proposed terms. But someone was quite willing to accept a contribution from the foreigner. And, wonder of wonders, the contribution was followed by new successes in the negotiations. Of course, the bribe had little to do with the new progress. The time delays simply allowed the internal problems to be resolved.

Some firms have been able to use local contacts to analyze the bargaining environment for them. The contacts may be local citizens; they may be foreigners with long experience in the country. Frequently, useful "interpreters" of the negotiating culture have been found among the lawyers, consultants, and accountants in the local business community. Sometimes the resident foreign middleman, who negotiates complete concession agreements and then transfers them to foreign investors, has saved the investor the problems of negotiating in an unfamiliar culture. His role may be of value to the investor, as well as to the host country. In other cases, however, middlemen have been unscrupulous profiteers whose agreements are likely to be subjected to particular scrutiny when their contacts in government have lost power.

A REMINDER

Much discussion of concession agreements deals with the bargaining relationship as "distributional," or as a "zero-sum game." The view is based on the assumption that there is a fixed package of benefits from the investment that are to be parcelled out between the investor and the government. To an extent this is true. But for many of the bigger issues and for some of the smaller ones it is completely misleading.

An important but difficult task for the negotiator is to keep in mind in the heat generated by spirited bargaining the possibility that it may be better to reach some agreement short of the ideal rather than having the negotiations break down. It is even possible that retreat on a particular point may not cost one's side anything, but may benefit one's opponent, who may be willing to yield on another point in exchange.

The nature of the bargain that can be struck between investor and host country depends, to a significant extent, on the economic and political factors discussed in previous chapters. But relative bargaining powers establish only a range of possible outcomes. Within that range, much depends on the negotiating skills of the parties involved. In the past, even the best of negotiating skills in the developing countries could be ineffective due to the paucity of information available to the government teams. As the developing countries attempt to cooperate with other developing countries to obtain stability in raw material markets, many are gaining access to a quantity of information never before available to them.[32]

NOTES

1. See, e.g., the *Concession Agreement between the Government of Liberia and the National Iron Ore Company, Ltd.* (March 13, 1958).

2. The Liberian Government first began to take a serious look at its concessions policy in 1967. See Raymond Vernon et al., "Proposed Program on the Government of Liberia's Concession Policy" (mimeo., April 1967), cited in Carl S. Shoup et al., *The Tax System of Liberia* (New York: Columbia University Press, 1970), p. 67; F. Rouhani, "Recommendations Concerning Co-Ordination of the Administration of Concessions" (Government of Liberia, mimeo., July 1970). See also "Liberia, Firestone's Taxes," *West Africa,* September 29, 1972, p. 1304; and Bobby Nardoo, "Export Success With High Quality Iron Ore Takes Sparkle From Gold and Diamonds" in "Liberia, Special Report," *The Times* (London), April 17, 1973, p. iv.

3. See, e.g., *Production-Sharing Contract between P.N. Pertambangan Minjak Nasional and Phillips Petroleum Company* (1968).

4. See *Agreement between the Government of the Republic of Indonesia and A. Soriano y Cia* (December 4, 1969). See the Indonesian Commission Four, *Report on Deviations in Forest Exploitation and the Lumber Trade* (1970).

5. The Indonesian law relating to limited liability companies includes only 21 brief articles. Translation of the *Indonesian Commercial Code,* S.G. 23/1847 (Djakarta, Ministry of Justice), Third Title, Third Chapter, Articles 36–56, "Concerning Limited Liability Companies."

6. Soedjatmoko, "Foreign Private Investment in a Developing Nation: An Indonesian Perspective," in Virginia S. Cameron, ed., *Private Investors Abroad—*

Problems and Solutions in International Business in 1969 (New York: Bender, 1969), pp. 322–23. See also Jean Lalive, "Negotiations with American Lawyers— A Foreign Lawyer's View," in 1965 volume of *Private Investors Abroad.*

7. See *Contract of Work between Republic of Indonesia and P.T. Kennecott Indonesia* (November 1, 1969), Art. 13(d)(D)(iii): "Operating Expenses shall include, inter alia, the following amounts: . . . (6) amounts for royalties and other payments including those to Affiliates for patents, designs, technical information and services. . . ."

8. *Contract of Work between the Government of Indonesia and the Indonesian Nickel Development Company, Ltd.* (April 1969).

9. See, e.g., *Agreement between the Government of Indonesia and A. Soriano y Cia* (December 4, 1969), Art. I: "In furtherance of the general policy of optimal integration, the establishment of log-processing plants such as sawmills, veneer plants and plywood plants is contemplated" (para. 3).

10. Roger D. Fisher, *International Conflict for Beginners* (New York: Harper and Row, 1969), p. 15.

11. Ibid., p. 16.

12. Decree 3528, Art. 2, U.S. Dept. of Interior, *Mineral Trade Notes* 70 (October 1973): 19.

13. *New York Times,* June 24, 1969, p. 53. See "Competitive Bidding for Mineral Leases," *Natural Resources Journal* 8 (October 1968): 650.

14. Marvine Howe, "De Beers Widens Angola Gem Hold," *New York Times,* May 31, 1971, p. 23.

15. Kenneth W. Dam, "Oil and Gas Licensing and the North Sea," *Journal of Law and Economics* 8 (October 1965): 51.

16. "Dominican Republic; Decree No. 3528," *Mineral Trade Notes* 70 (October 1973): 21.

17. *Mineral Trade Notes* 70 (November 1973): 7.

18. The following discussion on negotiating strategies and techniques draws, in part, on the following studies: Chester Karrass, *The Negotiating Game* (New York: World Publishing Company, 1970); Thomas Schelling, "An Essay in Bargaining," *American Economic Review* 46 (June 1956): 281, Wayne C. Minnick, *The Art of Persuasion* (Boston: Houghton Mifflin, 2d. ed. 1968); James White, "Material for a Course on the Negotiating Process" (mimeo., University of Michigan, undated).

19. See generally, Chester Karrass, op. cit.

20. For a description of a real, but disguised case, see Picard Printing Products (A), Harvard Business School case, I.C.H. 9–374–227.

21. Roger D. Fisher, op. cit., p. 17.

22. Raymond Vernon, "Indonesia's Policies toward Foreign Direct Investment," p. 5 (mimeo., September 15, 1969).

23. See Willard A. Hanna, "Petroleum as Panacea," *Field Staff Reports: Southeast Asia series,* Vol. XIX, no. 11 (1971).

24. The problem presented by state enterprises is usually framed in terms of the conflict between autonomy and accountability. The difficulty is one of providing sufficient flexibility for the public corporation to permit it to operate nonbureaucratically while ensuring its accountability to the government or

parliament. See R. Owodunni Teriba, "Accountability and Public Control of Public Corporations—The Experience of Western Nigeria," in D.J. Murray, ed., *Studies in Nigerian Administration* (London: Hutchinson Educational, 1970).

25. See Chapter 3, footnotes 44, 45, 46 and accompanying text.

26. *Contract of Work between the Government of Indonesia and P.T. Kennecott Indonesia* (November 1, 1969).

27. *Agreement between the Government of Indonesia and Aluminum Company of America* (1969), Art. 23.

28. *Contract of Work between the Government of Indonesia and P.T. Pacific Nikkel Indonesia* (February 17, 1967).

29. Gold Coast, Fact-Finding Committee on the Timber Industry in the Western Province of the Gold Coast, *Timber Industry* (Accra: Government Printing Department, 1951).

30. Ibid., p. 5.

31. See L. Michael Hager, "Taxation of Foreign Investment in Liberia," *Liberian Law Journal* 1 (December 1965): 165 ff.

32. On the problem of host country access to critical information, see David N. Smith, "Information-Sharing and Bargaining: Institutional Problems and Implications," in Gerald W. Garvey, ed., *The Political Economy of International Resource Flows* (Princeton, N.J.: Princeton Univ. Press, forthcoming).

Chapter Seven

The Search for Stability

To this point, we have viewed mineral negotiations primarily in terms of a single foreign firm bargaining with a single government. Although this simple model provides a useful way of examining the concessions process, the model does not reflect all of the relevant facts. An understanding of the problems facing the minerals investor and mineral producing countries requires a more complex construct. The number of parties making their interests felt in any concession arrangement is now seldom limited to two.

It is true, of course, that for the host government and for the investor the basic issues of structuring a suitable agreement, of shaping appropriate financial and development provisions, of developing adequate mechanisms for settling disputes, and of organizing an effective negotiating team remain much as in the past. But major change is occurring as producing countries search for new ways of increasing their bargaining power. The successful efforts of some oil-producing countries to increase their bargaining powers through OPEC has generated attempts on the part of countries producing other minerals to join forces. Moreover, in a search for stable prices, producing countries are extending their interests into the markets of consuming countries. Involvement in processing and marketing abroad appear to offer benefits to countries that in the past have limited their activities to extracting raw materials at home. At the same time, and partly in response to the actions of the producing countries, the governments of the consuming countries are increasingly reluctant to rely entirely on private firms for supplies of critical raw materials from abroad. Previous attempts to stockpile essential materials and to rely on national companies to defend the national interest are being augmented by efforts to organize the consuming countries. The goal is to ensure regular supplies of raw materials at reasonable prices.

These moves by producing countries are reminiscent of the earlier transformation of the private raw material firms into multinational enterprises. In the quest for inexpensive and regular sources of materials to supply manufacturing or distribution facilities at home, private firms ventured abroad. The first successful efforts at finding foreign sources led to other attempts; managers were anxious lest their fortunes be dependent on only a few supply points. But since sources for many minerals came in large units, especially in those days when a concession might cover half a country, success in obtaining multiple sources frequently generated the need for more outlets to dispose of the vastly increased production. Thus, firms began to seek markets in other countries. The attempts to reduce risk and to balance supply and outlets, coupled with the need to counter moves made by competitors in potentially attractive areas, led to the multinational thrust of the raw material firms.

Early in the process, firms in some industries began to join together in consortia to share the risks incurred in developing large deposits of raw materials. The consortia played an important role in addition to that of risk-sharing; membership in a consortium could ensure that a firm could keep an eye on competitors. In the years before World War II, the firms formed explicit cartels in some industries. Even later, when the cartels had been challenged by antitrust action, the opportunities to observe each other's actions firsthand in a network of joint projects reassured each member that its competitors were not bidding aggressively on new sources, not developing new technologies that would not be available to all, and not pricing in ways that could upset stability in the markets.

The goals of mineral-producing countries in the 1970s are, in many respects, similar to the goals of the private firms in earlier decades. In the search for stable markets, some producing nations are moving toward increasing involvement in the processing and distribution of their raw materials. In some cases this movement is leading them, as processors or marketers, into the countries that provide the principal outlets for their raw materials.

Involvement in processing and distribution is not the only route followed by producing countries in their search for stability. In some industries a number of producing governments are joining together in attempts to cooperate in the sale of their raw materials. The consortia of producing countries seek to exercise some joint control over the price and volume of the raw materials that they sell to other countries. They aim to increase the bargaining power of producing governments in dealing with the international raw material firms. Their efforts are geared toward capturing some of the benefits of oligopoly that have accrued to the private enterprises in the past.

The efforts of producing-country governments to reach outside national boundaries to gain stable outlets and higher prices will inevitably result in changes in the relationship between host country and foreign investor in extractive industries. Results from steps taken thus far suggest that the efforts will have some success in some industries. Stability may be enhanced, at least temporarily, and bargaining power may shift even more to the producing countries.

The successful arrangements will almost certainly be copied by other countries and in raw material industries where they have not yet been attempted. But the chances of success are not equal in all industries. And some of the promised stability may be elusive.

COOPERATION AMONG THE
PRODUCING COUNTRIES

Much of the history of efforts of producing countries to cooperate in selling their raw materials offers little promise that such arrangements can do much to improve the bargaining power and market stability of the producing countries. But the success of OPEC and the limited accomplishments of the International Tin Council and the International Coffee Agreement in the 1960s and early 1970s have raised the possibility that such organizations may indeed be able to attain at least some limited goals.[1]

Most cooperative efforts among the producing countries have had as their original aims the reduction of variance in the price and demand for their raw materials or the increase in revenues earned from exports. Some, such as the international tin agreements, have attempted to use a buffer stock to stabilize prices. In the tin agreements, the buffer stock was backstopped by export quotas. Other attempts at influencing the market, such as the coffee agreement, have relied heavily on export quotas as a mechanism to influence price by restricting supply. Still other arrangements such as CIPEC, the copper-producing countries' organization, did not originally rely on quotas or buffer stocks, but served primarily as a vehicle for the exchange of information among member countries, particularly in their negotiations with multinational firms.[2] Better information, it was hoped, would improve the bargaining position of individual countries.

Although producing countries have had some success with cooperative arrangements for petroleum, coffee, and tin, it is difficult to conceive of more differently structured industries. The intergovernmental organizations reflect these differences. Despite the differences, the successes of the petroleum- and coffee-producing countries have probably resulted to a great extent from one common feature: the willingness of the raw materials purchasers to cooperate with the governments of the producing countries.

Agreements among producers, be they the commodity agreements arranged by governments or cartel agreements established by private companies, all have the same Achilles' heel. If the incentive for a member to break the agreement is not counterbalanced by an equally strong penalty and enforcement mechanism, the life of the agreement is likely to be short. For exports to be controlled successfully, control over capacity may, in some cases, also be essential. If one member has excess capacity, there may be an overwhelming temptation to undercut the prices of the other members in order to take advantage of the high prices that result from the cartel. The periodic crises of the international cartel of scheduled airlines, IATA, point to the problems of maintaining a cartel based on price, but without capacity controls.

In theory, at least, export and capacity controls for raw materials would be relatively easy to institute and to police if the number of producing countries was very small. But a small number of producing countries seems to be neither an essential nor a sufficient ingredient for success. Among industries where successful arrangements have been concluded, only in the tin industry can the producers be counted on the fingers of both hands. Four tin suppliers—Malaysia, Indonesia, Bolivia, and Thailand—account for the majority of free-world production.[3] In contrast, the number of significant oil exporters has grown to at least fifteen countries. OPEC itself had thirteen members in 1975.

The tin industry, where the number of major suppliers was small, was an unusual one. If cooperative efforts were to be successful, most arrangements would have to include a large number of producing countries. But even in the rare cases where there were few producers, success was not guaranteed; for years the many attempts to organize cocoa producers failed, although only four countries produced over 70 percent of world exports.[4]

The International Coffee Agreement has provided encouragement that some success can be obtained in industries where there is a large number of producers. Significantly, from the first effective agreement in 1962 the coffee arrangement was based on the explicit cooperation of the importing countries. Initially, it appeared that the reluctance of the United States to join the agreement might lead it to falter, but in 1963 that country cooperated by ratifying the agreement. When the world's most important importer of coffee agreed to help enforce the terms of the arrangement, a critical element of success was added and the agreement went into effect.

Until 1973 the agreement relied on quotas to limit the coffee exports of each of its producing members. The producers and the consumers met yearly to determine the overall quota for the coming twelve months. This quota was then allocated among the exporting countries. Adjustments were made in the quarterly quotas to reflect new market and production information.

The coffee arrangements called on the importing countries to help enforce the restrictions on supply. The importers agreed to limit their purchases of coffee from nonmember countries and obligated themselves to demand certificates of origin for coffee they purchased. The importers were enlisted to control the direct shipping by exporting countries of coffee beyond their quotas and the transshipping of coffee from one country to another to avoid the quota restrictions. As long as the consuming countries cooperated in policing the arrangement, a country that decided to break away from the agreement or violate the export quotas would have found it difficult to obtain markets for its coffee. For a number of years, cooperation from the consuming countries provided the adhesive that held together the arrangement among a large number of producing countries with divergent interests. The enforcement mechanism on the part of the consuming countries was sufficiently strong to counteract the weak restrictions that the agreement placed on production capacity in the producing countries.

To be sure, the apparent success of the coffee agreement often disguised some serious internal stresses. From time to time the meetings of producing and consuming countries to determine quotas generated major crises for the agreement. Disputes developed among the producing countries as to who was to get what proportion of the quota, and disputes were common as the exporting and the importing countries disagreed about the size of the overall quota. These conflicts threatened periodically to pull the arrangement apart. A further series of threats to the agreement arose over the exports from producing countries of soluble coffee, since these exports appeared to provide an escape from the quotas and posed a threat to the processing industries in the consuming nations.

The 1968 version of the coffee agreement collapsed in late 1972, with less than a year to run. Afterwards it was questionable whether conflicting interests could again be accommodated to permit the renegotiation of some kind of effective arrangement. The usual disputes about quota size and allocations were intensified by the problems of instability and the uncertainties created by the changing relationship of some of the countries to the European Common Market as that organization was enlarged. The nature of the basic disputes was underlined by the membership in a London-based sales organization, Cafe Mondial, Ltd., that was established following the breakdown of the agreement. This organization represented Brazil, Colombia, Angola, and the Ivory Coast. It appeared for a time that the Central American producers might join, but the hopes came to naught and the other African growers were threatening to cut prices to find new markets.[5]

Despite the difficulties, the 1962 Agreement and its successors must be rated as reasonably successful. As one observer noted, "Ten years of a commodity agreement is a long time."[6] During the period of the agreement, the income of the producing countries was almost certainly higher and more stable than it would have been had the agreement not existed.

The OPEC arrangements were very different from the International Coffee Agreement. Not only had OPEC not succeeded in establishing export quotas by 1975, but also the explicit cooperation from the importing countries, which had been the key to success in the coffee agreement, was missing. The structure of the oil industry in the period around 1970 was such, however, that the producing countries did not need the signatures of the consuming country governments. The needed cooperation from the "consumers" was actual and implicit, through the international oil firms.[7]

Of course, the structure of the coffee industry differs dramatically from that of the petroleum industry. Although the coffee industry has been characterized by many independent growers and little vertical integration on the part of international companies, the international oil industry has been dominated for most of its history by a relatively small number of vertically integrated multinational firms. To the producing countries, these multinational enterprises have been the "consumers" of the crude oil that the countries supply. To have ties to the consumers, the producing countries needed only the implicit cooperation of the international firms that extract, process, and sell their oil. This they obtained in the late 1960s and held into the early 1970s.

The cooperation of the international oil firms did not have to be made explicit, since such cooperation was a natural result of interests shared with the producing countries. The integrated oil companies found cooperation more attractive than alternative actions that would divide the oil producers. This cooperation was forthcoming from the firms for a number of reasons.

First, the vertically integrated structure of the firms and the low marginal costs associated with oil production reduced the temptation of the oil firms to respond to the offers of an oil-producing country willing to undercut OPEC's terms. Unlike an unintegrated coffee roaster, an oil firm with production and transport facilities in place in particular countries might not be tempted to accept crude oil offered by a rebellious supplier at a discount.

For the petroleum firm, a shift in sources may result in little savings when the discounted price of the new crude oil is compared to the marginal costs in existing facilities. The slow response of the main integrated firms to discounts would leave the oil-producing countries relatively little incentive, at least in the short run, to offer the companies terms that are slightly below those which the organization of producing countries was supporting.

But the more important reason for implicit cooperation on the part of the international oil firms is probably the search for stability on the part of managers of the firms. In an oligopoly such as the international oil industry, a major threat to a firm is the possibility that some member of the oligopoly may obtain a source of oil cheaper than the others and begin to cut prices. If the price elasticity of demand facing the industry is low, the manager of a particular firm is much more anxious to ensure that he face a cost structure similar to those of his competitors than he is that the overall cost structure be the lowest possible. After all, higher costs can simply be passed on to the customer, at least within wide limits. Thus, an arrangement such as OPEC, which promises an equalization of costs among the companies, need not be viewed as a serious threat to the companies. Managers in search of stability are not likely to oppose a new deal, as long as the producing countries do not demand so much that sales fall precipitously.

The established oil companies thus found no reason to oppose the OPEC policy that all producing countries negotiate similar terms with the oil companies. As a tool toward this end, OPEC developed model petroleum agreements. When new producers appeared on the horizon, OPEC eagerly provided negotiating assistance to ensure that those countries did not seriously undercut the prevailing terms in the industry. In this way, OPEC provided assistance to Liberia when its government was negotiating offshore exploration rights in the late 1960s. For perhaps the first time in its history, Liberia was able to negotiate contracts that were up to international standards for the industry. A possible result, of course, is that Liberia may not quickly gain a large share of the international market if commercial oil is discovered there. But the government will get a good return on any oil it does export. The security of the oil companies has also bee assured. In Liberia, where non-oil firms were bidding to enter the oil business, none would receive terms dramatically more favorable than those faced by oil firms elsewhere. The traditional firms retained their stable environment without having to follow the successful concessionaires into the new area, as has been so common in other industries when a new area has been opened, especially when some of the entering firms have been outsiders to the oligopoly.

From efforts to promote standardization of agreements, OPEC moved to collective bargaining with the oil companies. The response of the American-based international oil companies to a possible united front among the producing countries was to seek permission from the U.S. government to negotiate with competitors in a bloc against the host governments. In 1971 the American government granted the firms immunity from antitrust actions to allow the companies to collaborate among themselves in negotiations with OPEC. Relief from antitrust restraints probably assured that the interests of the companies and OPEC were even closer than before. As long as the firms could negotiate together, no one company was likely to reach a secret deal to the detriment of the other firms. After a round of negotiations, all firms would be saddled with similar costs. If the result was higher payments to the producing countries, they could within limits simply be passed on by the oil companies to the consumers.

Unlike the members of the International Coffee Agreement, the OPEC members by 1975 had not attained their original goal of agreeing on export quotas. Until the early 1970s the production levels in the individual producing countries had been determined almost entirely by the decisions of the individual firms. The political demands of the 1973 Middle East War led Arab oil-producing countries to impose restrictions on the output of the firms. In 1974 some non-Arab oil-producing countries began to experiment with restrictions in oil production. Others did not cooperate in the restrictions, and allowed their production to expand to fill the gap. Whether the sporadic efforts on the part of some countries, after 1973, to withhold oil from the market would be successful was doubtful. Without a quota system, OPEC could do little to control supply. For the moment, output levels in many producing countries continued to be determined by the decisions of the private firms.

The OPEC arrangement, as limited as it was, has not been invulnerable. Perhaps the greatest threat, paradoxically, was a further reduction in the strength of the vertically integrated oil companies. Should oil again be in surplus after the "crisis" of 1973 and 1974, the appearance of major new buyers who are not driven toward vertical integration could tempt some member countries to offer cheap oil to increase their sales. Such buyers, without huge production facilities in place, would presumably respond to offers of low-priced oil. The temptation to expand output at lower prices by selling more to outsiders at a discount could break the unity of interests between the oil companies and producing countries. There was, it is true, not much temptation for some of the producing countries to expand output immediately after the 1973–74 price rise and before these countries were able to absorb new revenue. But the surplus years of the 1960s witnessed such moves as countries began to experiment with lower prices to independents along with taxing structures designed to reward producing companies that increased their output in the particular country. A crack in the solidarity of the OPEC countries appeared in the fall of 1975, when Ecuador announced that its oil sales would not be governed by OPEC's prices. As with coffee, the potential for quarrels over each country's share of the market could develop if export quotas were to be sought within OPEC. Much would depend on the actions of Saudi Arabia and Iran, whose reserves were sufficiently large that either could easily drive down prices or, by withholding oil, support prices in the short run.

In addition, the advent of cheaper nuclear power, or energy from other sources, or oil outside of OPEC could lead to an increase in the price elasticity of demand for OPEC oil. In fact, the decline in demand as prices for oil rose in 1973 and 1974 indicated that demand was more responsive to price than many observers had assumed, even though substitution is not quick and easy. If higher prices for oil should mean serious loss of sales to the companies, continual pressure for more host country revenue would mean that this money would come out of the purses of the international companies rather than out of the pockets of consumers. Again, the community of interests between producing country and company would be broken.

There were other threats to unity, as the oil producers began to disagree among themselves. Some of the oil-producing countries had, in 1974, become concerned about the impact of high oil prices on the poorer nations, largely in response to complaints from these poorer countries. Members of the Organization of African Unity had hoped that their support of the Arab cause in the Middle East War of October 1973 would have guaranteed them oil at a reduced cost. The Arab countries refused to sell at reduced prices but agreed to establish a $200 million fund for soft loans to black African states at about 1 percent interest.[8] Saudi Arabia, in an open conflict with other OPEC members, expressed concern about the disruptive effect of high oil prices on the economies of Western European countries and Japan, as well as developing countries in Asia, Latin America, and Africa. Saudi Arabia urged a reduction of prices; other OPEC members favored price increases.[9]

Until one of the potential threats materializes, the pattern of implicit co-operation between producing countries and the vertically integrated companies will probably mean that OPEC can succeed even if the shortage of oil of 1973 and 1974 turns out to be a temporary phenomenon. But the threats to OPEC's stability appeared major.

In contrast to the complexities of oil and coffee, the International Tin Agreement is, on the surface, a model of simplicity. Even though all major consuming countries except the United States have been members of the agreement, tin has provided a case in which the explicit or implicit cooperation of the raw material purchasers has probably not been a critical ingredient for success.

The special feature of the tin industry is, as noted previously, the small number of important producing countries. Four producers account for the bulk. As of 1975 an agreement needed to include only Malaysia, Indonesia, Bolivia, Australia, Nigeria, Thailand, and Zaire to capture practically all the world's supply of tin. With so few producers it has been feasible for the producers themselves to police the arrangement, without the need for cooperation from consuming countries. In addition, the small total value of all the tin traded and the ease of storing tin without spoilage and within reasonable physical constraints has permitted the financing of a buffer stock that could exercise a significant influence on supply, and thus prices.

But even the tin arrangement has been subject to internal disputes. The costs of production in the various member countries have been very different. Bolivia, for example, has been a higher-cost producer than Malaysia. When quotas have been used to restrict production, the agreement has called for them to be allotted among the producers on the basis of recent production levels. Low-cost producers were always aware of the possibility that they would probably gain a larger share of the tin market if they were to leave the agreement rather than submit to quotas. Still, in 1973 the threat of unstable prices without the agreement appeared to be sufficient to keep all the major producers within the arrangement.

Commodity agreements among the producing countries have been fragile, and it appears that most will inevitably fall apart, to be renegotiated another day under new rules. Probably in no industry are all the conditions of a really stable producer's cartel met. To hold together an arrangement that would assure high, stable prices, the producing countries would perhaps have to be few in number and have similar production costs. The demand for the product would probably have to be fairly price inelastic, with few close substitutes.[10] And the product would come in only a few standard grades to ease price-setting. Tin probably comes as close as any product to meeting these criteria. Where all these conditions are not met, the cooperation of consumers can help to hold together an agreement. Yet the interests of the ultimate consumers tend to diverge from those of the producers. Alliances erode as the governments of importing countries respond to the interest of their consumers or as the industry structure shifts, changing the position of the international firms. The divergence of interest adds to the instability of arrangements such as those for coffee, and may shorten the period during which agreements such as OPEC can be effective.

Yet even though dramatic success may be possible only under very special conditions, or with the cooperation of consumers, producing countries may accomplish a good deal under less favorable conditions. Take copper as an example. In the early 1970s there appeared to be little chance of explicit cooperation on the part of importing countries toward developing a quota system, or indeed toward developing any rigorous arrangement among producing countries. In the 1930s there had been sufficient strength on the part of the oligopolistic private firms to sustain prices through a cartel of private enterprises. During this period the companies themselves agreed on quotas, but the producing countries had little strength. The company cartel did not last. Although in the 1950s the number of major exporters was small, this was changing rapidly by the 1970s. New technology, especially large-scale equipment, made possible the exploitation of many ore deposits that were previously uneconomical. As a result, many new producers were entering the market.

In the 1970s a number of other conditions made a strong agreement among the copper-producing countries difficult. The firms were not sufficiently vertically integrated, and the cross-elasticity of demand between copper and aluminum was too high for there to be a clear community of interests in high prices between the producing countries and the international copper firms. In addition, high prices appeared to increase considerably the role played by reclaimed scrap copper. At the same time the consuming country governments saw little reason to support an agreement that would lead to high prices for such an important industrial input. Moreover, like the interests of the coffee producers, the interests of the various copper-producing countries differed considerably. The many countries that were discovering that they had usable copper ores in the late 1960s and early 1970s were eager to attract investors and to obtain a share of the market. The traditional producers wanted to retain their old shares. Any single formula for quotas or for common terms with the companies was likely to be rejected by one group or the other. If the formula left the traditional producers with their markets, the new producers would view the share they received as unjust. The new producers would realize that they would be gaining markets without an agreement. Similarly, the traditional producers would fight quotas that resulted in any significant reduction in their shares. At best, only a very unstable alliance appeared possible.

In fact, in late 1974 four copper countries appeared poised to go it alone, with a buffer stock and production cutbacks. But the cooperating countries, with 65 percent of world copper exports, represented a declining portion of world trade in copper, and other countries, such as Papua New Guinea, had indicated that they would not join in the production cuts.

Even though an arrangement such as those for coffee, tin, or oil appeared not to be in the cards for copper in the early 1970s, an organization of copper-producing countries could nevertheless serve some needs in the producing countries. As we noted earlier, the terms of agreements in the new copper regions differ from the norms established in the traditional copper-producing areas. Part of the difference was a result not of a conscious attempt to undercut the traditional suppliers but of ignorance on the part of the newly entering countries. In the late 1960s in Indonesia, for example, the government negotiators did not have detailed information on terms in other countries. In 1971 in Malaysia the government called in consultants who brought with them detailed descriptions of the terms in nearby countries and in the traditional copper-producing nations only after the negotiations for a copper mine in Sabah had been going on for months. An effective organization of producing countries could have reduced the erosion of terms created in the new producing countries. The OPEC model could have been followed, at least in helping the new entrants.

CIPEC, the organization of copper-producing countries created in 1967, had as members, in 1973, Chile, Peru, Zaire and Zambia. Even though it tried to play a minor role in encouraging suppliers not to fill the copper gap that resulted from the efforts of some European countries to block the sale of Chilean copper from expropriated mines, CIPEC had generally not been aggressive in assisting the negotiating teams of new copper-producing countries. This is so even though it would have been in the interests of the traditional producing countries to provide this assistance. Despite the failure of the organization to assist new producers, some of CIPEC's individual members offered help when asked. Peru, for example, sent a team to Papua New Guinea in 1973 to assist the government with an evaluation of Kennecott's proposals in preparation for negotiations for deposits near the West Irian border.[11] The assistance being provided in 1974 by an economist associated with CIPEC to Papua New Guinea in connection with the renegotiation of the Bougainville Copper Agreement suggested that CIPEC might soon pursue a more active role in the new producing nations.

The role that an organization such as CIPEC can play in assistance is important to the producing countries. The information gap on the part of new producers has been only partly filled by consultants who operate independently. Good ones who are willing to work at the relatively low fees offered by the producing countries or international organizations are rare. Even they have difficulty in assembling agreements from other countries. Intergovernmental organizations, such as CIPEC, could help lubricate the mechanism for this form of information-transfer with rosters of available consultants and details of arrangements in other countries. OPEC has succeeded in this area; few other organizations of raw-material producing countries have done well in this role.

In fact, most organizations of producing countries must depend on exchange of information and assistance rather than the more dramatic quotas, buffer stocks, and united fronts. Although the appeal of OPEC's increase in oil prices was leading governments of countries producing other commodities to attempt to emulate OPEC's strategy, the conditions required for success were typically absent. In 1974, for example, bauxite producers joined forces with a view to following OPEC's model. Unlike the oil producers, however, the integrated aluminum firms had little incentive to cooperate with the producers. The high cross-elasticity of demand between copper, aluminum, and plastics meant that cost increases could probably not be easily passed on by the firm to the consumer. And there were many alternative sources of aluminum. In fact, the companies took steps to demonstrate that they were developing technologies for making aluminum from ores other than bauxite.[12] Should the cost of bauxite be increased, they were suggesting, the bauxite producers just might find themselves without a market. And the governments of consuming countries had little interest in increased prices for aluminum products. It is not surprising that the increase in royalties imposed by Jamaica and Guyana in 1974 were, in the end, only a small percentage of the price of most final products.

There have been suggestions that existing international organizations, such as the United Nations, should step in to fill the gap in information and assistance that the producing countries have so frequently failed to provide each other. Such a unit is unlikely to be successful until the developing countries recognize the importance of providing such information to each other. The weakness of organizations such as CIPEC and the iron ore producers' organization suggest that recognition of the value of assistance has not yet grown sufficiently. Although the benefits to the producing countries from arrangements that provide only assistance are not likely to be as great or as dramatic as those that derive from arrangements that involve customer cooperation, they are still likely to be significant for the producing countries. This is true whether initiative comes from among organizations of producing countries or from international agencies such as the United Nations.

DOWNSTREAM INTEGRATION

Although participation of customers may allow cartel arrangements among producer countries to be effective, cooperation is not forthcoming in many industries. In some cases, to accomplish similar goals, producing country governments have themselves begun to undertake processing and marketing so that they can control their outlets. Through such extensions of their activities, countries have attempted to reach the stage of the industry where prices are relatively secure and to obtain outlets that can be tied to using the products of the particular producing country. In some cases they have hoped to break the control of the international firms over outlets. This integration has taken various forms, but the aim of stable markets has, as we have noted, been similar to that of private firms driven to integrate vertically.

Some of the most dramatic steps have been taken in the oil industry, where some national oil companies from the producing countries have integrated forward into refining and distribution without the participation of the private international firms. The Iranian national oil company, NIOC, reached an agreement with the Indian government for participation in a refinery located in India. The Indonesian oil company, Pertamina, has negotiated a joint venture in distribution in the country's major market, Japan. Saudi Arabia, in a more complex proposal, suggested that it invest in facilities in the United States in exchange for exemption from the U.S. oil import quotas.[13] And, in 1973, Iran announced its intention to obtain a share in an international oil company's refining, petrochemical, and service station operations in the United States.[14] Although the efforts had not succeeded by late 1975, they were continuing.

To the extent that a country can supply its products to a tied facility, it may avoid the vagaries of a fluctuating market for the raw material. Oligopolistic pricing based on brand loyalty, restriction of outlets, location of distribution facilities, and so on may lead to more stable markets for the processed product than exist for the raw material. With controlled outlets, even in times of surplus the producing country may be able to retain its export volume. In many cases vertical integration may lead to sales that are more constant in volume and price than would obtain if the producing country had to sell the raw material on an open market.

The attempts of the national oil firms of the producing countries to fill the role of the international firms have other effects. The consuming countries have thus far tended to look favorably on efforts of the producing countries to integrate into the market. Presumably the ties would decrease the willingness of the producing country to cut off oil from the particular consuming country in times of scarcity or political conflicts. Should the oil flow be cut, the aggrieved consuming country would have a hostage, in the form of the downstream investment.

While attempts of producing governments to integrate downstream into the consuming countries have been limited, and have been principally in the oil industry, attempts on the part of some governments to capture processing facilities in their own countries have served similar ends, in addition to increasing local value added.

If the processed raw material has a broader market or a less price-sensitive one than the unprocessed product, the country with processing facilities within its borders may face a potentially more stable market than the country that is dependent on facilities located abroad and perhaps closely held by a few companies.

Most efforts to attract processing facilities have focused on foreign private companies. More ambitious have been the plans of Jamaica, Trinidad and Tobago, and Guyana, which in 1974 were beginning efforts to build two aluminum smelters—one in Trinidad and Tobago and one in Guyana—to be jointly owned by the governments. The goal was to break the bargaining power held by the international firms that controlled most of the smelters in which bauxite from Guyana and Jamaica had to be processed.

The attempt of producing countries to reach downstream has not been limited to direct investment in processing facilities, at home or abroad. For a few raw materials the extension of interests to downstream operations has been based on an attempt to influence the preferences of the customer. The strategy of Colombia with regard to coffee provides an example of a country that has attempted to undertake part of the marketing effort for its products.

To differentiate its coffee in the minds of the final consumer, Colombia undertook an advertising campaign to convince the U.S. coffee drinker that he or she should specify Colombian coffee when buying coffee. To the extent that the strategy is successful, Colombia faces a lower cross-elasticity of demand for its coffee than it did as an undifferentiated supplier. Its product could be priced higher, even if subjected to export quotas under the coffee agreement.

Although such a strategy may work for consumer products like coffee and bananas, the opportunities are probably rather limited for most minerals. True, it appeared possible that the torch and lion of Iran's national oil company might fly over some New York service stations, or the mythical garuda of Indonesia over some of Tokyo's. But it does not appear feasible to convince a buyer of copper wire, for example, to specify that his wire should be made out of Peruvian copper. Still, promotion can be undertaken surprisingly successfully for a number of minerals, as the efforts of the Bismuth Institute suggest.[15] Brand names appear to play some role even for rather dull metals, perhaps especially where the particular metal accounts for only a small portion of the cost of some final product. Some Southeast Asian tin, for example, has long been marked with the brand of the smelter from which it came. Some brands have commanded a market premium as an assurance of predictable purity, even for a product for which objective standards of quality are available. The premium appeared to be worthwhile for buyers who did not want to be concerned with comparative shopping, experimentation, and assaying. The effort of seeking a cheaper alternative of similar quality did not seem worth the time and risk.

The attempts of the producing countries to integrate downstream, whether through control of processing or through efforts to create a differentiated product, are likely to present a challenge to the management skills of host governments. The problems of obtaining capital and technology are usually recognized. Whether the efforts to create regionally owned smelters in the Caribbean could overcome these barriers was uncertain in the mid-1970s. But less widely recognized is the fact that integration into downstream operations is likely, in many cases, to involve the producing country in the marketing function in some way or other. For successful downstream integration, the national company must be able to develop programs that will be effective in marketing the output of the processing facility. In some cases this will involve advertising to differentiate the product. With oil in surplus, the consumer must be loyal to the torch and lion rather than the tiger in the tank, or must value brand over price. In other cases service to the customer may be the key to success, as in sales of nickel, where technical assistance seems to be a part of the sales effort. With vertical integration, the demands placed on the management skills of the national enterprise from the producing country will be of a very different kind from those they have faced in the past. The need will be for broad-gauge managers who are able to deal with problems that have heretofore been left to the foreign firms. Negotiating skills will not be sufficient. Whether many governments will be able to obtain the management skills for themselves remains to be seen. If they can, the stability and bargaining power they can create will be significantly greater than at any time in the past.

ROLE OF CONSUMING COUNTRIES

Recognizing the importance of raw materials to their economies, governments of the consuming countries have been represented from time to time in the history of concessions. In the heydays of colonialism, the grand geographical designs of the European powers were augmented by the more mundane needs for raw materials. Gunboat diplomacy was not unknown in connection with efforts to obtain raw materials.

Occasionally the influences of governments from the consuming countries were more subtle. One weapon was the pocketbook rather than the sword. Firestone and the U.S. government had a common interest in developing sources of rubber other than those under the control of the British and Dutch in the 1920s. A loan to the Liberian government, with technical policing by U.S. government officials, was a part of the package that enabled Firestone to obtain large acreages in Liberia for rubber plantations. And the colonial powers were not averse to giving preference to their own companies over those from other countries when it came to concessions, as the struggles of American companies to gain concessions for tin in British-controlled Malaya demonstrated.

The postwar period saw a general retreat by the consuming countries from involvement in the concessions process in the developing nations. True, the retreat was not universal. Several European countries supported the development of national raw material firms to represent their interests. On the other hand, stockpiling provided a measure of security for countries such as the United States, and a means of influencing world prices of raw materials. From time to time, local embassies have defended the investors from the home country. The extent of the influence of consuming countries has varied. The French, for example, have been remarkably successful in retaining for French companies the rights to the raw materials in the ex-French colonies of Africa that have remained in the French orbit. It is notable that every major mining project in Gabon and Mauritania includes at least one French firm as a shareholder.

On the other hand, the occasional efforts of the U.S. government to intervene in recent years appear to have had limited success. Threats to cut off aid to governments that expropriate American property have been less than completely effective in stopping the practice.[16] Although American embassies have sometimes interfered in local negotiations, this interference has been more in the nature of assistance to American business firms than as a part of a broadly conceived strategy to develop or protect the nation's sources of raw materials. And when national strategy has been involved, as in the assistance to the major oil companies by the State Department in their Middle East negotiations, it is not obvious that the efforts reflected a clear idea of the national interest.[17]

While on the whole most of the postwar period was marked by a reluctance on the part of the governments of consuming countries to involve themselves deeply in the concessions process, there were signs in the early 1970s that the consuming countries' growing concern about their raw material sources would bring their influence to the negotiating table. Japan had initiated major efforts in the 1960s. Its reentry as a major buyer of raw materials had been associated with government participation. The availability of finance and foreign exchange permits for raw material development was clearly controlled by the Japanese government. And many developing countries can identify Japanese development assistance that was tied to the construction of infrastructure for a particular Japanese investor. The Japanese encouraged the formation of cartels to secure raw materials, such as iron ore from Australia, and investment consortia for gaining access to raw materials abroad. In both Malaysia and Ecuador, copper for the Japanese market was developed by a consortium of Japanese companies that included all the major Japanese smelters. Such activity would almost certainly have been illegal on the part of U.S. companies.

The interest of consuming countries was strengthened by the seeming scarcity of raw materials and the rising prices for those that were available in the early 1970s. A number of European governments had taken an interest earlier in developing national champion firms to secure reliable sources of raw material. These efforts could be reinforced as the reluctance of private firms to explore in "risky" areas continues to increase. In 1974 an economist with a major oil company expressed the problem clearly. He said that his company would no longer drill in areas where the likelihood of a quick contract renegotiation was high following a successful discovery. In his view, in many of the potentially attractive regions for drilling, the profits allowed after the renegotiation would not be large enough to provide an adequate return on the capital invested there, plus that required for unsuccessful wells in other countries. If that perception of the risks becomes widespread in private firms, two responses are possible. The producing countries may react to the slow-down in development by trying to assure the investor that his fears are unjustified. More reliance on laws of general application rather than *ad hoc* agreements could be one of the tools to be experimented with. However, if potential investors still consider the prospects too risky, the governments of consuming countries may take steps to insure continuing investment in raw material sources. The steps might include direct support of the private firms, funds to the potential producing countries so that they can develop the resources, or further development of national enterprises that do not have to show a market return on investment.

In the early 1970s some subtle shifts in the tone of international negotiations were taking place that were also influencing consumer-country investment. A number of industrial countries appeared to be less intent on representing some broader concept of the general good and had taken a few steps backward toward a narrow concept of self-interest in their dealing with other nations. During this period the success of the producer oil cartel on the price and political fronts led to proposals for a countervailing cartel of major consuming countries.[18] However, the new environment was proving to be a difficult one in which to promote cooperative efforts. And it was unclear that success in forming a united front would do more than freeze prices at their current levels, when the alternative might be lower prices in the future.

In 1973 the U.S. government sought to encourage efforts of OECD members to establish oil-sharing arrangements as insurance against threatened cutbacks in oil supplies from Arab nations. Because of significant variations in oil policies, and the hope of some consuming countries to do better alone, the agreement among OECD members was not forthcoming during the crisis.[19] Only after the crisis passed was there an agreement on how future crises would be handled. The feasibility of the terms were, of course, untested.

Important to attempts to coordinate consumer countries was the fact that one of the major consumers, Japan, was still struggling to establish raw material supplies as secure as the other major consuming countries had obtained. Its earlier efforts to rely heavily on long-term supply contracts had not proved satisfactory; as a result Japan was struggling to gain footholds with direct investment. Until Japan could feel that it was an equal, its interests might make it hesitant to support an arrangement among the consumers. Yet Japan's participation was essential to any united front.

Success of the consuming countries in establishing a united front in petroleum negotiations might lead to similar attempts in connection with other industries. Negotiations could increasingly involve the interests of the consuming countries as a group, as well as those of the firms and the producing countries. But it appeared in early 1974 that the interests of the consumers was to be represented not by a united front in most industries but rather by much more active participation of individual importing countries in the concessions process.

Examples of consumer-country involvement expanded rapidly in the early 1970s. In 1973 the Saudi Arabian government indicated that increased oil production might depend on the extent of industrialization of the Saudi economy. The government suggested that one condition for increased Saudi production might come to be major American aid in developing and diversifying the Saudi Arabian economy so as to increase the non-petroleum industries' share in the gross national product.[20] An agreement establishing a joint commission on economic cooperation was signed in mid-1974. While oil production was not mentioned in the accord, it was clear that U.S. authorities hoped that the agreement would provide an incentive to Saudi Arabia to increase oil production.[20] A somewhat similar arrangement was being contemplated between Iraq and

Japan in 1974.[22] And the French government was actively courting the favor of oil-producing countries. The tables were being turned. Rather than the United States threatening to withdraw aid from the producing countries, a producing country was threatening to withdraw oil, or at least not to provide more, unless increased aid was forthcoming.

In 1974 a bill was proposed in the U.S. Senate that would involve the U.S. government even more closely in the concessions process. The proposed act would require the registration of all oil concession agreements of firms engaged in U.S. commerce. They would be subject to the approval of the Federal Energy Administration no matter in which country the agreements were concluded.[23]

Whatever the form of involvement on the part of the governments of consuming countries—multilateral or unilateral, direct or through a state enterprise—that involvement appeared likely to grow as long as raw material supplies appeared expensive and chancy. No longer were the governments willing to let the price and security of their raw material supplies be determined by negotiations between the governments of producing countries and private firms. The cooperation of producing countries presented a challenge to which the governments of consuming countries felt obligated to respond.[24] The traditional policy of leaving the matter to private firms was no longer sufficient as it became increasingly clear that the private firms presented neither the power nor the convergence of interests with the consumer necessary to permit the firms to serve as bargaining intermediaries. Moreover, the entry of the government of one consuming country into the process generates a response from others. Governments have responded to each other's moves much as private firms have responded to each other's moves. Initiatives by the government of one consuming country are countered by other governments out of fear that a failure to respond would leave them exposed to higher prices or less reliable supplies.

THE ELUSIVE STABILITY

The concessions process promises to become more complex as the producing countries attempt to band together, as they extend their interests downstream, and as the consuming countries again become more active in asserting their interests. The arrangements for the extraction of raw materials will undoubtedly come to reflect these developments.

The attempts of the producing countries to extend their interests downstream may well result in a period of stable prices and markets in some industries. In many cases, however, the efforts to establish a vertical oligopoly in the hands of the producing country are probably coming too late. The attempts to establish stability represent efforts to reconstruct an oligopolistic position similar to that long held by the multinational firms. But oligopoly has to be built on barriers to entry. The international firms have relied on closely-held technology, control over markets, and access to large sources of investment funds. For many raw material industries, the barriers to entry in the downstream stages have been continually eroded. As the first chapter pointed out, technology that was once closely-held can become generally available, capital can be borrowed, and markets can open up with the entry of new firms. In fact it has been the erosion of the barriers that has increased the bargaining power of the producing countries. It is also their continual erosion that will limit the ability of the producing countries to establish themselves in many industries in the positions of power previously held by the international firms. For some governments, downstream integration will bring them into a highly competitive market. In these cases much of the purpose of integration will be frustrated. Stability appears always to be just beyond grasp.

Of course, the barriers to entry remain high at certain stages in some industries. The diamond marketing cartels are still effective, as is the hold of the aluminum firms over smelting operations. Where the producing countries have little chance of entering the downstream stages without destroying the barriers to entry that maintain the price structure, their interests may be better served by continuing to cooperate with the private firms. A significant piece of a larger cake may be worth more, at least in economic terms, than a very large portion of a much shrunken cake. Diamond-producing countries, for example, have generally found it more advantageous to cooperate with the private marketing cartels than to try to take over this function themselves.[25] Whether the politics of the developing countries will allow for arrangements that build on common interests between producing country and private firm, when such interests do indeed exist, is difficult to forecast.

The involvement of more parties in the concessions process offers both perils and promises to the stability of concession agreements. Negotiations among many parties rapidly become complex. The divergent interests and the political needs of each party multiply the possibilities of a breakdown in negotiations. Even though, in most cases, the private firm, the host government, and the consuming country are all served by conclusion of an agreement, the overlapping interests were easier to decipher in the simple negotiations between firm and government.

On the other hand, if the commitments of the parties become sufficiently complex, the arrangements may turn out to be stable simply because of that complexity. If the producing countries place facilities in the consuming countries that counterbalance those of the consuming countries in their own borders, threats to the arrangements that have been established may be perceived as undesirable by both parties. The situation may be analogous to international investment in oligopolistic manufacturing industries. Moves by one party against the interests of another member of the arrangement may be perceived as leading to unpredictable responses by the aggrieved member. Each member may be unwilling to disturb a working arrangement in ways that might generate an unforeseen result.

200 Negotiating Third-World Mineral Agreements

Within some such structures, private firms may find a comfortable home. Governments may be content to leave a part of the system in the hands of efficient managers who can handle the complex logistics. And the private firms may play other roles useful to governments. During the 1973 oil embargo, they were able to give a cloak of anonymity to oil that enabled untraceable supplies to continue to the embargoed countries. And if they could be encouraged to enter side-deals, with cut prices, the secrecy could create suspicions among the producing countries that could weaken the cartel. In such an industry, however, the private firms are unlikely to be the powerful, profitable enterprises of the days when the barriers to entry were high. They will, to an extent, be the pawns in moves made by the governments concerned. Although they will probably not be driven out of the oil business, their role in an industry dominated by governments will be less attractive than before. But there still appear to be bits of power left, such as in the technology of deep-sea drilling. On the whole, steps taken by some oil firms to diversify their interests out of petroleum while their cash flow is high may be a wise reaction to the threat of such developments. Whether they can find other energy or raw-material-based industries in which they can establish a new position of power is uncertain. Some seemed to be heading toward investments in other industries where the position of the private firms was eroding as rapidly as in petroleum. And some, especially in the United States, appeared to be running up against antitrust barriers.

In the mid 1970s, private firms in industries other than oil were not yet subject to the same pressures. Some would probably not be subjected to such forces for years. In fact new developments could restore advantages to some private firms. As the copper companies began to lose control in the traditional producing countries in the late 1960s, a new source of power developed, at least temporarily, as large-scale mining technology could be applied in new producing countries with low-grade ore. For aluminum firms a serious threat did not appear imminent in 1975. Despite the intentions of some producing countries, smelters owned by developing countries appeared to be a number of years away. If the moves of the bauxite countries drove the firms to alternative sources of aluminum, it appeared as if the firms' advantage in technology for developing laterite ores just might keep them in a position of some power. In fact, new developments such as deep-sea mining could restore a great deal of strength to mining firms. Those enterprises with the required new technology and with sources of capital could indeed turn out to be in a strong bargaining position again. But deep-sea mining negotiations are apt to be complex, involving new parties. Regardless of which organization turns out to be responsible for the ocean resources, it could have the weak negotiating skills of a developing country new to the field. Or it may turn out to be a powerful counterweight to companies with money and knowledge.

Even for the firms that retain some degree of strength, the future promises little stability. The rapid shifts in bargaining power, the involvement of more parties in the concessions process, and the new-found confidence of the producing countries guarantees some exciting days for government officials and business managers concerned with the minerals industry.

NOTES

1. The successes of OPEC in 1973–74 led a number of governments at a special UN General Assembly meeting to urge similar arrangements for other raw materials. "Raw Material Cartels Urged at UN Assembly," *West Africa,* April 22, 1974, p. 46. A 1973 UN Economic and Social Council resolution recognized that "one of the most effective ways in which the developing countries can protect their natural resources is to promote . . . cooperation . . . having as its main purpose to concert pricing policies . . . (and) to coordinate production policies. . . ." Several commodity groups took steps in 1974 to form cartels including timber, copper, bauxite, and iron ore. The immediate results of meetings among producers of various commodities appeared inconclusive. See "New Course Due on Copper Prices," *New York Times,* June 23, 1974, p. 65; "Embargo by Bauxite Producers Unlikely," *New York Times,* March 7, 1974, p. 55. For an important discussion of the issues, see the series of articles by Zuhayr Mikdashi, Stephen D. Krasner, and C. Fred Bergsten, "One, Two, Many OPEC's . . . ?" *Foreign Policy,* No. 14 (Spring 1974).

2. In late 1972, CIPEC members agreed not to take advantage of the vacuum created by the tying up of Chilean copper as a result of litigation brought by Kennecott in a Paris civil court to block a $1.33 million payment for Chilean copper shipments to France. Gene Smith, "Cerro Is to be Paid for Chile Copper," *New York Times,* December 2, 1972, p. 53.

3. "Tin," *Mineral Trade Notes* 69 (September 1972): 8–9. Malaysia, Bolivia, and Thailand account for some 70 percent of all tin entering international channels. Lester R. Brown, "Depending on Others for Minerals," *New York Times,* November 5, 1972, sec. 3, p. 11. There are, of course, other sectors— in which international arrangements are either non-existent or unsuccessful— where the number of major producing countries is small. Australia, Mexico, and Peru, for example, account for 60 percent of the exportable supply of lead.

4. In 1973 an agreement was reached, based on quotas to apply in nine countries that accounted for 95 percent of cocoa exports.

5. See Ursula Wassermann, "Breakdown in Commodity Agreements," *Journal of World Trade Law* 8 (May–June 1974): 337.

6. Edward Horesh, "Coffee Conflicts: 1," *West Africa,* November 27, 1972, p. 1592.

7. Morris A. Adelman, "Is the Oil Shortage Real? Oil Companies as OPEC Tax-Collectors," *Foreign Policy,* No. 9 (Winter 1972–73).

8. "No Cheaper Oil for African Lands," *New York Times,* June 9, 1974, p. 17.

9. "Oil Nations Face Dispute on Prices," *New York Times,* June 16, 1974, Sec. 1, p. 9.

10. There is also the consideration of substitute grades of ore. When representatives of bauxite-producing countries met in Guinea in 1974, Reynolds

Metal Company began test production of alumina from laterite ores in the U.S. See Gene Smith, "Reynolds Begins Tests of Laterite to Obtain Alumina," *New York Times,* March 7, 1974, p. 55.

11. "Tough Policy Recommended in PNG as Ok Tedi Negotiations Set to Resume," *Engineering and Mining Journal* 174 (July 1973): 34.

12. Gene Smith, loc. cit.

13. See "U.S. Studying Saudi Plan for Oil Investments Here," *New York Times,* October 3, 1972, p. 61; Clyde H. Farnsworth, "Oil-Consuming Countries Press for Pooling Accord," *New York Times,* October 3, 1973, p. 59.

14. "Iran, U.S. Oil Company Sign 50–50, 'Well-to-Pump' Deal," *International Herald Tribune,* July 26, 1973, p. 1.

15. "Bolivia: By-laws of the Bismuth Institute," *Mineral Trade Notes* 70 (September 1973): 13.

16. For background and results of some of the efforts, see Theodore H. Moran, "The Impact of U.S. Direct Investment on Latin-American Relations." Prepared for the Commission on U.S.-Latin American Relations, June 1974, pp. 16–20.

17. See "Multinational Petroleum Companies and Foreign Policy," Hearings before the Subcommittee on Multinational Corporations of the Committee on Foreign Relations, U.S. Senate, 93d Cong., 2d Sess. January 30, 1974.

18. See Robert Kleiman, "Draft of Pact by Oil-Importing Nations Pools Sovereignty," *New York Times,* September 30, 1974, p. 57.

19. Clyde H. Farnsworth, "U.S. Seeks to Spur Oil Sharing Accords," *New York Times,* September 12, 1973, p. 65.

20. William D. Smith, "Saudi Ties Oil Output to Industrializing," *New York Times,* September 12, 1973, p. 65.

21. B. Gwertzman, "'Milestone' Pact Is Signed By U.S. and Saudi Arabia," *New York Times,* June 9, 1974, p. 1.

22. "Officer of Iraq National Oil Says It Will Increase Output," *New York Times,* June 25, 1974, p. 51.

23. See proposal by Senator Church, Committee on Foreign Relations, U.S. Senate, "A Bill: Relating to Contracts and Other Agreements Involving the Purchase or Procurement of Crude Oil and Refined Petroleum Products from Nations Comprising the Organization of Petroleum Exporting Countries," 1974, to be entitled "Foreign Oil Contracts Act."

24. In 1974 the U.S. Senate Foreign Relations Subcommittee on Multinational Corporations held hearings on the feasibility of greater government participation in negotiations. E. Cowan, "Government Role in Oil Questioned," *New York Times,* June 7, 1974, p. 47.

25. The Central Selling Organization purchases diamonds and undertakes the market risks. To some extent the CSO may be successful because of consumer cooperation, at least in its gem sales: "its commodity is 'a pure luxury,' and one which, whatever its real qualities, people esteem largely because it *is* so expensive." "Diamond OPEC," *West Africa,* May 27, 1974, p. 627.

Illustrative Agreement

The agreement set forth below is intended to be illustrative of the type of contract that might be negotiated for the development of hard minerals. It indicates solutions that policymakers, negotiators, and draftsmen have formulated when faced with the problem of preparing a hard-mineral agreement.

It should be clear from what has been said before in this book that it is impossible to develop a model agreement that can be used at all times, in all places, for all minerals. In Chapter 1 we argue that the division of rewards will depend on the structure of the industry involved and the relative bargaining positions of the host country and the company. Chapter 2 proposes that the agreement may take one of several forms, depending in large part on the political decision as to how much the host country must exercise control over—or participate in—the company's operations.

Yet many of the basic policy considerations of both major and minor importance tend to emerge irrespective of the industry involved, the relative bargaining positions of the parties, or the form of agreement that the host country desires. The purpose of our illustrative agreement is to provide a starting point for the consideration of the issues that should be dealt with. If it serves merely as a checklist of provisions and policy considerations and an illustration of the interrelationship of various provisions, it will have served an important function.

We hope that this agreement will enable those charged with writing concession contracts to save valuable time in the drafting of provisions so that more attention can be paid to matters of policy rather than to the task of simply putting something on paper. And, indeed, there are at least *some* provisions—such as those relating to the submission of reports—that can be regarded as more or less standard and do not merit much further creative draftsmanship. In fact, no actual agreement is likely to be as long as our illustration. We have attempted to err on the side of covering many issues so that the negotiator can view the range of possibilities. The length of a particular agreement would reflect the state of the laws of general application in the host country and, to an extent, the legal traditions of that country and perhaps the home country of the investor. In many cases ten pages will suffice; in others, twenty or thirty may be required.

In structuring the agreement we have begun with an essentially standard form of concession, as opposed, for example, to a production-sharing or management contract format. We have, however, incorporated a number of innovations in the standard form which reflect recent trends in concession arrangements and which indicate the way in which concepts of principal-contractor, government participation in ownership of the operating company, and government participation in elements of the mineral development decision process can be melded together in a relatively simple fashion. The agreement deals with the various contractual relationships in such a manner that the implications of these relationships should become clear to all parties.

Since it is difficult to draft an agreement appropriate for all minerals, we have elected to take copper as the subject mineral and to assume that the host country is a new entrant in the copper industry. The agreement should be read in the light of comments on developments in the copper industry set forth in Chapter 1.

The model is structured on the assumption that the authority to enter mineral development agreements has been vested by the government in a state corporation (which we have termed here the National Mineral Development Corporation or NMDC) in which the government owns all the equity. This governmental arrangement is similar to that existing, for example, in Indonesia, where Pertamina—the state oil company—has power to enter into petroleum-development agreements with private companies, or in Lesotho, where the Lesotho National Development Corporation has the authority to carry out projects for the development of natural resources.

We have also assumed that, in accordance with national policy, the National Mineral Development Corporation has a 25 percent interest in United Copper Associates Joint Venture Company (UCAC), the locally incorporated company that will carry out the actual operations on behalf of NMDC, and that the balance of shares in UCAC is owned by a foreign corporation, Foreign Overseas Investors, Inc.

NMDC will receive dividends from UCAC in accordance with rights attaching to its equity ownership and will have representation on UCAC's board of directors. Provisions relating to NMDC's dividend rights and board representation might more usually appear in a separate contract, the NMDC—Foreign Overseas Investors, Inc. joint venture agreement. For convenience, and because the issues involved in the rights attaching to equity ownership and representation are of peculiar importance, we have included provisions relating to these issues in Part IV of the contract.

Although the power to grant mining rights is vested in NMDC, the government is made a party to the agreement so that provision can be made for direct payment of taxes to the government treasury, and also because there are certain‾ rights and obligations that attach to the government as distinct from NMDC (whether NMDC is to pay taxes on its income will normally be dealt with in the law establishing the state enterprise).

Figure A-1 diagrams the relationships among the parties involved in the illustrative agreement.

Variations on this structure are, of course, possible. A payment in lieu of taxes could be made to NMDC. This has been the practice in oil contracts in Indonesia, where payments have been made to Pertamina rather than to the government treasury. As another variation, the rights and obligations running to and from the government could be made the subject of an independent agreement between the government and UCAC. The 1971 Lesotho Maluti diamond concession arrangement, for example, is structured on: (1) a basic agreement between the government of Lesotho and Maluti Diamond Corporation (the operating company)—including such matters as income tax, employment, infrastructure, and repatriation of profits; and (2) an "Operating Agreement" between the Lesotho National Development Corporation and Maluti Diamond Corporation.

We have characterized the relationship between NMDC and UCAC as one between principal and contractor. The contractor label, as we have noted earlier, has some political appeal in that it reinforces the appearance, at least, of the government's control over its natural resources. The contractor characterization is one to which a number of countries are moving. Possible variations are: (1) the straight grant of concession (in which the concessionaire is given a right to the minerals in the ground as opposed to our format in which the company has a right to the minerals only after extraction and subject to the right of the government to take payment in kind); and (2) the use of a management contract whereby the contractor receives not the profits from the sale of the minerals but a commission based on net profits. The straight grant form is found in Ethiopian and Liberian agreements and is widely used elsewhere. The management contract device is used for copper contracts in Zambia and Zaire.

Part IV of the agreement incorporates provisions relating to stock ownership in the joint venture company (UCAC), representation of NMDC on the board of directors of UCAC, provision for the unanimous vote of the board of directors on certain matters, and provision for increasing ownership of equity over the 25-year term of the agreement.

Part V of the agreement includes provisions relating to income tax and other payments to the government. As we have structured the agreement, no royalty or tax payments will be made by UCAC to NMDC. NMDC will, of course, have a right to dividend payments from UCAC in its capacity as a shareholder in UCAC.

Several fiscal provisions deserve emphasis:

1. Special pricing provisions are included for the calculation of gross income.

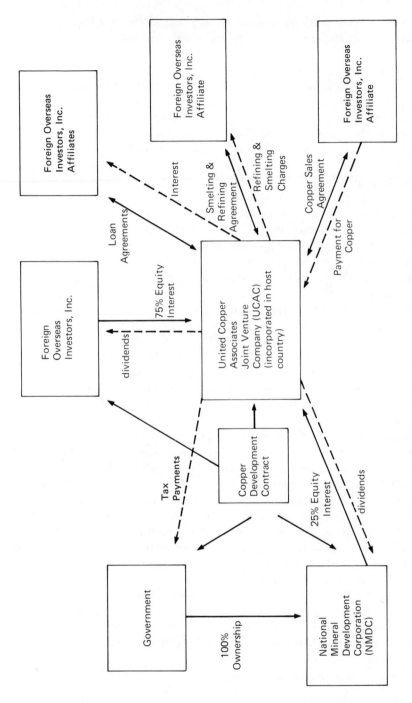

Figure A-1. Copper Development Project.

It is assumed for the purposes of this agreement that all or most of the company's sales of concentrates will be to affiliated parties. It has been necessary, therefore, to: (1) establish the principle that the sales price shall be deemed to be that which would govern transactions between independent parties; and (2) define how the independent or market price is to be established.

2. It has also been necessary to establish the principle that the costs of purchases from, and charges by, affiliated entities shall be deemed to be prices that would have been charged by independent parties. These costs relate not only to purchases of equipment, and payment of interest, rents, commissions, and fees, but also to the calculation of smelting and refining charges in the calculation of gross income. "Affiliate" is defined in Part I.

3. A special formula is included for calculating an acceptable debt-to-equity ratio for the purposes of allowing an interest deduction on loans. It is assumed, for the purposes of this agreement, that all or most of company's capital (excluding NMDC's contribution) will be from affiliates.

4. We assume for purposes of this agreement that the general income tax law does not deal sufficiently with problems of calculating gross and net income, and that some special provisions for the definition and calculation of gross and net income are necessary. It is also assumed that the general law (whether it is the income tax law or the mining concessions law) permits the inclusion of such special provisions in the contract. As developing countries adopt more sophisticated income tax laws, the need for special provisions becomes less acute. At least, however, those involved in the concessions process should determine that the various provisions in our Part V of the agreement are dealt with either in the general law or the agreement itself.

5. No provision for a general tax holiday or other investment incentive relating to mining activities is included in the agreement, since such matters are normally covered by an investment incentive act that defines the limits of offering tax incentives. We do, however, suggest a possible provision for granting tax incentives for the establishment of processing facilities, since this raises special problems of calculating the gross income from the processing operation. It is clear that tax incentives should not, in any case, be offered automatically (unless this is required by general legislation). (See the discussion below page 228.) Such matters as tax and royalty rates are also beyond the scope of the agreement, because they will either be established by general legislation or will be the subject of negotiations. It should be noted that, for reasons set forth in Chapter 3, deductions should not normally be the subject of negotiation.

Three types of dispute-settling and conflict-avoidance provisions are included. Provisions for relinquishment of land area and increasing equity participation by NMDC over time operate automatically. With regard to the tax and royalty structure, provision is made for review at periodic intervals. If unresolved conflict arises concerning revision or the economic feasibility of the establishment of processing facilities, these matters are subject to arbitration. Finally, provision is made for the traditional review of questions of interpretation and enforcement by an arbitral tribunal.

Comment on the content and function of various sections is included, in italics, at the beginning of each Part.

COPPER DEVELOPMENT AGREEMENT in respect of the
_____ Copper Project

between

The Government of _____ , and The _____ National
Mineral Development Corporation

and

Foreign Overseas Investors, Inc., and United Copper
Associates Joint Venture Company

Date:

INDEX TO CLAUSES

Preamble (Parties to Agreement)

Part XVIII: Settlement of Disputes

61. Method of Dispute-Settlement

Part XIX: Review of Contract Terms

62. Fiscal Provisions
63. General Review

Part XX: Domicile; Service of Process

64. General
65. Notices

Part XXI: Assignment

66. General

Part XXII:Agreement Period

67. General

Part XXIII: Right of Renewal of Agreement

68. General

Part XXIV: Governing Law

69. General

[Additional Provisions: Comment]

SCHEDULES

First Schedule—Contract Area.
Second Schedule—Map of Contract Area.
Third Schedule—Reports to Be Submitted.
    1. Reports to the Government and NMDC and Records to be Maintained
    2. Reports to be Confidential; Cost of Reports
    3. Inspection
    4. Exploration and Exploitation Reports

COPPER DEVELOPMENT AGREEMENT—[————]
COPPER PROJECT

This agreement is made this ____ day of ____, 19__ between the Government of _____ and the _____ National Mineral Development Corporation, parties of the first part, and Foreign Overseas Investors, Inc., and United Copper Associates Joint Venture Company, parties of the second part.

Whereas

(A) The United Copper Associates Joint Venture Company (hereinafter referred to as the Company) has applied to the National Mineral Development Corporation (hereinafter referred to as NMDC) under the (19— Mining Rights Act) for a copper development agreement in respect of certain lands specified in the First Schedule to this Agreement and has filed with NMDC a security deposit, assuring the due and faithful carrying out by the Company of the Company's obligations under this Agreement; and

(B) The Government and NMDC have agreed to enter into a copper development agreement with the Company,

The parties agree as follows:

PART I: DEFINITIONS

[Part I includes definitions of terms that are used frequently throughout the agreement or demand special attention.

Since many of the company's transactions may be expected to be with affiliated entities, a special definition of Affiliated Party is provided, together with a special definition of Control (which forms part of the Affiliated Party definition). The term Affiliated Party is used particularly in Part V with reference to the power of the Department of Finance to reallocate income and alter deductions for the purpose of calculating net taxable income.

The Agreement Period is defined as the term of the agreement set forth in Part XXII (twenty-five years), with the provision that the company's obligations extend beyond the term as defined in Part XXII if it has any obligations outstanding. It should be noted that, while the Agreement Period extends for twenty-five years, there are provisions for: (1) NMDC to gain total control of the company over the twenty-five-year period through increasing share ownership (Part IV); and (2) for review of fiscal and other provisions at stated intervals (Part XIX). Without these particular provisions, the host country might prefer to have a shorter agreement period with rights of renewal on renegotiated terms.

The Associated Minerals definition is important in restricting the types of minerals that can be mined under the agreement. In effect, the company is

restricted to mining copper, gold, silver, and such minor minerals as are commonly associated with copper. The term Associated Mineral is used in Part II, relating to the grant of rights to mine.

The Date of the Agreement is the starting point for many of the company's obligations and for the term of the agreement. The agreement extends for twenty-five years from the Date of the Agreement. Minimum working and expenditure obligations extend from the same date. If parliamentary or other approval is needed after signing before the contract becomes effective, the parties may wish to use the date of contract approval as the threshold date for obligations and rights.

Since this agreement involves the rights and obligations of the government and NMDC, special care must be given in specifying the agency that is to perform particular acts or to which the company owes particular duties. In some cases the host country draftsmen may wish to specify particular departments or ministries in place of the general term Government. In particular the agreement should specify the departments to which reports must be submitted.]

1. Meaning of Expressions in Agreement

In this Agreement the following expressions (except where the context otherwise requires) shall have the following meanings:

(a) *Affiliate, Affiliated Party,* or *Affiliated Parties*

    (i) Any corporation in which the Company holds 5% or more of the stock or which holds 5% or more of the Company's stock. A corporation affiliated by the same definition to an affiliated corporation of the Company is itself considered an Affiliate of the Company for the purpose of this Agreement;

    (ii) Any company which, directly or indirectly, is controlled by or controls, or is under common control with the company; or

    (iii) Any shareholder or group of shareholders of the Company or of any Affiliate and any individual or group of individuals in the employ of the Company or any Affiliate.

        For the purposes of this paragraph and the definition of Control, below, "company" and "companies" shall include corporations, partnerships, unincorporated associations, firms, and companies.

(b) *Agreement* or *this Agreement:* This contract, the Schedules thereto and any amendments agreed upon by the parties.

(c) *Agreement Period:* The term as set forth in Part XXII of this Agreement subject to the continuation of rights and obligations provided for in Part XVI of this agreement.

(d) *Associated Minerals:* those minerals of minor commercial significance commonly found in association with copper ore. In the event of disagreement between the Company and the Federal Government as to what constitutes an Associated Mineral, the Government's judgment shall prevail.

(e) *Contract Area:* That land area described in the First Schedule to this Agreement.

(f) *Control:* The possession, directly or indirectly, of the power to direct or cause the direction of the management and policies of a company exercised by any other company where a series of companies can be specified beginning with the parent company or companies and ending with the particular company, in which each company of the series, except the parent company or companies, is directly or indirectly controlled by one or more of the companies in the series.

(g) *The Company:* The United Copper Associates Joint Venture Company organized under the laws of [the host country], or its successor in interest.

(h) *Date of this Agreement:* The date on which this Agreement is signed by the parties.

(i) *The Government:* The Government of [the host country].

(j) *Income Tax Act, 19–:* The Income Tax Act, 19– (or its successor) as from time to time amended and in effect.

(k) *Market Value of the Ore:* The price ruling of the users' market, as defined in Section 25(c).

(l) *Mining Production Day:* the first day of commercial production from the mine.

(m) *The Mining Rights Act, 19–:* The Mining Rights Act, 19–, (or its successor), as from time to time amended and in effect.

(n) *The Minister of Mines* or *Ministry of Mines:* The Minister of Mines or Ministry of Mines of [the host country].

(o) *NMDC:* The National Mineral Development Company of [the host country], organized under the National Mineral Development Company Act, 1970.

(p) *The Project:* The Company's total operations under this Agreement.

(q) *The Project Facilities:* Facilities defined in Part VII of this Agreement.

(r) *Smelting Production Day:* The first day of commercial production from the smelter.

PART II: GRANT OF OPERATING RIGHTS

[The company is made a contractor to NMDC. Other possible relationships are discussed in Chapter 2.

The agreement grants the right to exploit only "copper and gold and silver and other Associated Minerals." Associated Minerals is defined in Part I. The company must report the discovery of any other minerals and must make a special application for the right to exploit these minerals or timber.

Note that Part VIII grants the company the right to use timber, water, stone, gravel, sand, and clay free of charge for purposes of the project.

Under this Part the company has a right of first refusal, in effect, with regard to exploiting other minerals (under new terms), but the government reserves the right to grant a lease to and/or enter into an agreement with another company if an agreement is not reached with this company. The government also reserves its own right of access to the contract area to make its own investigations.]

2. General: Appointment of Company as Sole Contractor

(a) In consideration of the Company's obligations under this agreement, NMDC hereby appoints the Company as the sole contractor for NMDC to conduct all of the operations hereinafter described, for the term set forth in Part XXII, and in relation to the Contract Area described in the First Schedule and in relation to such other areas as may be approved by NMDC.

(b) The Company shall, as sole contractor, (i) search for and mine copper and gold and silver and other Associated Minerals within the Contract Area, (ii) concentrate, smelt, and otherwise process such minerals within the Contract Area or elsewhere as specifically approved by NMDC and the Government, and (iii) subject to Section 25, relating to the determination of the prices of copper, gold, and silver, Section 42 relating to shipping, and Section 24 relating to the right of the Federal Government to the payment in kind, transport or sell or otherwise dispose of such minerals abroad.

3. Exploitation of Other Minerals or Other Natural Resources

In the event that any other mineral or natural resource is discovered in the Contract Area and the Company wishes to mine, develop, or otherwise exploit such mineral or other natural resource, the Company shall apply to NMDC for an additional agreement, or amendment to this Agreement to develop such mineral or other natural resource. Provided, however, that if, after six months from the date of such application, NMDC and the Company fail to reach an agreement with regard to the exploration and exploitation of such mineral or other natural resource, NMDC shall have the right to negotiate and conclude such an agreement with a third party.

4. Third-Party Agreements

In the event that NMDC enters into an agreement with a third party for the exploration and exploitation of some mineral or other resource within the

Contract Area other than those which are the subject of this Agreement, NMDC will exercise all reasonable precaution to minimize the impact of such third-party activities on the activities and operations of the Company under this Agreement. NMDC will also require that such third party or parties make fair and reasonable compensation to the Company for any loss of property rights sustained as a result of the establishment of additional operations and for any unamortized development costs to the extent that such development costs can be reasonably related to the discovery of such other mineral or other resources.

5. Government Right of Access

The Government and NMDC reserve the right of access to the Contract Area for the purpose of any subsoil investigation (or other reasonable investigation) they wish to make, provided that if damage results to the Company's property from such investigation, the Government and NMDC agree to provide fair and reasonable compensation to the Company for such damage.

6. Report of Discovery of Other Minerals

The Company shall, forthwith on the discovery of any mineral of economic value other than those minerals for which this Agreement is made, report in writing the discovery of such mineral to the Chairman of the NMDC.

PART III: COMPANY OBLIGATIONS

[This Part sets forth the company's major obligations relating to:

1. *Scientific methods of development.*
2. *Use of safety devices and precautions.*
3. *Fire prevention.*
4. *Pollution control (disposal of overburdens and tailings).*
5. *Commencement of operations.*
6. *Minimum expenditures.*
7. *The delivery of a guaranty bond if the company fails in its obligations relating to expenditures.*
8. *Submission of a performance bond at the outset of the agreement.*
9. *The relinquishment of sections of the contract area.*
10. *The establishment of a smelter if such establishment is economically feasible.*
11. *The submission of detailed reports (as specified in the Third Schedule).*

Note that Section 12, relating to minimum expenditures, does not permit inclusion of general overhead expenses that might be incurred in the home office.

In agreements where activities are divided into several distinct phases, it is usually appropriate to have minimum working obligations and expenditure obligations for each stage. Some agreements divide stages as follows: prospecting, construction, mining operations, processing.

Section 14 includes a test for determining the economic feasibility of establishing processing facilities, and requires that the standards for such tests, as set by an international agency, be used. Note that Part V includes an optional tax holiday provision relating to the establishment of smelting operations. (See Part XIII, Section 49, relating to the use of local processing facilities.) The test for establishing economic feasibility is discussed in Chapter 4.]

7. Responsibility: Scientific Exploration and Exploitation

(a) The Company accepts the rights and obligations to conduct operations and activities in accordance with the terms of this Agreement. The Company shall conduct all such operations and activities in a good and technical manner in accordance with good and acceptable international mining engineering standards and practices and in accordance with modern and accepted scientific and technical principles applicable to mining copper ore and to beneficiating, smelting, and manufacturing operations. All operations and activities under this Agreement shall be conducted so as to avoid waste or loss of natural resources, to protect natural resources against unnecessary damage, and to prevent pollution and contamination of the environment.

(b) The Company shall take all necessary measures to prevent and control fires and shall notify immediately the proper governmental authorities of any fire that may occur.

(c) The Company shall take measures to prevent damage to the rights and property of the Government or third parties. In the event of negligence or carelessness on the part of the Company or its agents or of any subcontractor carrying on operations or activities for the Company under this Agreement, they shall be liable for such injuries in accordance with the laws of [host country] generally applicable.

(d) The Company shall install and utilize such internationally recognized modern safety devices and shall observe such internationally recognized modern safety precautions as are provided and observed under conditions and operations comparable to those undertaken by the Company under this Agreement.

(e) The Company shall likewise observe internationally recognized modern measures for the protection of the general health and safety of its employees and of all other persons having legal access to the area covered by this Agreement. The Company shall comply with such instructions as may from time to time be given in writing by the Chief Inspector of Mines.

(f)   Insofar as such obligations are not otherwise covered by the terms of this Agreement, the Company shall comply with the terms of The Mining Rights Act, 19— and all other mining laws and regulations, from time to time in effect in [host country].

8. Overburden and Tailings

(a)   The Company shall not dispose of any overburden removed in the course of, or any tailings produced as a result of, its operations under this Agreement in an area or in a manner not previously approved for that purpose pursuant to the provisions of this Section, it being intended that such overburden and tailings shall be disposed of in a manner which is reasonably safe and results in as little damage or disturbance to the environment (having regard always to the need for the Company to carry out its said operations efficiently and economically) as possible.

(b)   The Company may at any time and from time to time hereafter submit to the Ministry of Mines a proposal for the disposal of such overburden and tailings, setting out the area or areas and manner in which it is proposed to dispose of the same. Forthwith upon receipt of such proposal the Ministry of Mines shall consider the same (having regard to the factors mentioned in paragraph (a) of this Section) and shall within two months of such receipt either—

   (i)   notify the Company that its proposal has been approved either without modification or with such modifications as are set out in the notification; or

   (ii) submit to the Company an alternative approved proposal for the disposal of the said overburden and tailings, setting out the area or areas and manner in which the same are to be disposed of thereunder.

(c)   In the event that the Ministry of Mines does not approve the Company's proposal without modification, the Company may at any time thereafter refer to arbitration as hereinafter provided in this Agreement the question of the disposal of the said overburden and tailings. Upon such arbitration the arbitrator or arbitrators shall have regard to the factors mentioned in paragraph (a) of this Section and shall either approve the Company's proposal or approve that of the Ministry of Mines in either case with modifications as he or they consider proper.

(d)   Notwithstanding that the same may have been disposed of in an area and in a manner approved as hereinbefore provided in this Section, the Company shall make compensation for any loss suffered by any indigenous or other local inhabitant resulting from any damage done (whether to land, anything on land, water, or otherwise) or any interference with any right to use land or water caused by the disposal by the Company of any overburden removed in the course of, or tailings produced as a result of, its operations under this Agreement.

(e) The Company shall not, save as is hereinbefore provided in this Section, be liable for any loss, damage, disturbance, or interference caused by the disposal of the Company of any of the said overburden or tailings and, save as aforesaid, neither the Government nor any governmental authority or person shall be entitled to any remedy in respect thereof. Nothing in this paragraph shall exclude any liability for negligence.

(f) In addition to complying with the present provisions of Mining Rights Act, 19–, as amended and other laws of general application relating to safety and protection, the Company:

(i) shall, when any dump for overburden and tailings established by it for the purpose of its operations under this Agreement ceases to be utilized for such purpose, ensure that in order to facilitate the rapid regeneration of vegetation thereon such dump is left with a reasonably flat upper surface; and

(ii) shall, within a reasonable time after any such dump ceases to be utilized as aforesaid, carry out experiments for the determination of whether vegetation can be established thereon and use its best endeavours to establish thereon vegetation of a type which can be so established.

But the Company shall not be required to do any further or other acts or carry out any furthur or other works for the rehabilitation or restoration of any of the areas affected by its operations under this Agreement.

9. Use of Subcontractors

The Company will have control and management of all of its activities under this Agreement and will have full responsibility therefor and assume all risks thereof in accordance with the terms and conditions of this Agreement. Without in any way detracting from the Company's responsibilities and obligations hereunder, the Company may engage subcontractors, whether or not Affiliates of the Company, for the execution of such phases of its operations as the Company deems appropriate. The records of such subcontractors shall be made available to the Government and NMDC inspectors as provided in Schedule Three.

10. Cooperation by Government

NMDC, the Government and all its agencies will cooperate fully with the Company and will grant it all necessary rights and will take such other action as may be desirable to achieve the mutual objectives of this Agreement.

11. Commencement of Program

The Company shall begin a program to commence as soon as possible following the Date of this Agreement, but no later than six months from the Date of this Agreement, to consist of construction of facilities for the project, exploitation activities, and operation of the project.

12. Working Obligations and Minimum Expenditures

(a)   The Company shall, within (three) years of the Date of this Agreement, spend in [host country] not less than $＿＿ per acre of land held in the Contract Area for expenses directly connected with the Company's operations and activities under this Agreement. Such expenses may not include general organizational overhead and administrative expenses incurred abroad.

(b)   If at the expiration of (18 months) from the Date of this Agreement or any time thereafter it appears to NMDC that the Company has seriously neglected its obligations with respect to minimum expenditures as provided in this Section, NMDC may require the Company to deliver a guarantee in the form of a bond or banker's guarantee in a sum which shall not exceed the total outstanding expenditure obligations remaining unfulfilled. Such guarantee may at the end of the said three-year period be forfeited to NMDC to the extent that the Company may have failed to fulfill its expenditure obligations.

(c)   In connection with the Company's obligations under this Part, the Company shall submit to NMDC within two months from the expiration of (eighteen months) from the Date of this Agreement a report setting forth the items and amounts of expenditures during the said eighteen-month period. In addition, the Company shall submit to NMDC within two months from the expiration of (three) years from the Date of this Agreement a report setting forth the items and amounts of expenditures during the said (three) year period. The Company shall support such reports with documentation.

(d)   The Company shall submit to NMDC as security for performance of its obligations under this Agreement a bank letter of credit in the amount of (Five hundred thousand U.S. dollars) (U.S. $500,000) within 30 days of the Date of this Agreement.

Fifty percent of said security deposit shall be released and put at the disposal of the Company after the expiration of twelve months from the Date of the Agreement if NMDC is satisfied that the Company has satisfactorily performed its obligations under this Agreement.

The remaining 50 percent of the security shall be released and put at the disposal of the Company at the expiration of the second twelve-month period from the date of this Agreement if NMDC is satisfied that the Company has satisfactorily performed its obligations under this Agreement.

In the event that the Company defaults in the making of minimum expenditure or in undertaking its working obligations or prematurely terminates its operations, or fails to make payments required under this Agreement to NMDC or the Government, or otherwise defaults in its obligations, all or part of such security deposit shall be forfeited to the Government or NMDC, as the case may be, in accordance with the penalty provisions of Part XV of this Agreement.

13. Relinquishment

(a) Subject to the Company's obligations and liabilities under this Agreement, the Company may by written notice to NMDC relinquish all or any part of the Contract Area at any time during the Agreement Period.

(b) The Company shall, after consultation with NMDC, relinquish, within one year of the Mining Production Day, all land within the Contract Area which the parties determine is not needed by the Company for its exploration and exploitation activities under this Agreement.

14. Processing Facilities: Economic Feasibility Test

(a) Within —— years from the Date of this Agreement the Company shall establish processing, smelting, and manufacturing facilities, hereinafter referred to as Processing Facilities, in [the host country] if then found economically feasible. The parties agree to consider jointly this economic feasibility at the end of each three year period following the Date of this Agreement. If and when any of such processing facilities are constructed, the parties agree to discuss thereafter and consider, in good faith, the feasibility of subsequent additional processing facilities which may be in the form of increases in the capacity of then existing facilities or the establishment of facilities previously not in existence.

The test for establishing the economic feasibility of establishing Processing Facilities in [the host country] shall meet the standards for such tests as set by [the World Bank] [the U.S. Agency for International Development]. In considering the economic feasibility of establishing Processing Facilities, the parties shall consider the economic viability of establishing such facilities, including a fair rate of return on investment to the Company, and the potential contribution that the establishment of such facilities may make to the economic development and general welfare of [the host country]. In no event shall the test for economic feasibility be limited to a comparison of the projected profitability to Foreign Overseas Investors, Inc. of the investment in such facilities in [the host country] with investment in such facilities in another country.

(b) Every three years following the Date of this Agreement, the Company shall submit to NMDC copies of studies relating to the feasibility of establishing processing facilities in the [host country]. Such studies shall meet the standards set by [the World Bank] [the Agency for International Development] for such feasibility studies made by independent evaluators.

15. Reports

The Company shall submit reports as provided in the Third Schedule to this Agreement.

PART IV: THE JOINT VENTURE RELATIONSHIP

[This part includes provisions concerning the joint venture relationship between NMDC and Foreign Overseas Investors, Inc. As noted earlier, these provisions might more appropriately become part of a separate, and more detailed, joint venture agreement between these two parties. Included here are provisions relating to the proportional equity ownership to be held by the two parties and the methods by which payment for the shares is to be financed. Section 16 suggests the following modes of payment for NMDC's shares: 40 percent to be granted NMDC outright as a premium for the granting of the contract to the company; 20 percent to be paid for by NMDC in cash within a fixed number of months; and 40 percent to be paid for out of future dividends.

Section 17 provides a schedule for increasing equity ownership for NMDC over a twenty-five-year period. Section 18 defines the process by which the price of shares is to be determined. We have opted here for a formula based on actual market value as determined by an independent arbitrator. Other fixed standards, such as book value or cost of assets, could be used. Each formula, of course, has different cost implications. Section 20 provides for proportional board representation and includes a list of subjects requiring the vote of a special majority.

Only a few of the more important provisions that might appear in a full-fledged joint venture agreement are included here.]

16. Equity Ownership in Joint Venture Company

(a) The initial equity capital in UCAC shall be owned in the following proportions—NMDC: 25 percent; Foreign Overseas Investors, Inc.: 75 percent.

(b) The cost of NMDC's initial shares in the Company shall be paid for as follows:

(i)   40 percent of NMDC's initial 25 percent shareholding shall be granted to NMDC in consideration of its granting the mining and exploitation rights referred to in this agreement.

(ii) 20 percent of NMDC's initial 25 percent shareholding shall be paid for by NMDC within ____ months of the signing of the agreement.

(iii) 40 percent of NMDC's initial 25 percent shareholding shall be paid out of future dividends received by NMDC from the Company's operations under this agreement. Provided, however, that at least 75 percent of NMDC's dividends each year shall be used for the purpose of paying for said shares until the cost of the shares is fully paid.

(c)   The cost of the initial shares to be held by Foreign Overseas Investors, Inc. shall be paid for as follows:

(i)   cash in the amount of U.S. $ _____.

(ii) equipment valued at U.S. $ _____.

17. Changes in Ownership Structure

The parties agree that it shall be the policy of the Company that at the end of (25) years, or before, 100 percent of the equity ownership of the Company shall be held by NMDC and/or the Government, and/or [host country] nationals.

To this end, the parties agree that Foreign Overseas Investors shall transfer its equity shares to NMDC or its nominee so that total authorized equity shall be held in accordance with the following schedule:

	First Party	*Second Party*
Initial share ownership	25%	75%
8 years from date of incorporation	30%	70%
15 years from date of incorporation	50%	50%
20 years from date of incorporation	70%	30%
25 years from date of incorporation	100%	0%

With regard to the foregoing provision, it is agreed that, if the NMDC is unwilling or unable to purchase shares as scheduled, such shares shall be offered to [host country] nationals.

[For joint ventures in which the foreign partner may continue to provide access to overseas markets or may continue to provide technology (neither of which the local partner can otherwise obtain access to) the following provision might be used:

The parties agree that it shall be the policy of the Company that at the end of (15) years, or before, 49 percent of the equity ownership of the Company shall be held by NMDC and that NMDC shall at the end of (15) years have the option to purchase additional shares from the Second Party in accordance with the following schedule:

	First Party	Second Party
Initial shares ownership	*25%*	*75%*
5 years from date of incorporation	*30%*	*70%*
10 years from date of incorporation	*49%*	*51%*
15 years from date of incorporation	*70%*	*30%*
20 years from date of incorporation	*100%*	*0%*

Provided, however, that should NMDC exercise its option, after the 10th year from date of incorporation, to purchase shares in excess of 50 percent, the Second Party shall have an option to require that the First Party purchase the Second Party's total equity ownership.]

18. Payment for Shares
(a)   NMDC shall pay for shares purchased from Foreign Overseas Investors in cash or out of future dividends received from the Company.
(b)   If NMDC elects to pay for the shares from future dividends, [75 percent] of the dividends to which NMDC is entitled each year shall be used as a credit against its outstanding obligation to Foreign Overseas Investors until such shares are fully paid for.

The price of shares sold by Foreign Overseas Investors to NMDC shall be [the actual market value] as determined by an [independent accountant] [arbitrator] selected by mutual agreement by the parties. In determining the actual market value of such shares the [arbitrator] shall take into account, as one element, a price formula based on 10 times the pro-rata annual profit based on the previous [3] year's earnings. The prices of shares shall be paid in the currency of _____

[Other possibilities include a price based on the book value of the shares or the original cost of the assets.]

19. Transfer of Shares
Neither party shall sell, pledge, or otherwise dispose of its shares in the Company to other parties without the prior written consent of the other party to this Agreement.

**20. Direction and Management of the
    Joint Company**
(a)   The Company shall have a Board of Directors consisting of ____ directors. Initially ____ of the directors shall be nominated by the NMDC and ___ of the directors shall be nominated by Foreign Overseas Investors. Each party shall vote all of its shares for the election and main-

tenance in office of the persons so nominated and for persons nominated by the two parties at subsequent elections. The Chairman of the Board of Directors shall be elected by the directors jointly.

(b) The initial representation of the parties on the Board of Directors shall reflect the initial proportions of equity owned by each party.

(c) Representation on the Board shall always be proportional to the ownership of shares held by each party, provided, however, that neither party shall ever have less than ____ representatives on the Board.

(d) All decisions of the Board of Directors, other than the categories of decisions listed in paragraph (e) of this section, shall require an affirmative vote of at least 51 percent of the directors.

(e) All decisions relating to the matters listed below shall require an affirmative vote of a special majority of the total number of the members of the Board of Directors. Such special majority shall be at least ____.
[This figure will be the total number of directors representing the party with the largest number of nominees on the Board plus one.]
Decisions requiring the vote of a special majority are those relating to:
 (i) increase or decrease in authorized capital;
 (ii) transfer of shares;
 (iii) the sale of a substantial portion of the assets of the Company;
 (iv) the issue of new shares;
 (v) the choice of and terms of employment of auditors for the Company;
 (vi) appointment and terms of employment of officers of the Company;
 (vii) dividend policy;
 (viii) changes in this Agreement;
 (ix) contracts with any shareholder or any Affiliate of a shareholder;
 (x) the borrowing or lending of money or the guaranteeing of the debts of others.

21. Technical Committee

The representatives of NMDC on the Board of Directors of UCAC will be assisted by a Technical Committee selected by NMDC. Such Committee shall have the same access to information relevant to the operations and activities of UCAC as members of the board of directors have. In particular, the Technical Committee shall have the same access to reports and accounts, and right of inspection, as provided for NMDC in the Third Schedule to this Agreement.

22. Dividends Policy

[The government and NMDC may wish to include here a provision requiring the company to pay out a certain percentage of profits each year as dividends. The wisdom of such a provision will depend in part on business judgments and whether profits in early years should be used for expansion or otherwise.]

PART V: TAXATION

[It is assumed in this part that the Company's income tax liability is governed by an Income Tax Act. Note that the Income Tax Act is defined in Part I as "the Income Tax Act, 19– as from time to time amended and in effect." This means that the tax rates and provisions governing this Agreement are not frozen and may be altered to the extent that the general income tax law is amended. Practice in other countries varies as to whether the income tax rates and terms are frozen for the whole or part of the term of the contract. Increasingly, at a minimum, contracts are including provisions requiring the parties to renegotiate financial provisions after the lapse of a certain period. (See Part XIX of this agreement). No attempt is made here to spell out the various deductions that might be taken from gross income. This problem is discussed in detail in Chapter 3.

There is a provision that allows the government to take payment of taxes in the form of ore. The value of this ore is to be calculated at a value no higher than would result from the methods used by the company in the preceding year. Thus, if the company prices ore at low prices to its affiliates, the government can also receive ore at that price. So there is an incentive for the company to use fair prices.

In addition to the income tax, provision is made (1) for the imposition of a copper tax of general applicability to the copper industry, should such a tax be enacted; and (2) an export tax on net income before tax. In part VI we suggest the possibility of imposing additional financial obligations: a nonrefundable premium (see Part IV, Section 16(b)(i) for one possible premium device); a security deposit (see Part III, Section 12(d) for a suggested use of a performance bond in connection with minimum work and expenditure requirements); land rent; and royalty.

In connection with the determination of gross income and net taxable income we include special provisions relating to affiliate transactions (Section 25). With regard to the fictitious debt problem, we suggest a provision to cover the complicated situation in which affiliation is virtually impossible to decipher and include an optional provision for disallowance of interest paid to affiliates. The principle established is that the debt-to-equity ratio will not exceed common practice in the area. Then a specific limit is set. Other alternatives are discussed in Chapter 3.

It is assumed that the general income tax law includes appropriate provisions relating to the method of payment of tax and the documentation that must accompany tax payments (see Section 28).

While in Chapter 3 we recommend a careful consideration of the tax holiday problem, in some cases tax incentives for establishing processing facilities may be appropriate. In Section 27 we suggest one way of dealing with this problem. The section indicates how profits are to be divided between mining and smelt-

ing operations so that profits are not unfairly shifted into the tax-free smelting operations.

As noted earlier, this Part might more appropriately be the subject of a separate agreement between the government and the company.]

23. Taxation Based on Income

(a)   The Company shall, for the Agreement Period, pay to the Government an income tax in accordance with the provisions of this Agreement and the Income Tax Act, 19—; an export tax in accordance with the provisions of Subsection (b) below; and any other tax generally applicable to the copper industry which the Government may from time to time enact. Provided, however, that all such taxes shall be nondiscriminatory within the copper industry within [host country]. All such taxes shall be payable in respect of the Company's income arising from all mining, concentration, smelting, and refining and other operations carred out in [host country] or elsewhere in relation to the Company's activities under this Agreement.

(b)   The Company shall, for the Agreement Period, pay to the Government an export tax in the amount of [10 percent] of the Company's net income before tax, received from the sale or other disposal of copper and all Associated Minerals. Such net income before tax shall be calculated in accordance with the provisions of the Income Tax Act, 19—, and this Agreement in the same manner as the calculation of the tax provided for in paragraph (a) above.

(c)   Subject to the provision of Section 24 relating to payment in kind, payment of the export tax shall be made at the same time, and under the same terms and conditions, as provided for the payment of income tax under the Income Tax Act, 19—.

24. Government Election to Take Payment in Kind

(a)   The Government may, in lieu of any or all of the taxes prescribed in this Part, elect to receive a part of the copper concentrate mined by the Company. Such election may be made by the Government giving not less than four calendar months' notice to the Company, and when made shall continue for such period as was stated in the notice given by the Government. Delivery of copper which the Government has elected to take shall be effected at such times and points of delivery as may be agreed upon by the parties.

(b)   When the Government takes payment in kind, the Company shall be deemed to have paid taxes in an amount equal to the value of the ore delivered to the Government. The value of the ore delivered to the Government shall be calculated on the basis of the Market Value of the Ore where that market value will not exceed the market value arrived at by using the same principles that the Company used in calculating the market value of ore sold to its Affiliates during the taxable year preceding the year in which the Government takes payment in kind.

(c)   Any balance of taxes due with respect to the tax period in question shall become due and payable on the date set for payment of income tax under the Income Tax Act, 19–.

25. Gross Income and Net Income: Pricing, Deductions, Transactions with Affiliates

(a)   In the calculation of gross income under this Agreement and the Income Tax Act, 19–, the income from the sale or other disposal of ores, or concentrates or other products therefrom, shall be deemed to be the income obtained from the sale of such ores, or concentrates or other products when the price agreed upon is not less than that prevailing in the users' market for transactions covering similar qualities, quantities and time periods, less expenses, namely freight, insurance, and other shipping expenses and customs duties, necessary to place the products in the foreign markets.

(b)   If the price agreed upon should be below that ruling in the users' market, the latter price shall be applied to determine the income, less the expenses stated in the preceding paragraph.

(c)   The price ruling in the users' market for contained copper in ores, concentrates or other products, shall be based on the price at which the principal copper producers in non-Communist countries sell their principal production of electrolytic copper wirebars on period contracts, on the basis of delivery c.i.f. main European port to the major non-Affiliated European fabricators and consumers of copper (which price, as of the date of this Agreement, is the official London Metal Exchange cash seller's price for electrolytic copper wirebars), or, if wirebars cease to be the principal shape in which such producers sell, as aforesaid, their electrolytically refined copper, then the price at which they sell as aforesaid their principal production of the new principal shape plus or minus such premium or discount if any as is appropriate to adjust prices based on the new principal shape to prices based on wirebars.

(d)   The price ruling in the users' market for contained gold or silver shall be based on the price of gold or silver received by the principal smelters in _____ or on the basis of the gold and silver prices quoted on the free bullion market in London, whichever is higher.

(e)   To determine the value of the unit of ore or concentrate or other product ruling in the users' market, the contained copper, gold, and silver will be valued at the prices indicated in the previous two paragraphs, calculated as the average of the daily prices for the 30-day period immediately following the date of delivery of the ore, concentrate, or other product to the smelter. Such value will be reduced by the costs of smelting and/or refining required to convert the ore, concentrate, or other product to electrolytic copper wirebars.

(f) Smelting and refining charges shall not be in excess of the charges which would have applied had the transaction or transactions occurred between non-Affiliated parties.

(g) The burden of showing that the charges do not exceed the charges which would have applied between non-Affiliated parties shall be on the Company. As evidence of the appropriateness of the charges, the Company may submit copies of sales contracts under which major _____ smelters purchase from non-Affiliated suppliers ore, concentrate, or other products of comparable quality and quantity and under comparable conditions.

(h) Pursuant to the right of the Director General of Income Tax under Section ____ of the Income Tax Act, 19–, to reallocate income and to alter adjusted income with regard to transactions between persons one of whom has Control over the other, the Director General shall have the right to disallow, for the purposes of calculating net taxable income, payments made by the Company to Affiliate Parties. Such payments shall include, but shall not be limited to, payments of interest, rents, commissions, and fees.

[The following provisions impose restrictions on the rate and amount of interest that may be deducted. Reference should be made to the discussion, in Chapter 3, of interest payments to affiliates and the problem of fictitious debt. In most cases the policy of not recognizing debt paid to affiliates is the most appropriate one for developing countries. The following provisions cover the somewhat unique–and complicated–situation where, as in the case of Japanese investment, the degree of affiliation among companies and banks is such that affiliation is difficult to trace. In the case of such investors, a policy that differentiates between debts to affiliates and other debts may be impossible to administer.]

(i) For the purpose of this Agreement, interest paid by the Company on loans will be allowed as a deduction from gross income in the calculation of adjusted income. Provided, however, that a deduction for the payment of interest shall be permitted only to the extent that the rate of interest does not exceed the rate that would have been paid in a comparable transaction between non-Affiliated Parties. In no case shall the interest and other charges connected with the loan exceed the Central Bank discount rate in _____ plus 2.5 percent.

Provided further, that a deduction for interest shall be allowed only to the extent that the corresponding debt does not cause the ratio of debt to debt plus equity to exceed the ratio of senior debt to total indebtedness plus equity which is customary for the financing of comparable copper mining operations in [Southeast Asia and Oceania.]

(j)   The parties agree that the ratio of senior debt to total indebtedness plus equity which is customary for the financing of comparable copper mining operations in [Southeast Asia and Oceania] is, at the Date of this Agreement, [two to three].

(k)   In exercising his power to alter adjusted income, the Director General of Income Tax may, if similar services or goods could not normally be provided or sold by non-Affiliated parties, allow as deductions only the actual costs of the goods or services. The Company shall submit the calculation of such costs, with a description of the method employed in allocating overhead or other fixed costs to the goods or services.

26. Other Taxes, Charges, and Fees

The Company shall be free from all other taxation, charges, and fees payable to the Government or to any governmental authority in [the host country] in relation to such mining, concentration, smelting, or refining and other operations carried out in [host country] in relation to the Company's activities under this Agreement, excluding the following:

(a)   any premium, land rent, royalty, or other payment due to NMDC or the Government in accordance with the provisions of this Agreement;

(b)   taxes, charges, and fees for services rendered by governmental authorities on request or to the public or commercial enterprises generally, provided that such taxes, charges, and fees are reasonable and non-discriminatory;

(c)   subject to the provisions of Sections ____ and ____, taxes, fees, and charges of general application including, but not limited to, custom duties applicable under the Customs Act of 19–, as from time to time amended and in effect, stamp duties, registration fees, and license fees provided that they are at rates no higher than generally applicable in [the host country].

27. Tax and Duty Exemption

[In Chapter 3 we warn against the unnecessary use of tax incentives. If the host government, after careful analysis, decides that some incentive is necessary in connection with the establishment of processing facilities, the following type of provision might be used.]

The Company shall be exempt from the following payments for the period specified for each exemption:

[Pursuant to the Investment Incentives Act, 19–,] income taxes payable in respect of income resulting from any smelting and refining operations carried out in [the host country] in relation to minerals produced under this Agreement or any other mineral so processed in [the host country], for a period of [3] years commencing with the Company's Smelting Production Day.

In calculating the income resulting from any smelting or refining operations carried out by the Company in [the host country], the following formula shall be utilized:

The gross income from the smelter shall be based on the price of the contained commercial metals in the users' market less the costs of refining required to convert the product of the smelter to the finished metals and less the freight, insurance, and other shipping expenses and customs duties necessary to place the products in the foreign markets.

The net income from the smelter shall be the gross income less the value of the copper concentrate as calculated in Section 25 (a) through (d) and less the costs directly associated with the operation of the smelter. In calculating the costs directly associated with the smelter, there shall be assigned a proportional part of the total overhead connected with the operations of the Project Facilities provided for in this Agreement that shall not be less than the proportional part that the investment in the smelter represents in the total investment in the Project Facilities provided for in this Agreement.

28. Tax Returns and Accounting Procedures

(a) The Company shall submit accounting and income tax returns for the full term of this Agreement, including any periods of tax exemption, in accordance with the provisions of the Income Tax Act, 19–.

(b) Unless otherwise provided in this Agreement, the provisions of the Income Tax Act, 19–, shall govern the Company's liability for payment of income tax and export tax to the Government.

(c) In determining the Company's net taxable income as defined in the Income Tax Act, 19–, sound, consistent, and generally accepted accounting principles as usually used in the copper mining industry shall be employed, provided, however, that where more than one accounting practice is found by the Government to prevail with regard to any item, the Government shall determine which practice is to be applied by the Company with regard to the particular item.

(d) The Company shall maintain books of account stated in _____ currency in accordance with generally accepted accounting principles. All payments to the Government shall be calculated in [United States dollars] and paid in [United States dollars] or in such other currencies as may be mutually acceptable to the Company and the Ministry of Finance or any Government agency which is a successor in function thereto. The Company shall within a period as provided by the prevailing law and regulations furnish annually to the Government audited financial statements consisting of a balance sheet and statement of income prepared in accordance with generally accepted accounting principles together with production statistics in reasonable detail. The accounts shall be audited by a firm of accountants acceptable to the Government.

(e) The Company shall permit the Government, through a duly authorized representative, to inspect at all reasonable times the books of account and records of the Company relative to any shipment, sale, utilization, or other disposition of any ore. The Company shall take reasonable steps to satisfy the Government either by certificate of a competent independent party acceptable to the Government or otherwise to the satisfaction of the Government as to all weights and analyses of ore. Due regard shall be given to any objection or representation made by the Government as to any particular weight or assay of ore or other matter which may affect the amount of tax payable under this Agreement. The books of account and records of the Company referred to in this Section shall be maintained in the Company's _____ office.

(f) Notwithstanding any provision in the general company or tax law to the contrary, the Government shall have [7] years in which to complete its audits of Company accounts.

PART VI: OTHER FINANCIAL OBLIGATIONS

[Provision might be made here for one or more of the following: a nonrefundable premium *to be paid to NMDC (in consideration of the grant of the concession);* a security deposit *(to be forfeited if certain obligations are not met or to be credited against future tax or royalty obligations if obligations are met);* a land rent *based on a certain sum per acre;* a royalty, *based on value or unit of production or some other standard, to be paid to NMDC or the government. The feasibility of such payments, and their amounts, will vary from case to case. For one type of premium payment, see Part IV, Section 16(b)(i) above. See reference to a security deposit in the preamble and in Part III.]*

29. Premium

30. Security Deposit

31. Land Rent

32. Royalties

[Parts VII, VIII, and IX (Sections 33–40) define the company's project facilities; provide for the company's access to public and private land (with compensation to owners if necessary); provide for the company's right to establish accessory

works; guarantee the company's right to take and use water, gravel, sand, clay, stone and timber; require the establishment of medical facilities and schools and the coordination of the project with state and regional planning authorities; and guarantee the right of the government and third parties to access to certain of the company's facilities.]

PART VII: PROJECT FACILITIES; PROJECT MANAGEMENT

33. Project Facilities

(a)   Project facilities shall include the mines, processing facilities, port facilities, aircraft landing facilities, and transportation, communication, water supply and other necessarily related facilities as set forth below, for which the Company is, subject to the rights of third parties, hereby granted all necessary licenses and permits to construct and operate in accordance with such reasonable safety regulations relating to design, construction, and operation as may be in force and of general applicability in [host country].

(i)   the mines and other operating facilities: development of mines will require opening of roads, bridges, and storage areas, and may entail construction of aerial tramways, conveyor belts, pipelines, and other transportation facilities;

(ii)   port facilities: these facilities will require docks and storage areas and possibly, in addition, piers, jetties, harbors, breakwaters, terminal facilities, loading and unloading equipment, and warehouses;

(iii)   additional roads: these will include roads to provide access to housing for Company personnel and to port and aircraft landing facilities;

(iv)   a communications system: communications between points in the Contract Area may include radio, telephone, and telegraph systems;

(v)   water supply: provision for water supply may require pumping stations, purification systems, and distribution lines;

(vi)   in addition, the project may require other buildings, workshops, warehouses, storage areas, sewage-treatment systems, systems for tailings, plant waste and sewage disposal, foundries, machine shops, repair shops, and all such additional or other facilities, plant and equipment as the Company shall consider necessary for its operations or to provide services or to carry on activities ancillary or incidental to such operations.

(b)   All Project Facilities shall be the property of the Company and may be mortgaged, pledged or otherwise encumbered by it subject to the provisions of Part XXI relating to Assignment and Part XVI relating to Termination of the Contract.

34. Control of Operations

The Company shall have full and effective control and management of all matters relating to the operation of the Project including the production and marketing of its products in accordance with sound, long-term policies. The Company may make expansions, modifications, improvements, and replacements of the Project Facilities, and may add new facilities, as the Company shall consider necessary for the operation of the Project or to provide services or to carry on activities ancillary or incidental to the Project. All such expansions, modifications, improvements, replacements, and additions shall be considered part of the Project Facilities.

PART VIII: OCCUPATION OF SURFACE AND OTHER RIGHTS

35. General

(a)   Right to use land.

    (i)   Subject to the provisions of this Agreement, the Company shall have the right to enter and occupy any land within the Contract Area for the purpose of undertaking operations and activities under this Agreement. Provided, however, that with regard to land within the Contract Area which is privately owned, the Company shall comply with the provisions of subsection (iv) below.

    (ii)   Subject to the provisions of subsections (iii) and (iv) below, the Company shall have the right to occupy and utilize for the duration of this Agreement, or for a lesser period, the surface of such suitable areas outside the Contract Area as may be necessary for the construction and operations of roads, ports, railways, and pipelines necessary for its activities and operations under this Agreement.

    (iii)   With regard to public lands lying outside the Contract Area, the Company shall apply to the Government for the right to use such land. The right to use such land shall not be unreasonably denied by the Government. The Company shall apply to use such public lands by making application to the Ministry of Mines which shall conclude with the Company the terms and conditions under which the easement or other rights sought may be exercised, including the annual land rental to be charged.

    (iv)   With regard to private lands lying either within or without the Contract Area, the Company may, in the event that it is unable to reach a satisfactory agreement with the private owner or owners as to the terms on which it may enter and occupy the land in question, bring the matter to the attention of the Ministry of Mines by filing a petition. Such petition shall set forth the facts of the case and shall specify as exactly as possible (i) the land it requires, (ii) the name or names of the owners and/or occupants of the land if this can be reasonably ascertained, (iii) the use to which the Company intends to put the land, and (iv) the type of occupancy (lease, right-of-way, or easement) which the Company seeks.

The Ministry of Mines shall issue a notice to the owners and occupants of the land to present themselves on a day and at a time to be specified therein. Such day shall not be more than sixty (60) days or less than thirty (30) days from the date of said notice. On the appointed day the Minister of Mines or his representative shall hear the Company and the owners and occupants of the land and, after considering proofs and arguments on both sides, shall determine and assess the amount to be paid to the owners and/or occupants of the land for loss of the right to use the land for the period of the lease, right-of-way or easement and for damages arising out of the loss or destruction of goods and property because of rights granted to the Company. In the event of any dispute as to the nature and extent of the interests in or ownership of the land or the amount of compensation payable by the Company or if the decision of the Minister of Mines or his representative is unacceptable to any of the parties concerned, the case may be brought before a court of competent jurisdiction in (host country). In such case, the Company may file an indemnity bond, in an amount designated by the Minister of Mines, and may enter upon the land immediately subject to later determination by the court of competent jurisdiction of the exact amount payable.

(v)   Provided, however, that no lease, right-of-way, or easement shall be granted if it substantially interferes with operations of another previously granted contract.

(vi)   No blasting or other dangerous operations may be conducted within ( ) feet of any public works or permanent building without the previous consent of the ( ) and subject to such conditions as he may impose.

(b)   Accessory works and installation.

(i)   Subject to the provisions of section (a) above and the prompt payment of adequate compensation to any person whose rights are thereby affected and to the approval of the appropriate authority, the Company shall have the right to construct, maintain, alter, and operate

(1) industrial buildings and installations including mining, crushing, milling, ore refining, leading and pumping stations, warehouses, storage places and storage tanks;

(2) subject to the prior approval in writing from the Minister of _____ wharves, shipping terminals, ports, or port sites;

(3) facilities for shipping and aircraft;

(4) living accommodation and amenities, including hospitals,

(5) schools and recreational facilities, for the Company's employees and workmen;

(5) other buildings, installation, and works necessary or useful for the effective carrying out of the Company's operation and activities under this Agreement.

(ii) The construction of any railroad or electric power generating facilities shall require the prior approval of the Ministry of _____ which approval shall not be unreasonably denied. The Company shall submit the proposed plans for such railroad or electric power generating facility to the Minister of _____.

(iii) In the case of lands required for sidings, stations, yards, and other rail transportation installations, the right-of-way of the Company's railroads shall be in accordance with rules laid down by _____.

(c) Right to take and use water. Subject to the approval of the Minister of _____ previously obtained in writing and to such conditions (other than conditions imposing a charge for the use of water) as he may impose, the Company may appropriate and use, free of charge, any water found within the Contract Area and any water within the public domain within three miles of the Contract Area for purposes necessary or useful to the Company's operations and activities under this Agreement. Provided, however, that the Company shall not deprive any lands, villages, houses, or watering places for animals of a reasonable supply of water insofar as such water has, through custom, been utilized for such lands, villages, houses, or animals. Nor shall the Company interfere with any rights of water enjoyed by any persons under the law of [host country].

(d) Right to take and use gravel, sand, clay, or stone. Subject to the approval of the Minister of _____ previously obtained in writing and to such conditions as he may impose, the Company may appropriate and use, free of charge, gravel, sand, clay, or stone found within the Contract Area for purposes necessary and useful to Company's operations and activities under this Agreement. Provided, however, that such gravel, sand, clay, or stone shall be sold only with the prior approval of the Minister of Mines and subject to such conditions as he may impose (including conditions relating to fees to be paid to the Government) and provided further that upon termination of this Agreement any excavation shall be filled in or leveled and left by the Company as far as may be reasonably practical in its original condition and, if so required by the Minister of Mines, fenced or otherwise safeguarded as circumstances may require.

(e)   Right to take and use timber. The Company shall have the right to cut, appropriate and use the brushwood, undergrowth and timber (except protected trees) which may be found within the public domain within the Contract Area, subject to the general forestry laws of [host country]. Such cutting, appropriation, and use shall be permitted only to the extent necessary to the operations and activities of the Company under this Agreement. Such cutting, appropriation, and use may be for the purpose of facilitating ingress and egress into and from the Contract Area, for the purpose of clearing land for the erection of machinery, plant and buildings connected with Company's operations and activities, and for the purpose of construction required for Company's operations and activities.

Provided, however, that such timber shall be sold by the Company only with the prior approval of the Minister of _____ and subject to such conditions as he may impose (including conditions relating to fees to be paid to the Government).

PART IX: ADDITIONAL INFRASTRUCTURE AND OTHER FACILITIES

36. Medical Facilities

The Company shall furnish such free medical care and attention to all its employees and families of employees and to all Government officials working in the area covered by this Agreement as is reasonable and shall establish, staff, and maintain a dispensary, clinic, or hospital which shall be reasonably adequate under the circumstances. Provided, however, that whenever the Company employs more than [150] laborers in any one region it shall maintain a dispensary or hospital headed by a medical doctor.

37. Employee Accident Compensation

The [Workmen's Accident Compensation Law] of [host country] shall apply to accidents occuring to employees of the Company.

38. Schools

The Company shall provide, free of charge, primary and secondary school education for the children of all employees. Rules, regulations, and standards established by the Ministry of Education shall be followed.

39. Local and Regional Benefits

To maximize the regional economic and social benefits which the Project can generate, the Company shall also:

(a)   coordinate all of its studies of the Project's infrastructure requirements with local and Government infrastructure studies undertaken by the national and local Governments and interested local, foreign, and international public and private entities with a view toward integration of the infrastructure of the Company's operations with that of the state, region, and country; and

(b)   assist and advise the Government in its planning of the infrastructure and regional development which the Company may deem useful to the Project and to existing and future industries and activities in the region of the Project.

**40. Government's and Third Parties' Rights
to Use Company's Facilities**

(a)   The Company shall:

    (i)   transport the passengers and carry the freight of the Government and all mail of the public and Government on its railroads to the extent that such transport and carriage does not unduly prejudice or interfere with Company's operations hereunder;

    (ii)   transport the passengers and carry freight of third parties on its railroads to the extent that such transport and carriage does not unduly prejudice or interfere with Company's operations hereunder. Provided, however, that the transportation and carriage of such third-party passengers and freight shall be on such reasonable terms and reasonable charges as the Company may impose;

    (iii)   allow the public and the Government to use free of charge any roads constructed and/or maintained by the Company, provided, however, that such use shall not unduly prejudice or interfere with the Company's operations hereunder;

    (iv)   allow the public and the Government to use the Company's wharf and harbor installations, machinery, equipment services, and facilities on such reasonable terms and reasonable charges as the Company shall impose. Provided, however, that such use shall not unduly prejudice or interfere with the Company's operations hereunder;

    (v)   allow the Government and third parties to have access over the Contract Area, provided that such access does not unduly prejudice or interfere with the Company's operations hereunder;

    (vi)   allow the Government to place, free of charge at its own expense, telegraph and telephone wires on the poles of the lines of the Company, provided that such installation does not unduly interfere with the Company's efficient use of such poles and lines;

(vii) allow the Government and third parties to explore for and exploit minerals and other substances within the Contract Area in accordance with Part II of this Agreement.

[Parts X, XI and XII (Sections 41–47): Parts X and XI suggest ways of maximizing the economic development impact of the agreement. Parts X and XII require the company to use local goods and services (including shipping and bank loans) where they are available on terms generally comparable to terms for goods and services from abroad. (See Part XIII, Section 49, relating to the use of local processing facilities.) Part XI establishes a schedule for the training and employment of local nationals. Economic development provisions are discussed in Chapter 4.]

PART X: LOCAL PURCHASING: PROMOTION OF NATIONAL INTERESTS

41. Services and Supplies

The Company and its subcontractors shall purchase goods and services in [host country] if there are available in [host country] goods and services of suitable and reasonably comparable quality, and at no higher price than goods available from abroad, provided that in comparing prices of goods available in [host country] to the prices of imported goods there shall be added customs duties not to exceed 20 percent and other expenses incurred up to the time the imported goods are landed in [host country].

42. Shipping

The Company shall use ships of [host country] ownership and registration for the transport of all ore or concentrates or other products leaving [host country] to the extent available.

PART XI: EMPLOYMENT AND TRAINING OF [HOST COUNTRY] NATIONALS

43. [Host Country] Manpower: Employment of [Host Country] Nationals

(a) The Company shall employ [host country] personnel, to the extent available, and upon terms which are acceptable to the Company, in all classifications of full-time employment, for its operations in [host country]. Provided, however, that the following percentages of all positions in each employment classification shall be held by [host country] nationals within the periods stated beginning with the Date of this Agreement. The classifications of employment for the purpose of this

Part shall include the following: managerial, technical, professional, administrative, clerical, skilled labor, and unskilled labor.

	3 years	*5 years*	*8 years*
Unskilled labor	100%	100%	100%
Skilled labor	50	75	100
Clerical & supervisory	50	75	90
Technical	50	75	85
Management; Professional	50	75	85

The Company's failure to achieve said percentages will be considered a breach of contract in accordance with Part XV of this Agreement except where the Company can justify such failure on grounds acceptable to the Government. It is further understood that the Company shall not be restricted in its employment, selection, assignment, or discharge of personnel; provided, however, that subject to the foregoing requirements, the employment and the terms and conditions of such employment and the discharge or disciplining of [host country] personnel shall be carried out in compliance with laws and regulations of [host country] which at the time are of general application.

(b)   The Company shall provide direct [host country] participation in the Project through the inclusion of [host country] nationals in the management of the Company and among the members of its board of directors in accordance with Section 20 of this Agreement.

44. Training
(a)   The Company shall provide for the training of suitable persons of [host country] citizenship in order to qualify them for skilled, clerical and supervisory, technical, and management and professional posts in the Company's operations and activities in [host country].

(b)   Education Grants. The Company shall establish and cooperate in a program of scholarships for [host country] nationals and grants to educational institutions of [host country].

45. Non- [Host Country] Personnel
(a)   Subject to the provisions of Sections 43 and 44 of this Part, the Company and its subcontractors may bring into [host country] such non-[host country] personnel as in the Company's judgment are required to carry out the operations efficiently and successfully, and at the Company's request (which shall be accompanied by information concerning the education, experience, and other qualifications of the personnel concerned), the Government shall cause all necessary per-

mits (including entry and exit permits, work permits, visas, and such other permits as may be required) to be issued without delay and without hampering the continuous and efficient performance of the Company under this Agreement. In this connection the Company shall have the right periodically to submit manpower requirement plans and the Government will thereupon issue the necessary permits for all personnel covered by any such plan subject only to completion of the required security checks.

(b)   There shall at all times be equal treatment, facilities, and opportunities for all employees in the same job classification regardless of nationality.

PART XII: FINANCING

46. General

The Company shall have sole responsibility for financing the project and determining the terms on which said financing shall be obtained, including the extent to which the financing shall be accomplished through issuance of shares of, or borrowing by, the Company.

47. [Host Country] Bank Loans: Right of First Refusal

Provided, however, that for the purpose of financing the Local Currency costs of any of the operations of the Company or its subcontractors, [host country] banks shall be given a right of first option to grant such loans at rates and on conditions no less favorable than the rates and conditions of loans available from other sources.

PART XIII: IMPORTS AND EXPORTS

[This part exempts the Company from tax on imports of materials necessary to the project. The exemption does not apply if comparable goods are available in the host country on generally comparable terms. The Company is also exempted from export duties, (except for the export tax provided for in Part V). The Company must use local processing facilities if they are available on terms generally comparable to terms available abroad.]

48. Imports

(a)   This Agreement shall constitute a license for the Company and its subcontractors to import free from all import duties and other customs levies, by any route and any means of transport, into and for use in [host country] all equipment and materials, such as machinery, supplies, and equipment, necessary for the operation of the Project. Without limitation, the foregoing shall also include all machines, machine-units, tools or appliances, and their parts, vehicles (except sedan cars), aircraft, vessels, and other means of transport, raw materials (for export production), ancillary supplies, office equipment, building material for plants, office buildings, employee housing, schools and hospitals, and other machinery, supplies, and equipment needed for the operation of the Project. This license shall extend on the same terms to personal effects (including household and living equipment and goods) belonging to foreign personnel (and their dependents) employed in the Project and especially provided from abroad, to the extent that such personal effects have been in use prior to importation; such use shall be not less than for the period required by the prevailing customs regulations.

(b)   Re-exports. Any items imported by the Company or its subcontractors for use in connection with the Project and no longer needed for such use may be sold outside [host country] and re-exported free of all customs duties and levies. No imported items shall be sold domestically except after compliance with customs and import laws and regulations which shall at the time of such sale be in effect and of general application throughout [host country].

(c)   The exemption from import duties and the license to import set forth in this part shall not apply to any goods which are available in [host country] of suitable and reasonably comparable quality, and at no higher price, provided that in comparing prices of goods available in [host country] to the price of imported goods there shall be added customs duties not exceeding 20 percent ad valorem and other expenses incurred up to the time the imported goods are landed in [host country].

(d)   The decision of the [Director of Customs] as to whether any article comes within the import duty and licensing exemption set forth in this part shall be final, subject, however, to the Company's right to submit any dispute to arbitration in accordance with Part XVIII of this Agreement. The Government, through the [Director of Customs] or his agent shall have the right to inspect and inventory any articles imported by the Company for which the Company claims import duty exemption.

(e)   Articles which are dutiable under laws and regulations governing customs and not exempted from duty under this Article shall be subject to the payment of the appropriate duty in accordance with the Custom Act, 19— as from time to time amended and in effect.

(f)   If the Company or any contractor or subcontractor, as the case may be, intends to sell or transfer any articles which have been imported free of duty under this Part, a declaration shall be made to the [Director of Customs] before such sale or transfer is effected, and, unless such goods are sold or transferred to another company or contractor entitled to the same exemption, such import duty shall be paid as may be assessed by the [Director of Customs] in accordance with the customs laws and regulations as from time to time in effect.

(g) If the Company applies any article which has been imported free of duty under this Article to a nonexempt purpose, a declaration shall be made to the [Director of Customs] within thirty days of such initial use of nonexempt purposes and such import duty shall be paid as may be assessed by the [Director of Customs] in accordance with the laws and regulations governing customs.

(h) In order to enjoy the benefits granted by this Part all articles which are imported and for which a duty exemption is claimed must, as far as possible, be marked with the name or marks of the Company in a manner difficult to delete.

49. Exports

(a) The Company shall, subject to the conditions set forth in Part V, have the right to export and sell free of customs duties all products obtained from the operations under this Agreement subject to its prior fulfillment of the needs of [host country] purchasers, and its customers may take such products out of the country.

Provided that the Company shall, in accordance with Section 41, use existing processing facilities in [host country], if the charges, recoveries and services therefor are competitive, after due regard has been given to any savings in transportation costs that would result from processing in [host country]. In the event that such recoveries and services are not competitive, then the Company shall have the right to process abroad, it being understood and agreed, however, that the Company will not so process abroad if it is economically feasible to construct the requisite facilities therefor in [host country] pursuant to Section 14 of this Agreement and thereafter process its products on a basis which would be competitive with charges, recoveries, and services which would be competitive with those processing facilities abroad which it otherwise would have used, after due regard has been given to any savings in transportation costs that would result from processing in [host country].

(b) It is understood and agreed that exemption from customs duties shall not liberate the Company, its contractors and subcontractors, or its agents and personnel from the obligation to fulfill all customs formalities necessary for statistical verification and other purposes.

50. Cooperation

All imports and exports of articles under this Agreement shall be handled simply and expeditiously and the Government will, at the Company's request, cooperate with the Company in making appropriate arrangements between the Company and the customs authorities to this end.

[Parts XIV, XV, XVI and XVII (Sections 51-60) relate to the company's right to suspend operations in certain circumstances; the government's power to revoke the agreement for cause (with definitions of what constitutes default); the company's rights and obligations on termination of the agreement; and the definition of force majeure *(justifying temporary curtailment of company activities).*

The company may suspend operations for short periods if economically justifiable, but suspension of activities beyond two months can be considered a breach of obligations, and the government can consider this a default under Part XV. Part XIV must be read in connection with Part III Section 12 relating to working obligations and minimum expenditures, and Part XV Section 52 relating to the government's power to revoke the contract if the company does not produce a minimum tonnage of copper concentrate a year, after the first commercial shipment.

It should be noted that since provision is made for NMDC to obtain 100 per-cent ownership of operations after 25 years, all Company property will become the property of NMDC. Section 55(b) (allowing the company to withdraw normal stockpiles and liquid assets) would become operative only if the contract terminates before NMDC gains substantial ownership.

Since the problems of default and termination are not dealt with specifically in the text, reference is made here to the following: G.R. Delaume, "Excuse for Non-Performance and Force Majeure *in Economic Development Agreements,"* Columbia Journal of Transnational Law *10 (Fall 1971): 242; and Peter Eigen, "Default, Termination and Surrender," paper prepared for the Interregional Workshop on Negotiation and Drafting of Mining Development Agreements, dated 12 October 1973 (U.N., ESA/RT/AC.7/15).]*

PART XIV: SUSPENSION OF OPERATIONS

51. General

At any time and from time to time after the Date of this Agreement, the Company may notify NMDC that the Company is suspending, in whole or in part, its operations because in the Company's judgment economic or other conditions make it necessary to do so. The Company may then suspend opera-tions and may continue such total or partial suspension of operations until, in the Company's judgment, such conditions no longer exist, provided, however, if the Company continues a total suspension of operations for longer than a period of two months, which is not made necesary by *force majeure,* the Government may treat such suspension as a default to be governed by the provisions of Sec-tion 52 of this Agreement. In any event, the Company will consult with NMDC and keep them fully informed regarding any suspension of operations under this Part.

PART XV: DEFAULT BY COMPANY

52. Government's and NMDC's Power of Revocation for Cause

In the event that

(i)   the Company fails to commence operations within six months as required by Part III of this Agreement or fails to meet its expenditure obligations within the period specified in Part III of this Agreement, or

(ii)   no commercial shipment of ore is made within [four] years of the Date of this Agreement, or

(iii)   any tax or other payment payable by the Company under this Agreement or the laws of [host country] shall be in arrears or unpaid for a period of six calendar months next after any of the days on or before which the same ought to have been paid, or

(iv)   the Company assigns to a third party the whole or part of the rights held by it under this Agreement without the previous written consent of NMDC as provided in this part, or

(v)   the Company has knowingly submitted to the Government or NMDC any false statements which were a material consideration for the execution of this Agreement, or

(vi)   the Company intentionally extracts any minerals other than copper ore, gold, silver, or Associated Minerals without express authorization by NMDC, or

(vii)   the Company fails to export ____ tons of copper concentrate or its equivalent in smelted or refined product in any year after the first commercial shipment, or

(viii) the Company fails to comply with any final decisions by the arbital tribunal in a controversy arising with either the Government or NMDC under this Agreement, or

(ix)   there be any other breach or nonobservance by the Compoany of any of the terms, obligations, or conditions of this Agreement, or of any law of [host country] not superseded by this Agreement, or

(x)   the Company shall make or enter into any agreements for composition with its creditors or shall go into liquidation, whether compulsory or voluntary (other than for the purpose of reconstruction), or if a receiver is appointed, or

(xi)   the Company fails to establish processing facilities in accordance with Section 14 of this Agreement.

The Government and/or NMDC may, subject to the provisions of this Part, revoke this Agreement.

53. Notification and Remedy

(a) In the event that the Government or NMDC deems it desirable to revoke this Agreement pursuant to this Part, the Government or NMDC shall give to the Company notice in writing specifying the particular breach or nonobservance complaint of and requiring the Company, within three calendar months of such notice (or within such extended time as the Government or NMDC may deem fair having regard to the circumstances of the particular case), to remedy the same or make reasonable compensation to the Government or NMDC, as the case may be, in a manner acceptable to the Government or NMDC.

(b) If the Company shall fail to comply with said notice, the Government or NMDC may, after the expiration of said three calendar months or extended time, revoke this Agreement, provided, however, that where there is any dispute between the parties as to:

(i) whether there has been any breach or nonobservance by the Company of any term, obligation, or condition of this Agreement, or

(ii) whether any breach or nonobservance is remediable or as to the manner in which it should be remedied, the Company may, within the above-mentioned three-month period refer the dispute to arbitration, and neither the Government nor NMDC shall exercise its power of revocation until the result of arbitration is known, and then subject to the terms of the award. Provided, however, that if the Company elects to refer the dispute to arbitration, it shall be diligent in prosecuting its claim before the arbital tribunal.

(c) Upon the revocation of this Agreement by the Government or NMDC all rights granted to the Company hereunder shall terminate, subject to, and without prejudice to, any obligation or liability imposed or incurred under this Agreement prior to the effective date of revocation and subject to, and without prejudice to, the rights and obligations of the parties under this Part.

54. Penalties

(a) Unless otherwise specifically provided for in this Agreement or any law referred to in this Agreement and notwithstanding NMDC's right of revocation under this Part, the penalty for any breach of this Agreement shall be damages which shall be fixed by agreement, or, if agreement cannot be reached, then damages or specific performance as fixed by the arbital tribunal.

(b) Notwithstanding the provisions of this Part, in the event the Company shall be in default in the making of any payment of money to the Government which the Company is required to make pursuant to Part V, the period within which the Company must cure such default shall be 30 days after the receipt of notice thereof. The penalty for late payment shall be an interest charge on the amount in default equal to [the New York prime interest rates in effect at the date of default plus ____ percent] .

PART XVI: TERMINATION BY THE COMPANY

55. Removal of Property at Termination

(a)   Upon the expiration or earlier termination of this concession or any part thereof and of any extensions or renewals thereof, the Company shall leave, in good and safe running order, the mine or quarry, all fixed assets such as buildings, roads, railroads, airstrips, harbors, and docks constructed by the Company under this Agreement, and all plants and equipment necessary for the continued operation of the concession, and the same shall revert to NMDC and shall become the property of NMDC without compensation to the Company.

(b)   Subject to any claims which NMDC or the Government may have against the Company, arising under this Agreement or otherwise, all normal stockpiles and other liquid assets used by the Company in connection with its operations and activities under this Agreement shall remain the property of the Company and may be freely withdrawn, exported, sold, or otherwise disposed of, without payment of any duty, provided, however, that NMDC shall have the first right to purchase at a fair price to be determined between the parties any such stockpiles or other liquid assets. In the event that NMDC fails to exercise such right of purchase within ninety days after the termination of concession, the Company may remove such stockpiles and other liquid assets.

56. Continuation of Rights and Duties

Rights and obligations which have come into effect prior to the termination of this Agreement and rights and obligations relating to transfer of currencies and properties which have not yet been completed at the time of such termination, shall continue in effect for the time necessary or appropriate fully to exercise such rights and discharge such obligations.

57. Infrastructure

At the end of the term as provided in Part XXII or upon termination of the Agreement as provided in this Part XVI, or when no longer needed by the Company, and at no cost to the Company, any such property of the Company in [host country] movable and immovable, as shall be in use for public purposes such as roads, schools, and hospitals, shall be transferred as a gift to the Government.

PART XVII: FORCE MAJEURE

58. General

Any failure by either NMDC, the Government or any of its instrumentalities or subdivisions, or by the Company, to carry out any of its obligations under this Agreement other than the Company's obligation to make payments of money shall not be deemed a breach of contract or default if such failure is caused by *force majeure*. If, through *force majeure,* the fulfillment by either party of any terms and conditions of this Agreement is delayed, curtailed or prevented, then, anything in this Agreement to the contrary notwithstanding, the time for carrying out the activity thereby affected and the term of this Agreement specified in Part XXII shall each be extended for a period equal to the total of the periods during which such causes or their effects were operative. For purposes of this Agreement, *force majeure* shall include wars, insurrections, civil disturbances, blockades, embargoes, strikes and other labor conflicts, riots, epidemics, earthquakes, storms, floods, or other adverse weather conditions, explosions, fires, lightning, orders or directions of any government *de jure* or *de facto* or instrumentality or subdivision thereof, and acts of God or the public enemy. Provided, however, that only such loss, damage, or injury as could not have been avoided by the taking of proper precautions, due care or such reasonable alternative measures as aforesaid shall be regarded as the consequences of any failure caused by *force majeure*. It is understood that in no event may the Government or any of its instrumentalities or subdivisions, invoke as *force majeure* any act (or failure to act) on its part.

59. Notice

The party whose ability to perform its obligations is affected by *force majeure* shall, as soon as possible after the occurrence, notify the other party thereof in writing, stating the cause, and the parties shall endeavor to do all reasonably within their power to remove such cause and resume activities; provided, however, that neither party shall be obligated to resolve or terminate any disagreement with third parties, including labor disputes, except under conditions acceptable to it or pursuant to the final decision of any arbital, judicial, or statutory agencies having jurisdiction to finally resolve the disagreement. As to labor disputes, the Government and the Company will cooperate in a joint endeavor to alleviate any conflict which may arise.

60. Disputes

Any differences regarding interpretation or application of this Part, including differences concerning the period by which the terms of this Agreement and of rights and obligations thereunder should be extended, shall, if not otherwise amicably resolved, be determined through means of settlement stipulated under Part XVIII.

*[*Parts XVIII and XIX *(Sections 61–63) relate to the settlement of disputes and contract revision. The dispute-settlement provision relates to the construction, meaning, or effect of the contract, to questions arising out of the contract, and to rights and obligations under the contract. This provision is broadly enough drafted to cover disputes relating to the economic feasibility of establishing processing facilities (Part III, Section 14) or contract revision (Part XIX). Provision is made for reference of disputes to the International Centre for Settlement of Investment Disputes; the rules of the Centre are to be used. Other dispute-settling agencies could, of course, be used. If the particular agency does not have its own rules of procedure, they should be included in the contract. Parties must be nationals of states that have signed the Convention on the Settlement of Investment Disputes to use the Centre.*

Part XIX provides for periodic review of fiscal and other provisions with regard to the review of the tax rate or profit-sharing; the parties are to take into consideration the economic value of the concession and the terms of other agreements negotiated in the prior five years by the host government, the investor, or third parties with regard to the mineral in question.

It may be noted that some countries do not permit dispute settlement by external agencies.]

PART XVIII: SETTLEMENT OF DISPUTES

61. Method of Dispute-Settlement

(a)   If at any time during the continuance of this Contract or thereafter there shall be any question or dispute with respect to the construction, meaning, or effect of this Contract, or arising out of this Contract or concerning the rights or obligations hereunder, either party shall have the right to refer the dispute to the International Centre for Settlement of Investment Disputes for settlement by conciliation and/or arbitration as hereinafter provided. Any of the parties to such dispute may commence conciliation or arbitration proceedings by giving notice to the other party and to the Secretary-General, International Centre for Settlement of Investment Disputes (including in such notice a statement of the question or dispute and of the claim or contention of the person giving the notice).

(b)   The Rules of Conciliation and Arbitration of the International Centre for Settlement of Investment Disputes shall govern the conciliation and arbitration. The place of conciliation or arbitration shall be such as may be agreed by the parties and in default of agreement shall be as provided in the Rules of the Centre.

(c)   Pending the issue of a decision or award, the operations or activities that shall have given rise to the arbitration need not be discontinued, but if the decision or award recognizes that a complaint was justified, provision may be made in the award for such reparation or compensation in respect of such continued operations and activities as shall be decided by the arbitrator to be appropriate.

(d) The decision of the arbitrator shall be final and binding upon the parties to this Contract and upon any person who participated as a party in such arbitration proceedings, and he shall comply in good faith with the decision.

(e) Should the International Centre for Settlement of Investment Disputes be replaced by, or its functions substantially devolve upon or be transferred to, any new international body of similar type and competence, the function of the Arbitration Tribunal of the International Centre for Settlement of Investment Disputes provided by this Article shall be exercisable by the chief officer of such international body without further agreement among the parties hereto.

(f) This Agreement shall be construed in accordance with the laws of [host country].

(g) If the services of the Centre are unavailable to the parties to this Agreement, then such unsettled dispute shall be referred to the International Chamber of Commerce to be settled under the rules of procedures of the said Chamber of Commerce.

PART XIX: REVIEW OF CONTRACT TERMS

62. Fiscal Provisions

(a) The Parties shall, at five-year intervals from the effective date of this Agreement, review the terms of sections _____ of this Agreement (fiscal) to determine whether sections _____ shall be amended to provide for an allocation of [net profits] differing from the allocation provided for in said Article.

(b) In undertaking such review, the Parties shall bargain in good faith with a view toward providing a fair and equitable division of profits in light of the economic factors prevailing at the time of the review.

(c) In undertaking such review the Parties shall be guided by, but not limited to, consideration of the following factors:

    (i) the economic value of the concession,

    (ii) terms of other copper agreements negotiated by the government within the five-year period preceding the date of review,

    (iii) terms of other copper agreements negotiated by Foreign Overseas Investors, Inc. within the five-year period preceding the date of review,

    (iv) terms of other copper agreements negotiated by third parties to the extent that such agreements can be reasonably compared to this Agreement.

63. General Review

(a)   The Parties shall, at _____ year intervals from the effective date of this Agreement, review the Agreement (excluding those sections covered in Section 62 above) to determine whether, in the light of changed circumstances, the Agreement should be amended.

(b)   The Parties agree that they shall each carry out such review in good faith and shall give due regard to the legitimate interests of the other party.

[Parts XX, XXI, XXII, XXIII and XXIV (Sections 64–69) relate to the company's domicile, service of process, assignment of the company's rights and obligations, the agreement period, the right of renewal, and the law governing the contract.

The agreement is to run for twenty-five years. Since NMDC is to purchase 100 percent equity ownership by the twenty-fifth year, a right of renewal would not be appropriate here. An optional provision is included to cover circumstances in which the government or its agent does not acquire full control.]

PART XX: DOMICILE; SERVICE OF PROCESS

64. General

The Company shall be domiciled in [host country] and subject to the jurisdiction of courts in [host country] which normally have jurisdiction over corporations. The Company shall maintain in [host country] an office or agent for receipt of service of process or notification or other official or legal communication.

65. Notices

(a)   Notices for the purpose of this Agreement shall be sufficiently served if delivered or sent by registered post:

   (i)   in the case of NMDC to the _____.
   (ii) in the case of the Government, to the _____.
   (iii) in the case of the Company, to the manager of the _____ office.
   (iv) in the case of Foreign Overseas Investors, Inc. to _____.

(b)   All notices, requests or other communications required by, provided for in, or relative to this Agreement shall be in writing. Cables and telegrams shall be considered as written communications, but they shall be confirmed by letter.

PART XXI: ASSIGNMENT

66. General

(a)   The Company shall not assign, or purport to assign, the concession or any part thereof granted under this Agreement or any rights, privileges, liabilities or obligations granted or imposed by this Agreement, or any interest in the concession without the previous consent in writing of NMDC (except that the consent of NMDC shall not be required where the assignment is to another company in which the Company holds 100% of the equity, provided that NMDC shall be informed of any such assignment within thirty days of the assignment).

(b) NMDC shall not give its consent unless it is satisfied:
    (i)   that the proposed assignee is itself of good reputation or is a member of a group or groups of companies of good reputation or is owned by a company or companies of good reputation;
    (ii) that there is likely to be available to the proposed assignee either from its own resources or through other companies in the group of which it is a member, or otherwise, sufficient technical knowledge, experience and know-how and sufficient financial resources to enable it effectively to carry out a program satisfactory to NMDC for the operations hereunder; and
    (iii) that the proposed assignee is in all other respects acceptable to NMDC. NMDC may impose such conditions on the assignment as it considers appropriate.

(c) The assignee shall have all the rights and privileges and shall assume all the liabilities and obligations of the assignor with respect to what is assigned without relieving the Company or Foreign Overseas Investors, Inc. of such liabilities and obligations unless the Government and NMDC expressly consent to such a release.

(d) For the purposes of this Part the term "assign" shall include the admission to partnership of any third party in the activities and operations of the Company under this Agreement and shall include the mortgaging of any rights, privileges, liabilities, or obligations granted or imposed by this Agreement.

PART XXII: AGREEMENT PERIOD

67. General
Subject to the provisions herein contained, this Agreement shall continue in force until the expiration of [twenty-five] years following the Date of this Agreement, [subject to renewal for such term or terms and on such terms and conditions as provided in Part XXIII]. It is understood and agreed that at any time the Company shall propose a substantial new investment in the Project or shall require an extension of the term of this Agreement in order to facilitate additional financing, long-term sales contracts or otherwise, and in any event at least five years prior to such expiration date, the Government will give sympathetic consideration to a request by the Company to extend the term of this Agreement to permit continuation of the Project on the basis of long-term plan-

ning and sound mining and operating practices and to assure continuing employment of those devoting their time and efforts to the success of the Project.

PART XXIII: RIGHT OF RENEWAL
OF AGREEMENT

[A right-of-renewal provision will ordinarily not be appropriate in a situation, such as contemplated in this illustrative contract, in which (1) the contract is to run for 25 years; (2) NMDC is to gain total control of the company within 25 years (see Part IV); and (3) provision is made for review of fiscal and other provisions at stated intervals (see Part XIX). In circumstances where a right of renewal is appropriate, the following type of provision might be included.]

68. General
(a) This Agreement may be renewed for an additional term of ＿＿ years on the same conditions except those relating to income taxation, royalty payments, land rent, and other provisions relating to the Company's financial obligations to the Government and NMDC.
(b) This Agreement may be renewed for a second additional period of ＿＿ years on such terms as are agreed upon by the parties.
(c) Provided, however, that such rights of renewal are subject to the Company's fulfillment of its obligations under this Agreement.

PART XXIV: GOVERNING LAW

69. General
This Agreement shall be governed by the laws of [the host country].

ADDITIONAL PROVISIONS: COMMENT

[The inclusion of particular subjects in a concession agreement will depend on a number of factors, including the comprehensiveness of general legislation and the concerns of each party. If the general income tax act is comprehensive in its coverage, mere reference to that act may be sufficient. The same may be true of a mining code, exchange control act, or company law, for example.

If an investor is concerned about his right to remit profits, he may request a provision on foreign exchange. If he is concerned about his freedom to market the ore or processed product, or to enter into long-term contracts, he may request a provision on marketing.

Opinions differ among investors concerning the advisability of a provision dealing with nationalization and the right to speedy and effective compensation. Some feel that it is useful to have a provision guaranteeing compensation in the event of nationalization. Others feel that such a provision might encourage the nationalization they seek to avoid. Some countries have been willing to include provisions guaranteeing that the government will not nationalize for a specific period.]

FIRST SCHEDULE: CONTRACT AREA

The Contract Area includes the following:

SECOND SCHEDULE: MAP OF CONTRACT AREA DESCRIBED IN FIRST SCHEDULE

THIRD SCHEDULE: REPORTS TO BE SUBMITTED

1. Reports to the Government and NMDC and Records to be Maintained

(a) With respect to the Company's obligation to pay taxes on net income, the Company shall submit such information and documents as required in the Income Tax Act, 19–.

(b) With respect to the Company's exploratory and mining activities, the Company shall submit such information and documents as required in Section 4 below.

(c) In addition, the following shall be delivered to NMDC:

    (i) True copies of all sales, management, commercial, and financial agreements concluded with Affiliates and independent parties and all other agreements concluded with Affiliates, to be submitted within one month after conclusion.

    (ii) Monthly reports setting forth the quantities and qualities of ore produced, shipped, sold, utilized, or otherwise disposed of and prices obtained.

(d) The Company shall furnish to NMDC and the Government all other information of whatever kind which the latter may request in order that NMDC and the Government may be fully apprised of the Company's exploration and exploitation activities.

(e) All information furnished to the Government shall be in [English] and, in the event that such information is a translation from the original, shall be certified true translation. All financial data shall be recorded in [U.S. dollars].

(f) The Company shall maintain all original records and reports relating to its activities and operations under this Agreement including all documents relating to financial and commercial transactions with Independent Parties and Affiliates in its principal office in [host country]. These records and reports shall be opened to inspection by NMDC and the Government through an authorized representative during normal working hours. Such reports and records shall be maintained in the [English] language and all financial data shall be recorded in [U.S. dollars].

(g) The provisions of this Schedule shall apply to the Company's coparticipants, Affiliates, contractors, and subcontractors to the extent that such coparticipant, Affiliate, contractor, or subcontractor carries out operations and activities in furtherance of the Company's obligations, activities and operations under this Agreement.

2. Reports to be Confidential; Cost of Reports

(a) Any information supplied by the Company shall (except with the consent in writing of the Company which shall not be unreasonably withheld) be treated by all persons in the service of NMDC and the Government as confidential, but NMDC and the Government shall nevertheless be entitled at any time to make use of any information received from the Company for the purpose of preparing and publishing aggregated returns and general reports on the extent of ore prospecting or ore mining operations in [host country] and for the purpose of any arbitration or litigation between NMDC and/or the Government and the Company.

(b) All records, reports, plans, maps, charts, accounts, and information which the Company is or may be from time to time required to supply under the provisions of this Agreement shall be supplied at the expense of the Company.

3. Inspection

Any person or persons authorized by the NMDC or the Government shall be entitled at all reasonable times to enter into and upon any part of the premises of the Company and inspect its work, activities, and operations to insure the proper implementation by the Company of the provisions of any law applicable to the work, activities and operations of the Company, including the provisions of this Agreement and any regulations and decisions issued for the implementation of any applicable law.

4. Exploration and Exploitation Reports

(a) The Company will keep the NMDC and the Government, through the _____, advised concerning the Company's operations through submission of progress reports, beginning with the first quarter following the Date of this Agreement, as to the progress and results of the Company's development operations and activities under this Agreement.

(b) The Company shall file with the _____ a summary of its geological and metallurgical investigations, all geological, geophysical, topographic, and hydrographic data obtained from the general survey and exploration and a sample representative of each principal type of copper-bearing mineralization encountered in its investigations.

(c) Exploration Reports. Quarterly reports relating to any exploration activities shall include:

    (i)   the results of geological and geophysical investigations and proving of ore deposits in the exploration area and the sampling of such deposits;

    (ii)   the results of any general reconnaissance of the various sites of proposed operations and activities under this Agreement;

    (iii)   information concerning the selection of routes for roads and railways from the mining areas to a suitable harbor for the export of the ore;

    (iv)   information concerning the planning of suitable townsites, including information of suitable water and power supplies for the townsites and other facilities;

    (v)   such other plans and information as to the progress of operations in the exploration area as the [Department of Mines] may from time to time reasonably require.

(d) Exploitation Reports.

    (i)   the Company shall submit to the [Department of Mines] a monthly statistical report beginning with the first month following the commencement of mining operations which shall set forth the number and location of the workings on which work was begun during the preceding month; the number of workmen employed thereon at the end of the month, a list of the equipment at the workings at the end of the month and a brief description of the work in progress at the end of the month and of the work contemplated during the following month.

    (ii)   the Company shall furnish to the [Department of Mines] quarterly reports beginning with the first quarter following the commencement of the exploitation period concerning the progress of its operations in the Contract Area. This report shall specify in full:

        (1)   those workings in which ore is considered to have been found, regardless of whether the deposits are deemed to be commercial or not (together with all data relative to the estimated volumes of the reserves, the kind or kinds of such ore encountered, and the analyses thereof); the number and description of workings which have been placed in commercial production and the full particulars concerning the disposition of such production; the number of workmen employed on each such working as of the work in progress

at the end of the quarter in question and of the work contemplated during the ensuing quarter.

(2) the work accomplished during the quarter in question with respect to all installations and facilities directly or indirectly related to its exploitation program such as, but not limited to, those accessory works and installations described in Part VIII hereof, together with the work contemplated for the ensuing quarter with respect to the same installations and facilities and indicating actual and estimated investment in such installations and facilities made, committed, or to be committed with respect to such installations and facilities.

(3) the Company shall furnish to the [Department of Mines] an annual report beginning with the first complete year following the First Mining Day which shall include:

(A) the number and description of the workings which were in progress at the end of the year preceding the year in question (with a showing as to which are in commercial production); the number and description of workings abandoned during the year; the production of each of the workings, regardless of whether in commercial production or not, with a full description of the kind and quality and analysis of ore produced from each working; the number of workings on which activities are continuing at year end, but which have not gone into commercial production.

(B) the total volume of ores, kind-by-kind, broken down between volumes mined, volumes transported from the mines and their corresponding destination, volumes stockpiled at the mines or elsewhere in [host country], volumes sold or committed for export (whether actually shipped from [host country] or not), volumes actually shipped from [host country] (with full details as to purchaser, destination and terms of sale), volumes refined, processed and/or manufactured within [host country] with full specifications as to the intermediate products, by-products, or final products, outturned within [host country] (with full showing as to the disposition of such intermediate products, by-products or final products and of the terms on which they were disposed); and

(C) work accomplished and work in progress at the end

of the year in question with respect to all of the installations and facilities related to the exploitation programs, including, but not limited to those referred to in this Schedule herein, together with a full description of all work programmed for the ensuing year with respect to such installations and facilities including a detailed report of all investment actually made or committed during the year in question and all investment committed for the ensuing year or years.

(4) Monthly and quarterly reports shall be submitted in quadruplicate within thirty days of the end of the month or quarter in question, as the case may be. Annual reports shall be submitted in quadruplicate within ninety days of the end of the year in question.

Index

About the Authors

David N. Smith, Assistant Dean for International Legal Studies at the Harvard Law School, holds a B.A. degree from Harvard College and an LL.B. degree from the Harvard Law School. He is a former legal advisor to the Ministry of Justice, Northern Nigeria, and a former Assistant Attorney General in the New York State Department of Law. His research and writing have included work on the relationship between law and economic and social development as well as developing country policies toward foreign investment. He has served as a consultant to a number of governments in their negotiations with foreign investors.

Louis T. Wells, Jr., Professor at the Harvard Graduate School of Business Administration and Faculty Associate of Harvard's Center for International Affairs, holds a B.S. in Physics from Georgia Tech and an M.B.A. and a D.B.A. from Harvard University. His research in the field of international business includes work on choice of production technology in developing countries, the use of joint ventures by multinational firms, and investments by firms from one developing country in other developing nations. He has served as a consultant to a number of governments in their negotiations with foreign investors.